University of St. Francis
GEN 792 W983
Best broadcasts of 1938/39-

3 0301 00024745 8

This book may be kept

Best Broadcasts of 1940-41

Best Broadcasts
of 1940-41

Selected and Edited by

MAX WYLIE

Radio Department
N. W. Ayer & Son, Inc.

New York WHITTLESEY HOUSE *London*

McGRAW-HILL BOOK COMPANY, INC.

LIBRARY
College of St. Francis
JOLIET, ILL.

Copyright, 1942, *by the* McGraw-Hill Book Company, Inc.

"We Hold These Truths!" copyright by the Office of Facts and Figures. "An American Crusader," copyright, 1941, by Robert E. Sherwood from The Free Company over the Columbia Broadcasting System. Raymond Gram Swing material, copyright by Raymond Gram Swing; this excerpt reprinted by special permission of Tom Stix. Fred Allen material, copyright by Fred Allen; this composite broadcast reprinted by special permission of Mr. Allen. Fibber McGee and Molly, copyright, 1941. Quiz Kids, copyright, 1941. Published by special permission of James Parks. Rudy Vallée Program, copyright by Rudy Vallée; reprinted by special permission of Rudy Vallée. Jack Benny program, reprinted by special permission of Jack Benny; the Jack Benny Program is written by Ed Beloin and Bill Morrow. Maudie's Diary; the included reprint, an original by Albert G. Miller, is from a series of the same name based on stories written for *The Saturday Evening Post* by Sarah and Graeme Lorimer. "Honest Abe," copyright by the Columbia Broadcasting System; reprinted by special permission of the author, E. P. Conkle. "Roadside," copyright by the Columbia Broadcasting System; reprinted by special permission of the author, Lynn Riggs. "And Six Came Back," from Six Came Back, the published diary of David L. Brainard, edited by Bessie Rowland James, copyright, 1940, and used by special permission of the Publishers, The Bobbs-Merrill Company. "The Little Wife," reprinted by special permission of the copyright owner and author, William March. "Moll Flanders," from the series, "Invitation to Learning"; reprinted by special permission of the Columbia Broadcasting System and Random House, copyright owners. "Elementals," an original story by Stephen Vincent Benét, published by Farrar & Rinehart, Inc.; reprinted by special arrangement with the author and the copyright owners. "Vic and Sade," "Lone Journey," "Against the Storm," "Ma Perkins," copyrights by the Procter & Gamble Company of Cincinnati, Ohio. "The Light of the World," copyright held by General Mills, Inc., Minneapolis. "Justice Rides the Range," copyright owner, Falstaff Brewing Corporation, St. Louis, Omaha, New Orleans.

Notice: This book is copyrighted, and no part
or section thereof may be reprinted, rebroadcast,
or performed for any purpose whatever by any person, without permission of the copyright owners.

SECOND PRINTING

PUBLISHED BY WHITTLESEY HOUSE
A Division of the McGraw-Hill Book Company, Inc.

Printed in the United States of America by the Maple Press Co., York, Pa.

792
W983

Contents

ᶩᶩ

18754

CONTENTS

Best Broadcasts of 1940-41

Radio Address to the Nation, Dec. 9, 1941

by FRANKLIN D. ROOSEVELT

FRANKLIN D. ROOSEVELT.—The sudden criminal attacks perpetrated by the Japanese in the Pacific provide the climax of a decade of international immorality.

Powerful and resourceful gangsters have banded together to make war upon the whole human race. Their challenge has now been flung at the United States of America. The Japanese have treacherously violated the long-standing peace between us.

Many American soldiers and sailors have been killed by enemy action. American ships have been sunk, American airplanes have been destroyed.

The Congress and the people of the United States have accepted that challenge.

Together, with our free peoples, we are now fighting to maintain our right to live among our world neighbors in freedom and in common decency, without fear or assault.

I have prepared the full record about past relations with Japan, and it will be submitted to the Congress. It begins with the visit of Commodore Perry to Japan 88 years ago. It ends with the visit of two Japanese emissaries to the Secretary of State last Sunday, an hour after Japanese forces had loosed their bombs and machine guns against our flag, our forces and our citizens.

I can say with utmost confidence that no Americans today or a thousand years hence, need feel anything but pride in our patience and our efforts through all the years toward achieving a peace in the Pacific which would be fair and honorable to every nation, large or small.

And no honest person, today or a thousand years hence, will be able to suppress a sense of indignation and horror at the

3

treachery committed by the military dictators of Japan, under the very shadow of the flag of peace borne by their special envoys in our midst.

The course that Japan has followed for the past ten years in Asia has paralleled the course of Hitler and Mussolini in Europe and Africa. Today, it has become far more than a parallel. It is collaboration so well calculated that all the continents of the world, and all the oceans, are now considered by the Axis strategists as one gigantic battlefield.

In 1931, Japan invaded Manchukuo—without warning.

In 1935, Italy invaded Ethiopia—without warning.

In 1938, Hitler occupied Austria—without warning.

In 1939, Hitler invaded Czechoslovakia—without warning.

Later in 1939, Hitler invaded Poland—without warning.

In 1940, Hitler invaded Norway, Denmark, Holland, Belgium and Luxembourg—without warning.

In 1940, Italy attacked France and later Greece—without warning.

In 1941, the Axis powers attacked Yugoslavia and Greece and they dominated the Balkans—without warning.

In 1941, Hitler invaded Russia—without warning.

And now Japan has attacked Malaya and Thailand—and the United States—without warning.

It is all of one pattern.

We are now in this war. We are all in it—all the way. Every single man, woman and child is a partner in the most tremendous undertaking of our American history. We must share together the bad news and the good news, the defeats and the victories—the changing fortunes of war.

So far, the news has all been bad. We have suffered a serious setback in Hawaii. Our forces in the Philippines, which include the brave people of that commonwealth, are taking punishment, but are defending themselves vigorously. The reports from Guam and Wake and Midway Islands are still confused, but we must be prepared for the announcement that all these three outposts have been seized.

The casualty lists of these first few days will undoubtedly be large. I deeply feel the anxiety of all families of the men in our armed forces and the relatives of people in cities which have been bombed. I can only give them my solemn promise that they will get news just as quickly as possible.

4

This government will put its trust in the stamina of the American people, and will give the facts to the public as soon as two conditions have been fulfilled: First, that the information has been definitely and officially confirmed; and, second, that the release of the information at the time it is received will not prove valuable to the enemy directly or indirectly.

Most earnestly I urge my countrymen to reject all rumors. These ugly little hints of complete disaster fly thick and fast in war-time. They have to be examined and appraised.

As an example, I can tell you frankly that until further surveys are made, I have not sufficient information to state the exact damage which has been done to our naval vessels at Pearl Harbor. Admittedly the damage is serious. But no one can say how serious until we know how much of this damage can be repaired and how quickly the necessary repairs can be made.

I cite as another example a statement made on Sunday night that a Japanese carrier had been located and sunk off the Canal Zone. And when you hear statements that are attributed to what they call "an authoritative source" you can be reasonably sure that under these war circumstances the "authoritative source" was not any person in authority.

Many rumors and reports which we now hear originate with enemy source. For instance, today the Japanese are claiming that as a result of their one action against Hawaii they have gained naval supremacy in the Pacific. This is an old trick of propaganda which has been used innumerable times by the Nazis. The purposes of such fantastic claims are, of course, to spread fear and confusion among us, and to goad us into revealing military information which our enemies are desperately anxious to obtain.

Our government will not be caught in this obvious trap— and neither will our people.

It must be remembered by each and every one of us that our free and rapid communication must be greatly restricted in war-time. It is not possible to receive full, speedy, accurate reports from distant areas of combat. This is particularly true where naval operations are concerned. For in these days of the marvels of radio it is often impossible for the commanders of various units to report their activities by radio, for the very simple reason that this information would become available to the enemy, and would disclose their position and their plan of defense or attack.

5

Of necessity there will be delays in officially confirming or denying reports of operations but we will not hide facts from the country if we know the facts and if the enemy will not be aided by their disclosure.

To all newspapers and radio stations—all those who reach the eyes and ears of the American people—I say this: You have a most grave responsibility to the nation now and for the duration of the war.

If you feel that your government is not disclosing enough of the truth, you have every right to say so. But—in the absence of all the facts, as revealed by official sources—you have no right to deal out unconfirmed reports in such a way as to make people believe they are gospel truth.

Every citizen, in every walk of life, shares this same responsibility. The lives of our soldiers and sailors—the whole future of this nation—depend upon the manner in which each and every one of us fulfills his obligation to our country.

Now a word about the recent past—and the future. A year and a half has elapsed since the fall of France, when the whole world first realized the mechanized might which the Axis nations had been building for so many years. America has used that year and a half to great advantage. Knowing that the attack might reach us in all too short a time, we immediately began greatly to increase our industrial strength and our capacity to meet the demands of modern warfare.

Precious months were gained by sending vast quantities of our war material to the nations of the world still able to resist Axis aggression. Our policy rested on the fundamental truth that the defense of any country resisting Hitler or Japan was in the long run the defense of our own country. That policy has been justified.

It has given us time, invaluable time, to build our American assembly lines of production.

Assembly lines are now in operation. Others are being rushed to completion. A steady stream of tanks and planes, of guns and ships, of shells and equipment—that is what these eighteen months have given us.

But it is all only a beginning of what has to be done. We must be set to face a long war against crafty and powerful bandits. The attack at Pearl Harbor can be repeated at any one of many points in both oceans and along both our coast lines and against all the rest of the hemisphere.

6

It will not only be a long war, it will be a hard war. That is the basis on which we now lay all our plans. That is the yardstick by which we measure what we shall need and demand; money, materials, doubled and quadrupled production—ever-increasing.

The production must be not only for our own Army and Navy and Air Forces. It must reinforce the other armies and navies and air forces fighting the Nazis and the war lords of Japan throughout the Americas and the world.

I have been working today on the subject of production. Your government has decided on two broad policies.

The first is to speed up all existing production by working on a seven day week basis in every war industry, including the production of essential raw materials.

The second policy, now being put into form, is to rush additions to the capacity of production by building more new plants, by adding to old plants, and by using the many smaller plants for war needs.

Over the hard road of the past months, we have at times met obstacles and difficulties, divisions and disputes, indifference and callousness. That is now all past—and, I am sure, forgotten.

The fact is that the country now has an organization in Washington built around men and women who are recognized experts in their own fields. I think the country knows that the people who are actually responsible in each and every one of these many fields are pulling together with a teamwork that has never before been excelled.

On the road ahead there lies hard work—grueling work—day and night, every hour and every minute.

I was about to add that ahead there lies sacrifice for all of us.

But it is not correct to use that word. The United States does not consider it a sacrifice to do all one can, to give one's best to our nation, when the nation is fighting for its existence and its future life.

It is not a sacrifice for any man, old or young, to be in the army or the navy of the United States. Rather is it a privilege.

It is not a sacrifice for the industrialist or the wage-earner, the farmer or the shop keeper, the trainman or the doctor, to

7

pay more taxes, to buy more bonds, to forego extra profits, to work longer or harder at the task for which he is best fitted. Rather is it a privilege.

It is not a sacrifice to do without many things to which we are accustomed if the national defense calls for doing without.

A review this morning leads me to the conclusion that at present we shall not have to curtail the normal articles of food. There is enough food for all of us and enough left over to send to those who are fighting on the same side with us.

There will be a clear and definite shortage of metals of many kinds for civilian use, for the very good reason that in our increased program we shall need for war purposes more than half of that portion of the principal metals which during the past year have gone into articles for civilian use. We shall have to give up many things entirely.

I am sure that the people in every part of the nation are prepared in their individual living to win this war. I am sure they will cheerfully help to pay a large part of its financial cost while it goes on. I am sure they will cheerfully give up those material things they are asked to give up.

I am sure that they will retain all those great spiritual things without which we cannot win through.

I repeat that the United States can accept no result save victory, final and complete. Not only must the shame of Japanese treachery be wiped out, but the sources of international brutality, wherever they exist, must be absolutely and finally broken.

In my message to the Congress yesterday I said that we "will make very certain that this form of treachery shall never endanger us again." In order to achieve that certainty, we must begin the great task that is before us by abandoning once and for all the illusion that we can ever again isolate ourselves from the rest of humanity.

In these past few years—and, most violently, in the past few days—we have learned a terrible lesson.

It is our obligation to our dead—it is our sacred obligation to their children and our children—that we must never forget what we have learned.

And what we have learned is this:

8

There is no such thing as security for any nation—or any individual—in a world ruled by the principles of gangsterism.

There is no such thing as impregnable defense against powerful aggressors who sneak up in the dark and strike without warning.

We have learned that our ocean-girt hemisphere is not immune from severe attack—that we cannot measure our safety in terms of miles on any group.

We may acknowledge that our enemies have performed a brilliant feat of deception, perfectly timed and executed with a great skill. It was a thoroughly dishonorable deed, but we must face the fact that modern warfare as conducted in the Nazi manner is a dirty business. We don't like it—we didn't want to get in it—but we are in it and we're going to fight it with everything we've got.

I do not think any American has any doubt of our ability to administer proper punishment to the perpetrators of these crimes.

Your government knows that for weeks Germany has been telling Japan that if Japan did not attack the United States, Japan would not share in dividing the spoils with Germany when peace came. She was promised by Germany that if she came in she would receive the complete and perpetual control of the whole of the Pacific area—and that means not only the Far East, not only all of the islands in the Pacific, but also a stranglehold on the West Coast of North, Central and South America.

We also know that Germany and Japan are conducting their military and naval operations in accordance with a joint plan. That plan considers all peoples and nations which are not helping the Axis powers as common enemies of each and every one of the Axis powers.

That is their simple and obvious grand strategy. That is why the American people must realize that it can be matched only with similar grand strategy.

We must realize for example that Japanese successes against the United States in the Pacific are helpful to German operations in Libya; that any German success against the Caucasus is inevitably an assistance to Japan in her operations against the Dutch East Indies; that a German attack against Algiers or Morocco opens the way to a German attack against South America.

9

On the other side of the picture we must learn to know that guerrilla warfare against the Germans in Serbia helps us; that a successful Russian offensive against the Germans helps us and that British successes on land or sea or in any part of the world strengthen our hands.

Remember always that Germany and Italy, regardless of any formal declaration of war, consider themselves at war with the United States at this moment just as much as they consider themselves at war with Britain and Russia. And Germany puts all the other republics of the Americas into the category of enemies. The people of the hemisphere can be honored by that.

The true goal we seek is far above and beyond the ugly field of battle. When we resort to force, as now we must, we are determined that this force shall be directed toward ultimate good as well as against immediate evil. We Americans are not destroyers—we are builders.

We are now in the midst of a war, not for conquest, not for vengeance, but for a world in which this nation, and all that this nation represents, will be safe for our children. We expect to eliminate the danger from Japan, but it would serve us ill if we accomplished that and found that the rest of the world was dominated by Hitler and Mussolini.

We are going to win the war and we are going to win the peace that follows.

And in the dark hours of this day—and through the dark days that may be yet to come—we will know that the vast majority of the members of the human race are on our side. Many of them are fighting with us. All of them are praying for us. For, in representing our cause, we represent theirs as well—our hope and their hope for liberty under God.

Speech before the Joint Session of Congress, Dec. 26, 1941

by WINSTON CHURCHILL

WINSTON CHURCHILL.—Members of the senate and of the house of representatives of the United States: I feel greatly honored that you should have thus invited me to enter the United States senate chamber and address the representatives of both branches of congress. The fact that my American forebears have for so many generations played their part in the life of the United States and that here I am, an Englishman, welcomed in your midst, makes this experience one of the most moving and thrilling in my life, which is already long and has not been entirely uneventful.

I wish indeed that my mother, whose memory I cherish across the vale of years, could have been here to see. By the way, I cannot help reflecting that if my father had been an American and my mother British, instead of the other way around, I might have got here on my own.

In that case, this would not have been the first time you would have heard my voice. In that case I would not have needed any invitation, but if I had it is hardly likely that it would have been unanimous. So perhaps things are better as they are. I may confess, however, that I do not feel quite like a fish out of water in a legislative assembly where English is spoken.

I am a child of the house of commons. I was brought up in my father's house to believe in democracy; trust the people, that was his message. I was to see him cheered at meetings and in the streets by crowds of working men 'way back in those aristocratic, Victorian days when, as Disraeli said, the world was for the few and for the very few.

Therefore, I have been in full harmony all my life with the tides which have flowed on both sides of the Atlantic, against privilege and monopoly, and I have steered confidently to-

II

wards the Gettysburg ideal of government of the people, by the people, for the people.

I owe my advancement entirely to the house of commons, whose servant I am. In my country as in yours public men are proud to be the servants of the state, and would be ashamed to be its masters. On any day, if they thought the people wanted it, the house of commons could by a single vote remove me from my office, but I am not worrying about it at all.

As a matter of fact, I am sure they will approve very highly of my journey here, for which I obtained the king's permission, in order to meet the President of the United States, and to arrange with him for all that mapping out of our military plans and for all those intimate meetings of the high officers of the armed services in both countries which are indispensable for the successful prosecution of the war.

I should like to say, first of all, how much I have b impressed and encouraged by the breadth of view and sense of proportion which I have found in all quarters c here to which I have had access.

Any one who did not understand the size and solidarity of the foundation of the United States might easily have expected to find an excited, disturbed, self-centered atmosphere, with all minds fixed upon the novel, startling, and painful episode of sudden war as it hit America.

After all, the United States have been attacked and set upon by three most powerfully armed dictator states. The greatest military power in Europe, the greatest military power in Asia—Japan, Germany, and Italy have all declared and are making war upon you, and the quarrel is open, which can only end in their overthrow or yours.

But here in Washington, in these memorable days, I have found an Olympian fortitude which, far from being based upon complacency, is only the mark of an inflexible purpose and the proof of a sure, well grounded confidence in the final outcome.

We in Britain had the same feeling in our darkest days. We, too, were sure that in the end all would be well. You do not, I am certain, underrate the severity of the ordeal to which you and we have still to be subjected.

The forces ranged against us are enormous. They are bitter, ruthless. The wicked men and their factions who have launched their peoples on the path of war and conquest know that they will be called to terrible account if they cannot beat down by force of arms the people they have assailed.

They will stop at nothing. They have a vast accumulation of war weapons of all kinds. They have highly trained and disciplined armies, navies, and air services. They have plans and designs which have long been contrived and matured. They will stop at nothing that violence or treachery can suggest.

It is quite true that on our side our resources in man power and materials are far greater than theirs. But only a portion of your resources are as yet mobilized and developed, and we, both of us, have much to learn in the cruel art of war.

We have, therefore, without doubt, a time of tribulation before us. In this same time, some ground will be lost which it will be hard and costly to regain. Many disappointments and unpleasant surprises await us. Many of them will affect us before the full marshaling of our latent and total power can be accomplished.

For the best part of 20 years, the youth of Britain and America have been taught that war was evil, which is true, and that it would never come again, which has been proved false.

For the best part of 20 years, the youth of Germany, of Japan, and Italy have been taught that aggressive war is the noblest duty of the citizen and that it should be begun as soon as the necessary weapons and organization have been made.

We have performed the duties incident to peace. They have plotted and planned for war. Naturally, this places us in Britain and now places you in the United States at a disadvantage which only time, courage, and untiring exertion can correct.

We have indeed to be thankful that so much time has been granted to us. If Germany had tried to invade the British Isles after the French collapse in June, 1940, and if Japan had declared war on the British empire and the United States at about the same date, no one can say what disaster and agonies might not have been our lot. But now, at the end of December, 1941, our transformation from easy going peace to total war efficiency has made very great progress.

The broad flow of munitions in Great Britain has already begun. Immense strides have been made in the conversion of American industry to military purposes, and now that the United States is at war, it is possible for orders to be given every day which in a year or 18 months hence will produce results in war power beyond anything that has been seen or foreseen in the dictator states.

Provided that every effort is made, that nothing is kept back, that the whole man power, brain power, virility, valor, and virtue of the English speaking world, with all its galaxy of loyal friends, are associated in a common community or state, we can be reunited by the simple but supreme God.

I think it would be reasonable to hope that the end of 1942 will see us quite definitely in a better position than we are now, and that the year 1943 will enable us to assume the initiative upon an ample scale. Some people may be startled or momentarily depressed when, like your President, I speak of a long, hard war.

Our peoples would rather know the truth, somber tho it may be, and after all, when we are doing the most blessed work in the world, not only defending our hearths and homes, but the cause of freedom in every land, the question of whether deliverance comes in 1942 or 1943 or 1944 falls into its proper place in the grand proportions of human history.

Sure I am that this day now, we are masters of our fate; that the task which has been set us is not above our strength; that its pangs and toils are not beyond our endurance, as long as we have faith in our cause and unconquerable will-power, salvation will not be denied us.

In the words of the sonnet, 'Ye shall not be afraid of evil tidings; his heart is fixed, trusting in the Lord.' Not all the tidings will be evil. On the contrary, mighty strokes of war already have been dealt against the enemy—the glorious defense of armies and people. Wounds have been inflicted upon the Nazi tyranny system which have bitten deep and will fester and inflame not only the Nazi body but in the Nazi mind.

The boastful Mussolini has crumpled already. He is now but a lackey and a serf, the merest utensil of his master's will. He has inflicted great suffering and wrong upon his industrious people. He has been stripped of all his African empire. Abyssinia is liberated.

14

Our armies of the east, which were so weak and ill equipped at the moment of the French desertion, now control all the regions from Teheran to Bengazi, from Aleppo and Cyprus to the sources of the Nile.

For many months we devoted ourselves to preparing to take the offensive in Libya. The very considerable battle which has been proceeding there for the last six weeks in the desert has been most fiercely fought on both sides.

Owing to the difficulties of supplies upon the desert flank, we were never able to bring numerically equal forces to bombard the enemy. Therefore, we had to rely upon superiority in numbers and qualities of tanks and aircraft—British and American.

For the first time, aided by these, we have fought the enemy with equal weapons. For the first time we have made them feel the sharp edge of those tools with which he has enslaved Europe. The armored forces of the enemy in Cirenaica amounted to about 150,000 men, of whom a third were German. Gen. Auchinleck set out to destroy totally that armored force and I have every reason to believe that his aim will be accomplished.

I am so glad to be able to place before you members of the senate and the house of representatives at this moment, when you are entering the war, the proof that with proper weapons and proper organization, we are able to beat the life out of the savage Nazis. What Hitler is suffering in Libya is only a sample and a foretaste of what we have got to give him and his accomplices wherever this war should lead us in any quarter of the globe.

There are good tidings also from the blue waters. The lifeline of supplies which join our two nations across the ocean without which all would fail—that lifeline is flowing steadily and freely in spite of all that the enemy could do.

The back of the British empire, which many thought 18 months ago was broken, is now incomparably stronger and is growing stronger with every month. Lastly, if you will forgive me for saying so, the best tidings of all, the United States—united as never before and who have drawn the sword for freedom and cast away the scabbard.

All these tremendous steps have led the subjugated peoples of Europe to lift up their heads again in hope; they have put aside forever the shameful temptation of resigning themselves to the conqueror's will.

Hope has returned to the hearts of scores of millions of men and women, and with that hope there burns the flame of anger against the brutal, corrupt invaders and still more fiercely burn the fires of hatred and contempt for the filthy Quislings whom they have suborned.

In a dozen famous ancient states, now prostrate under the Nazi yoke, the masses of the people await their hour of liberation when they too will once again be able to play their parts and strike their blows like men. That hour will strike and the people will proclaim that night is past and that dawn has come.

The onslaught upon us, so long and so completely planned by Japan, has presented both our countries with grievous problems for which we could not be fully prepared. If people asked me, and they have a right to ask me in England, "Why is it that you have not got an ample equipment of modern aircraft and army weapons of all kinds in Malaya and in the East Indies?" I can only point to the victory Gen. Auchinleck has gained in the Libyan campaign.

Had he diverted and dispersed our gradually growing resources between Libya and Malaya, we could have been found wanting in both places. If the United States has been found at a disadvantage at various points in the Pacific ocean, we know well that that is to no small extent because of the aid which you have been giving to us in munitions for the defense of the British Isles and to the Libyan campaign, and above all, because of your help in the battle of the Atlantic, upon which all depends and which has in consequence been successfully and prosperously maintained.

Of course, it would have been much better, I freely admit, if we had enough resources of all kinds to be of full strength at all threatened points, but considering how slowly and reluctantly we brought ourselves to large scale preparations today, we had no right to expect to be in such a fortunate position.

The choice of how to dispose of our hitherto limited resources had to be made by Britain in time of war and by the United States in time of peace, and I believe that history will pronounce that upon the whole—and it is upon the whole that these matters must be judged—the choice made was right.

Now that we are together, now that we are linked in a righteous comradeship of arms, now that our two considerable nations, each in perfect unity, have joined all their life energies in a common resolve, you will see milestones upon which a steady light will glow and brighten.

Many people have been astonished that Japan, in a single day, has made war against the United States and the British empire.

We all wonder why if this dark design, with its laborious and intricate preparation, had been so long filling their secret mind, they did not choose our moment of weakness 18 months ago. But, quite dispassionately, in spite of the losses we have suffered and the further punishment we will have to take, it certainly appears an irrational act. It, of course, only proves it correct to assume that they have made very careful calculations and think they see their way through; nevertheless, there may be another explanation.

We know that for many years past the policy of Japan has been dominated by secret sects of societies and junior officers of the army and navy who have enforced their will upon successive Japanese cabinets and parliament by the assassination of any Japanese statesman who opposed or who did not sufficiently further their aggressive policies.

It may be that these societies, dazzled and dizzy with their own dreams of aggression and the prospect of early victory, have forced their country into war against its better judgment. They have certainly embarked upon a very considerable undertaking.

After the outbreak at Pearl Harbor and the Pacific islands, in the Philippines, in Malaya, and the Dutch East Indies, they must now know that the stakes for which they decided to play are enormous. When we look at the resources of the United States and the British empire compared to those of Japan, when we remember those of China, which have for so long valiantly withstood invasion of tyranny, and, when also we observe the Russian menace which hangs over Japan, it becomes still more difficult to reconcile Japanese action with prudence or even sanity. What kind of a people do they think we are?

Is it possible they do not realize that we shall never cease to persevere against them until they have been taught a lesson which they and the world will never forget?

Members of the senate and members of the house of representatives: I'll turn for one moment more from the turmoil

17

and convulsions of the present to the broader spaces of the future. Here we are together, facing a group of mighty foes who seek our ruin.

Here we are together, defending all that to free men are dear. Twice in a single generation the catastrophe of world war has fallen upon us. Twice in our lifetime the long arm of fate has reached out across the ocean to bring the United States into the forefront of the battle. If we had stuck together after the last war, if we took common measures for our safety, this renewal of the curse need never have fallen upon us.

Do we not owe it to ourselves, to our children, to tormented mankind, to make sure that these catastrophes do not engulf us for the third time? It has been proved that pestilences may break out in the old world which carry their destructive ravages into the new world, from which, once they are afoot, the new world cannot escape.

Duty and prudence alike demand, first, that the germ centers of hatred and revenge should be constantly and vigilantly served and treated in good time and that an adequate organization should be set up to make sure that the pestilence can be controlled at its earliest beginnings, before it spreads and rages throughout the entire earth.

Five or six years ago, it would have been easy, without shedding a drop of blood, for the United States and Great Britain to have insisted on the fulfilment of the disarmament clauses of the treaties which Germany signed after the great war, and that also would have been the opportunity for assuring to the Germans those materials, those raw materials, which we declared in the Atlantic charter should not be denied to any nation, victor or vanquished.

The chance has departed; it is gone. Prodigious hammer strokes have been needed to bring us together today.

If you will allow me to use other language, I will say that he must indeed have a blind soul who cannot see that some great purpose and design is being worked out here below, for which we have the honor to be the faithful servant.

It is not given to us to peer into the mysteries of the future; yet, in the days to come, the British and American peoples will, for their own safety and for the good of all, walk together in majesty, in justice, and in peace.

We Hold These Truths

by NORMAN CORWIN *and* THE OFFICE OF FACTS AND FIGURES

eeeeeeeeeeeeeeeeeeeeeeeeeeeeeeeeeeeeeeeeeeeeeeeeee

VOICE.—We Hold These Truths!

MUSIC.—*Introductory passage: strong, heroic, but not arrogant; it sustains behind.*

HUSTON.—(*With quiet dignity; each space a pause*) This is a program about the making of a promise and the keeping of a promise.

This is a program about the rights of the people.

This is a program coming to you over the combined radio networks of the United States, bringing you the voices of Americans, bringing you the voice of the President of the United States.

This is a program for listeners in all zones of continental time, for listeners on ships away from home, for listeners in uniform, for listeners on the American islands in the two great oceans.

This is a program about a guaranty made to the people of America 150 years ago . . . a guaranty that has been kept through peace and war and peace and war . . . a guaranty we call the Bill of Rights.

BARRYMORE.—My name is Barrymore. I am one of several actors gathered in a studio in California, near shores that face an enemy across an ocean now Pacific in name only.

We are here tonight to join 130 million fellow Americans in praise of a document that men have fought for, that men are fighting for, that men will keep on fighting for as long as freedom is a strong word falling sweet upon the ear.

What we enact tonight has been enacted many times before in living flesh and blood. The people we portray have walked the world. The drama is the ancient one, the endless one, the struggle for men's rights to live their lives out peacefully and profitably in a decent world.

19

It may be many of us people here are known to many of you people there. For with us, honored to have a part in this program of commemoration, are some whose names you may have heard: names such as Edward Arnold, Walter Brennan, Bob Burns, Norman Corwin, Bernard Herrmann, Walter Huston, Marjorie Main, Edward G. Robinson, Corporal James Stewart, loaned to us for this occasion by the Army Air Corps, Rudy Vallee, and Orson Welles.

In New York City, waiting to join us, are Doctor Leopold Stokowski and a symphony orchestra; in Washington, the highest name in the land—the President of the United States, Commander in Chief of the Army and the Navy— Mr. Roosevelt.

But this is not a night of names, of personalities. Our names or any names are meaningless unless *your* names are added; unless you join us, you for whom the sacred rights were written and to whom their keeping is entrusted; you, the guardians of what has been bequeathed to you by millions like yourselves and by the toil of centuries as dark and menacing as this we live in.

You, the people of the federated states.

Music.—*Resolution of introductory passage . . . pause . . . slow arpeggio on harpsichord into (solo) passage of eighteenth century flavor, holding behind.*

Barrymore.—*(Over harpsichord)* One hundred fifty years is not long in the reckoning of a hill. But to a man it's long enough. One hundred fifty years is a week end to a redwood tree, but to a man it's two full lifetimes. One hundred fifty years is a twinkle to a star, but to a man it's time enough to teach six generations what the meaning is of liberty, how to use it, when to fight for it.

Music.—*Harpsichord sweeps up into a full orchestra movement of great energy: nervous, modern, metropolitan. After establishing, comes down to back the following.*

Stewart.—Have you ever been to Washington, your capital? Have you been there lately?

Well, let me tell you, it's a place of buildings and of boom and bustle, of the fever of emergency, of workers working overtime, of windows lighted late into the night.

It's a handsome city, proud of its sturdy name, proud of the men who've stopped there and made decisions; proud of its domes and lawns and monuments. (*Sneak in traffic background as music level drops*) Of course, too, Washington is like some other cities you have seen—has streetcars, haberdasheries, newsstands, coffee shops, and slums. At busy intersections there are neon traffic signs which, when the light's against you, say:

SIGN.—*Very flatly . . . like a sign* Don't walk.

STEWART.—And when the light changes . . .

SIGN.—Walk.

STEWART.—It's a tourist's city . . . (*Traffic level gradually out*) which is proper, when you think how much of history a busy guide can cover in a day and when you realize that the District of Columbia belongs to all the people of the states. The tourists know that here their voices have been heard from clear back home; that here their votes are put to work. The tourists go to see the sights they've seen a thousand pictures of . . . the sights so famous and familiar that they're thrilled to find they look just as they thought they'd look. Washington Monument, for example, or the Lincoln Memorial (*The city music is shut out . . . now Lincoln music*), where the seated and relaxed Abe Lincoln sits between two mighty murals of plain words, his own words.

LINCOLN.—(*On echo . . . slowly . . . out of stone*) With firmness in the right, as God gives us to see the right, let us strive on to finish the work we are in . . . to do all which may achieve and cherish a just and lasting peace among ourselves and with all nations.

MUSIC.—*Lincoln segues to city music.*

STEWART.—The city moves on busily outside the Monument . . . The tourist goes to see the Capitol, the White House, the museums; sees all about him statues and inscriptions . . . more sayings than he'd ever seen before . . . wise sayings . . . profound sayings. At the Union Station, for example:

DEPOT.—"A man must carry knowledge with him if he would bring home knowledge"—Samuel Johnson.

MUSIC.—*Filigree after each of these. We do not stop for them.*

STEWART.—The Archives Building.

ARCHIVES.—What is past is prologue.

STEWART.—The Supreme Court.

COURT.—Justice, the guardian of liberty.

STEWART.—But one of the best is in the Library of Congress.

LIBRARY.—"The noblest motive is the public good"—Vergil.

MUSIC.—*A respectful chord.*

STEWART.—The tourist thinks that over . . .

TOURIST.—"The noblest motive is the public good."

STEWART.— . . . and with this in mind, he climbs the marble stairs inside the library—to come at length upon a case containing a handwritten document:

TOURIST.—(*Reading slowly*) "The engrossed original of the Constitution of the United States of America."

STEWART.—He sees the manuscript is aging, that its words are worn, as though from use. The writing's dim; it's hard to make it out . . . it's getting on in years . . .

MUSIC.—*Mnemonic strings behind.*

VOICE.—(*Distant perspective, symbolic of the faded writing on the manuscript*) "We, the people of the United States, in order to form a more perfect Union, establish justice, insure domestic tranquility, provide for the common defense, promote the general welfare, and secure the blessings of liberty to ourselves and our posterity, do ordain and establish this Constitution for the United States of America."

STEWART (*Overlaps*)	VOICE
The words are dim—but not the meaning of words.	"Article One: Section One: All legislative powers herein granted shall be vested in a Congress of the United States, which shall consist of a Senate and House of Representatives.
The pens that put this down are dust—but not the marks they made.	
There was a time when this was shining parchment, when the text was easier to read, when the ink was not yet dry.	"Section Two: The House of Representatives shall be composed of members chosen every

Suppose that we, stopped here in modern Washington before this shrine, were to return, go back, go back a little north by east in time and space to one bright afternoon in Philadelphia . . . that fine fall day when deputies from 12 free states subscribed their names to a new blueprint of a new society.

second year by the people of the several States, and the electors in each State shall have the qualifications requisite for electors of the most numerous branch of the State Legislature. No person shall be a Representative who shall not have attained to the age of twenty-five years. (*Cross on word "Philadelphia in overlapping narration to*) . . . both of the United States and of the several States, shall be bound by oath or affirmation to support this Constitution. (*Voice fading rapidly on board . . . the writing becomes clearer*) . . .

" . . . Done in Convention by the unanimous consent of the States present, the seventeenth day of September in the Year of Our Lord, 1787 and of the Independence of the United States the twelvth. In witness whereof we have hereunto subscribed our names . . . George Washington, President, and Deputy from Virginia."

WASHINGTON.—Now, gentlemen, we are ready for your signatures: by geographical progression, north to south. The deputies from New Hampshire will please sign first.

LANGDON.—John Langdon.

GILMAN.—Nicholas Gilman.

WASHINGTON.—The delegates from Massachusetts . . .

STEWART
Good-looking men, these. Mostly lawyers. Two or three are surgeons.

GORHAM
Nathaniel Gorham.
KING
Rufus King.

23

Broom, there, Broom of Delaware, he did surveying for a while.

Sherman, who just signed, he was a shoemaker before he studied law.

That's Washington, calling the delegations.

The man behind Ben Franklin is Alexander Hamilton. Ben's getting old now. Eighty-one. Slept off and on throughout the whole convention. But when it was important to be awake, he was awake . . . and active.

There have been men assembled in a room before. But never to a greater purpose.

Well . . . here comes the last to sign, now.

WASHINGTON
The gentlemen from Connecticut, please.

JOHNSON
William Samuel Johnson.

SHERMAN
Roger Sherman.

WASHINGTON
And now our representative of New York.

HAMILTON
Alexander Hamilton.

WASHINGTON
The gentlemen from New Jersey.

LIVINGSTON
William Livingston.

BREARLEY
David Brearley.

. . . .

WASHINGTON
The gentlemen from North Carolina.

BLOUNT
William Blount.

SPAIGHT
Richard Dobbs Spaight.

WASHINGTON
The gentlemen from South Carolina.

RUTLEDGE
J. Rutledge.

PINCKNEY
Charles Cotesworth Pinckney.

WASHINGTON
The gentlemen from Georgia.

FEW
William Few.

BALDWIN
Abraham Baldwin.

JACKSON
Attest: William Jackson, Secretary.

SOUND.—*Now that the Constitution has been signed, the meeting lightens . . . music out . . . there is general and amiable talk, a little laughter, and this sustains behind the following:*

STEWART.—So: the Constitution has been drafted, signed, and presently will be submitted to the states for their approval. The convention is relaxed now . . . there are handshakes and felicitations . . .

Is everybody happy? Will they celebrate, do you suppose? Will Rufus King go home to Boston and be welcomed by a welcoming committee from the city? Will appreciative Virginians hoist James Madison to their shoulders and parade him through the streets shouting "father of the Constitution"? Will a thumping band march up and down the town making a noise like this?

MUSIC.—*Band for eight bars . . . cheering by cast.*

STEWART.—No. There will be no band. Will there be speeches?

ORATOR.—(*Fulsomely*) And I say to you, ladies and gentlemen: the heart of every man and woman—nay, of every *child* in each and every one of our 13 states, from the rockbound shores of Maryland to the golden sands of Georgia, should fill and swell with pride on reading the noble and glorious Constitution which our wise and prudent and farsighted representatives in solemn assembly have framed and submitted to our glorious states for their approval. *And I say to you . . .*

STEWART.—No. There will be no speeches. There will be no celebration. No confetti from the windows; fireworks; saluting cannon; roses strewn beneath the coaches of the delegates.

Instead—suspicion. Suspicion by the very men who fought the long fight so that there could *be* a Constitution drawn for the emancipated states: the farmers and the clerks, the hackmen and the artisans, the grease-grimed blacksmiths in their shops—these men who only lately put away their guns and powder in a good dry place—these men who won a war of freedom, but who know that freedom must be guarded to be kept . . . They are *suspicious*. They are talking on the common, in the tavern, in the parlor, in the foundry room.

SOUND.—*Under the foregoing, fade in hammering on an anvil . . it stops.*

25

LIBRARY 18754
College of St. Francis
JOLIET, ILL.

Smith.—Mmmmm. What else does it say?

Stewart.—That covers it. That's the whole thing.

Sound.—*A few more hammer strokes.*

Smith.—(*Half to himself, as though testing the word*) Con-stitution (*Three more strokes*) I don't like it.

Stewart.—Why?

Sound.—*More strokes. Then the hammer is put down.*

Smith.—C'mere with me. Come over to the door.

Sound.—*Footsteps on wooden floor. They stop.*

Smith.—See that spire?

Stewart.—Yes.

Smith.—That's the church I go to.

Stewart.—What about it?

Smith.—I like it. I'm a God-fearing man. I want to keep on going there.

Stewart.—Well?

Smith.—I don't want anybody telling me I have to pray *his* way.

Stewart.—Who'd think of doing that?

Smith.—It's been done. It's happened often.

Sound.—*Footsteps recrossing slowly to anvil.*

Smith.—Ever hear of state religion?

Stewart.—Yes.

Smith.—(*After a pause*) It's bad.

Sound.—*Hammering resumes.*

Smith.—I don't like it. Don't think we should have it.

Stewart.—We haven't got it.

Smith.—Nothing in that thing you read me guarantees we won't get it.

Sound.—*Hammering continues, crossing under.*

26

Music.—*Brief transitional passage "A," fading for*

Farmer.—You say this here Constitution gives us order and authority, hm?

Stewart.—Yes.

Farmer.—But we *had* order and authority under King George before the Revolution. Shecks, the *Romans* had order and authority under *Nero*, too . . . only the wrong kind, and too much of it.

Stewart.—Yes, but you can surely trust . . .

Farmer.—Trust the men who wrote that Constitution? Sure thing, sure thing, neighbor. But *they* won't always be around.

Stewart.—Well, you don't seem to understand. This is our *own* authority. Now if—

Farmer.—Fact it's our own don't make no difference. Constitution's fine far as it goes, but the time to talk authority is after you put it down in black and white that we're all free men, and *then* we'll give you all the authority you need to *keep* us that-away—and what's more, we'll back it up with guns. That fair enough?

Stewart.—The way you talk, you'd think . . .

Farmer.—The way I talk I think it all depends who's handing out authority . . . whether it's to keep men slaves or keep men free.

Music.—*"B."*

Woman.—(*Irritated*) Didn't think it was *necessary?* The *English* thought it was necessary 100 years ago! They've got a Bill of Rights! Where's *ours?*

Stewart.—Maybe they'll get around to that. Maybe they'll amend the Constitution later.

Widow.—How do *we* know they will?

Stewart.—Well, maybe they're planning . . .

Widow.—I don't like this "maybe" business. When my husband Robert got killed at Trenton there was no maybe about it. He got killed. He knew what he was fighting for, and he was glad to die for it. Now the fightin's over, I want to see it!

27

Music.—"*C.*"

Sound.—*Fade in effect of scraping brick, rapping it with trowel, etc.*

Bricklayer.—(*Grousing*) I dunno, Jerry. Sometimes I wonder whether you use your head for anything else'n to keep your ears apart.

Jerry.—I got my opinion, and I stick to it. Constitution looks good to me. I don't think it needs no adding to.

Bricklayer.—Hand me a brick there.

Jerry.—It's a foundation, that's what it is.

Bricklayer.—*Sure*, it's a foundation. That's just what I'm talking about. But do you build a foundation and then go away and not build the *house?* Do you clear the woods and then let the ground go barren?

Jerry.—Oh, piffle.

Bricklayer.—(*Outraged*) What a way to argue! Piffle? Is that all you can say? Hand me that brick there!

Music.—*Cue* 1.

Lawyer.—What's the hurry? Give them time. It's not an easy job to get a new country running right.

Merchant.—That's just the point! It's a lot easier to get it running wrong.

Music.—"*D.*"

Clerk.—Rights, rights, *rights*, man! Can't you get that through your head? Why shouldn't rights be written into the Constitution just as much as rules on how to meet and when to vote and how much a senator should get paid?

Music.—*Final of the sequence, holding under.*

Stewart.—Not they alone. Not only little men like them, whose names escape us, whose names will never be recalled . . . the men who left their bloody footprints in the snows of Pennsylvania and buried their comrades in the clearing back of the clump of evergreens: the little men who took it . . . gave it . . . stuck for the duration; saw it through. Not they alone are doubters, wondering and grumbling. No; there are big names, too—the names now bandied on the tongue but later to be illustrious, later to be sainted: Tom Jefferson, George Mason, Jimmy Madison, Pat Henry. Take Jefferson, for instance. Know what he says?

JEFFERSON.—A Bill of Rights is what the people are entitled to against any government on earth.

STEWART.—Take Patrick Henry!

HENRY.—I cannot give my oath to support this Constitution without a Bill of Rights!

STEWART.—Take Mason, the wealthy planter of Virginia, who'd rather plant a seed of liberty than 20,000 acres of tobacco:

MASON.—A government to be lasting must be founded in the confidence and affections of the people. Without a Bill of Rights this government will end either in monarchy or a tyrannical aristocracy. This Constitution has been formed without the knowledge of the people, and it is not proper to say to them, "Take this or nothing."

STEWART.—Well, then! The Constitution is in peril . . . this document so handsomely engrossed in Philadelphia. There are doubts about it—and suspicions. Will the states approve of it—approve by ratifying? Will they throw it out, or will they ratify, providing certain changes will be made?

MUSIC.—*Base of a pyramid, with a suggestion of suspense. It holds behind the following and builds progressively, as later indicated.*

STEWART.—The writing's fresh, still fresh upon the parchment. The text is clean, the ink is bold, the meaning clear. Only the *worth* of the Constitution is uncertain. All the points, the articles, the regulations are well put—but will they be well taken?

The states decide. Not one man, two men, three men, but the states united. They decide.

What says South Carolina?

SOUTH CAROLINA.—We ratify. But offer four amendments.

MUSIC.—*Short statement of motif 1 progressing with each repetition.*

STEWART.—What says Massachusetts, where she stands?

MASSACHUSETTS.—We ratify. But offer nine amendments.

MUSIC.—*Motif 2.*

STEWART.—New Hampshire, you?

NEW HAMPSHIRE.—We ratify. But propose 12 amendments.

MUSIC.—*Motif* 3.

STEWART.—Rhode Island?

RHODE ISLAND.—We ratify. But 21 amendments, please.

MUSIC.—*Motif* 4.

STEWART.—North Carolina?

NORTH CAROLINA.—Twenty-six amendments, and a Declaration of Men's Rights!

MUSIC.—*Motif* 5.

STEWART.—Virginia?

VIRGINIA.—We ratify, but we're suggesting 29 amendments, and a Bill of Rights!

STEWART.—New York?

NEW YORK.—Thirty-three amendments in full faith and credit—and we ratify!

MUSIC.—*Peak of the pyramid . . . triumphant.*

STEWART.—Now Congress may begin . . . may call itself "First Congress" . . . may go to work . . . may tackle the new job of running a democracy.

But it has one thing to remember:

A promise is a promise. The people have been promised changes; promised amendments; promised that their freedoms would be written down in black and white for all to see, for all to know, for all to live and prosper by.

It will take time. No quorum, to begin with. Bad roads. New York City hard to get to. There is some indifference, too. So the days go by. No quorum. Month of March goes by. No quorum. (*Pause*)

Well . . . patience. (*Pause*) Good things grow slowly. Good things don't come running when you whistle for them. Good things are always fought for; worked for; grown. The acorn to the oak is not an overnight procedure. God himself took several days to make the earth.

But one day they begin. They sit down in a drafty hall in New York City, and they go to work. At first they're busy with a hundred other things, but Madison keeps after them. He's a stickler for a Bill of Rights. Madison remembers what the people want.

Sound.—*Hammering, sawing, well off-mike . . . it keeps on at intervals beneath the following:*

Stewart.—By this time, carpenters are making changes in Federal Hall . . . adding more room. Place has to be enlarged. Government's growing. The representatives, all 55 of them, work through the noise. They are making some additions of their own.

They're working on the Bill of Rights.

Music.—*In suddenly . . . dark, restless agitato . . . andante (theme "X") . . . it holds under*

Narrator.—Do you think 55 representatives of the American people sat in a hall in New York City, in a drafty hall, and made up articles of freedom? Do you think the congressmen from 13 states made up those freedoms out of their own heads? Debated there, deliberated there, without assistance? All by themselves? From their own experience?

Oh, no. They had much help.

From many nameless and unknown. From dust in quiet places. From broken bones deep in the earth, deep in forgotten earth, mixed with the empty clay. From bleeding mouths; burned flesh; cropped ears; from numberless and nameless agonies.

The delegates from dungeons, they were there.

Martyr.—(*Low, a whisper*) I said that men were born equal, that is all I said.

Narrator.—The delegates from ashes at the bottoms of the stakes, they were there.

Second.—The king did not approve.

Narrator.—The gallows delegates, whose corpses lifted gently in the breeze; they, too.

Several.—(*Whispering in chorus . . . barely audible*) We, too, we too.

NARRATOR.—The exiled wanderers; the Christians killed for being Christians; Jews for being Jews; the Quakers hanged in Boston town; they made a quorum also.

SEVERAL.—Present. We are present.

NARRATOR.—The murdered men. The lopped-off hands. The shattered limbs. The red welts where the whip lash bit into the back.

Must you know what they said?

Must you know how they argued?

Must you be told the evidence, the silent testimony of the wraiths? Must it be told verbatim? Listen, then.

SOUND.—*Music stops . . . A woman's scream.*

NARRATOR.—That was an argument for an amendment.

SOUND.—*A man's groan.*

NARRATOR.—That was a speech in favor of an article of freedom.

SOUND.—*A shriek.*

NARRATOR.—That prayed the passage of a Bill of Rights. (*Music resumes*)

How much of all this must be told to be *believed?* Must it be drawn on diagrams? X marks the spot where decency was last observed? The dotted line shows how the victim staggered? The arrow points to blood?

The headsman, he was there in Federal Hall. The man who turned the rachets on the rack, he sat in the assembly, too.

Nero was there. Caligula, King Phillip, Torquemada, Cotton Mather, all the tyrants and the martyrs who had gone before, sat quietly, unseen, among the representatives, read from their memoirs expert testimonies, found their way into the records and between the lines.

All the long and bloody history of fanaticism: murder in the name of God; torture in the name of love: crucifixion in the name of safety to the crown.

VOICE.—(*Low*) My God, my God, why hast thou forsaken me?

NARRATOR.—He too sat in the Congress . . . the mild man with the scars in his hands and feet where the spikes went through. He was a consultant in the business at hand. Had He not died because the rulers of a realm denied free speech? Was

He not nailed up on a cross between two thieves because His preachments were considered treason? He, the Son of God, was He not executed over an issue of the Rights of Man?

Make no mistake about it—He was there . . . He sat beside James Madison and Elbridge Gerry and John Page in Federal Hall. Unseen He was, but voting.

The men of Congress were collaborated with. They added up the gains and losses, and the brave words spoken and the brave songs sung; they weighed the drawn and quartered flesh, they took into account the hemlock and the crucifix, the faggot and garotte. (*Pause*)

And then they framed amendments to the Constitution.

Out of the agonies, out of the crisscrossed scars of all the human race, they made a Bill of Rights for their own people —for a new, a willful, and a hopeful nation—made a Bill of Rights to stand against the enemies within: connivers, fakers, those who lust for power, those who make of their authority an insolence. The Congress of the 13 states, instructed by the people of the 13 states, threw up a bulwark, wrote a hope, and made a sign for their posterity against the bigots, the fanatics, bullies, lynchers, race haters, the cruel men, the spiteful men, the sneaking men, the pessimists, the men who give up fights that have been just begun.

The Congress wrote a 10-part epic of amendments.

MUSIC.—*Theme "X" up but does not finish . . . it brightens, flares up, broadens lyrically, and comes down to back the following:*

STRONG VOICE.—Amendment One. Congress shall make no law regarding an establishment of religion or prohibiting the free exercise thereof; or abridging the freedom of speech or of the press or of the right of the people peaceably to assemble and to petition the government for a redress of grievances.

LEGISLATOR.—Mr. Speaker!

SPEAKER.—Mr. Redburn.

ARNOLD

These are the voices of Virginians. They are debating Congress amendments on this mild December afternoon, this

LEGISLATOR (*Off-mike, speaking from the floor*)

I move this amendment be accepted in its present form, without qualification. It seems

fifteenth of December, 1791 . . . debating in the State Assembly in the capitol at Richmond.

Only one more state is needed now to ratify. Just one more state, and the amendments become law.

The victory is close at hand.

Virginia likes these articles. Virginia, the home of Washington and Jefferson, of Madison and Mason . . . Virginia has fought to win these rights for many years . . . has waited for this day.

This is December 15, 1791.

Virginia will ratify the Bill of Rights today, and freedom will take hold, take root, begin to burgeon in the rich earth of America.

Today! Today! The fifteenth of December!

to me that such an article well deserves to rank ahead of any of the other proposed amendments, being at once the most basic and the most comprehensive of all which Congress has seen proper to recommend to the country.

GREY

Mr. Speaker.

SPEAKER

Mr. Grey.

GREY

I support the motion of Mr. Redburn, especially in acknowledgement of the fact that this amendment is in letter and spirit, substantially what has already been assured to the citizens of our own commonwealth by the prior enactments of our assembly. Furthermore, Virginia may take a modest and (*fading*) a reasonable pride in that so many of her own sons have contributed greatly to the bill before us; also, in the fact that its conception and its execution was . . .

MUSIC.—*Theme "X" up to a happy conclusion. This is ratification. This is the long struggle ended.*

STEWART.—*Now!* Now the people of the states breathe easier! It's down in black and white: a contract. It's a deal between the future and themselves.

Americans don't make a promise lightly, or take it that way, either. A promise made by honest men to other honest men is like a handclasp and a vow; meant to be understood, meant to be remembered.

Ah, look about the country now; suspicion thaws like frost beneath the frank diplomacy of spring. The people read the new amendments slowly, pleasurefully, as they'd read a

34

letter from a son just set up in a business, who'd written home to tell how he was making good:

SOUND.—*Dinner sounds . . . crockery, cutlery.*

FARMER.—(*As though he'd discovered something*) Aha! Aha! Now that's more like it! That's more like it!

WIFE.—You've got your sleeve in the soup, dear. (*Pause*) What's more like what?

FARMER.—Listen to this: "Amendment Two. A well-regulated militia, being necessary to the security of a free state, the right of the people to keep and bear arms shall not be infringed."

WIFE.—That mean you can keep your gun?

FARMER.—That means if somebody gets into office and turns sour on the people that put him there, why he can't vex us with a standing army the way George did before the war. If we people of the states got arms, nobody's gonna order us to do things the majority of the country ain't voted for. Not without a fight.

WIFE.—Better eat that soup 'fore it gets cold. Shouldn't read when you eat, anyways. Put down the paper.

FARMER.—(*Grudgingly*) Oh, all right. (*Paper sound*)

WIFE.—(*After quite a pause*) That's a good law, ain't it, Jasper?

FARMER.—Yep.

SOUND.—*Cross-fade dinner sounds to sounds of the anvil, as in the previous sequence . . . the hammer stops.*

SMITH.—Go on. Go on reading it. Why'd you stop?

FRIEND.—Well, how can you hear me when you're hammering?

SMITH.—Concentration. Go on.

FRIEND.—(*Sighs*) "Amendment Three: No soldiers shall in time of peace be quartered in any house without the consent of the owner, nor in time of war, but in a manner to be prescribed by law."

SMITH.—Gives me elbow grease, just hearing things like that. Makes the old hammer handle easier.

35

FRIEND.—The way this sounds, you'd think we was expectin' another war. "In a time of war," this says. I thought we just been all through that a little while ago.

SMITH.—(*Laughing*) Why, the more these amendments make us free, the more they'll be hated by those who don't *want* freedom, because it spoils their game. Think nobody's going to try to break us up *because* we're united and agreed? Some people are just *ornery* that way. Wouldn't surprise *me* none if we had t'fight more wars.

FRIEND.—You mean to say we're maybe gonna have to fight all over again to keep our independence? Hope it don't get to be a habit.

SMITH.—I hope it *does*. It's a pretty good habit to get into— fighting for your rights. There's always somebody waitin' for a chance to steal valuables . . . and if *freedom* ain't a valuable, I don't know what is.

FRIEND.—(*Dryly*) Yeah. Well.

SMITH.—Go on. Read some more.

FRIEND.—"Amendment Four: The rights of the people to be secure in their persons, homes, papers, and effects, against unreasonable searches and seizures . . . (*Hammering resumes*) shall not be . . . (*stops momentarily in despair, then shouts to top the hammering*) . . . shall not be violated, and no warrants shall issue but upon probable cause, supported by oath and affirmation, and particularly describing the place to be searched and the persons or things to be seized . . .

"Amendment Five: (*Fading together with the hammering as trowel sounds come in*) No person shall be held to answer for a capital or otherwise infamous crime . . . " (*Etc. . . . etc.*)

MUSIC.—*Fades in.*

WIDOW.—(*In full*) I brought you these, Robert. I grew them myself, inside the house. Don't smell much, but they're awful pretty.

Everything's going on about the same at the house. (*Pause*) Except I'm a year older since I was here last.

Guess you don't have to worry any more, Robert. Guess you can rest in peace now. Looks like it's going to be all right. They didn't trick you . . . Looks all right, Robert.

36

STEWART.—The voices of Americans . . . in Maryland, in Pennsylvania, Connecticut, the Carolinas, Georgia . . . up and down the little seaboard nation, the voices of Americans together now, together in a new way, in a strange new way . . . a way that men have never lived together in before . . . (*Sneak in song*) Proud men, unsuspicious, trusting men, their fighting over and their living just begun, their building and their working and their singing just now getting started.

SINGER.—"Here strangers from a thousand shores,
　　　　Compelled by tyranny to roam,
　　　　Shall find, amid abundant stores,
　　　　A nobler and a happier home.

　　　　"Rejoice, Columbia's sons, rejoice!
　　　　To tyrants never bend the knee
　　　　But join with heart and soul and voice
　　　　For Jefferson and Liberty.

　　　　　　(*Fading behind following speech*)
　　　　"Here Art shall lift her laurel'd head,
　　　　Wealth, Industry, and Peace divine.
　　　　And where dark, pathless forests spread,
　　　　Rich fields and lofty cities shine."
　　　　　　(*Hum the chorus under*)

STEWART.—Shall this song make good its promise? Does this folk tune hold a truth? Shall strangers from a thousand shores be compelled by tyrannies to roam? Shall they find here, amidst abundant stores, a nobler and a happier home?

One hundred fifty years from this beginning, how much of what is said and what is sung and what is written down shall still be good?

This parchment of the Bill of Rights, with the word "Resolved" so plainly written on it, how long will it endure? Is it a passport to a greater day? Will future generations read it, sanction it, and pass it on? Will children's children live by it and work by it and profit by it?

Look it over. Look it over. It is new. The parchment shines. The text is easy reading. The words are not yet worn with trial and experience. The writing's fresh, the meaning's clear; the parchment gleams in the December sunlight like a burnished shield upraised against oppression:

37

JUDICIAL VOICE.—"Amendment Five: No person shall be held to answer for a capital or otherwise infamous crime, unless on a presentment or indictment of a grand jury, nor shall any person be subject for the same offense to be twice put in jeopardy of life and limb; nor shall be compelled in any criminal case to be a witness against himself, nor be deprived of life, liberty or property, without due process of law; nor shall private property be taken for public use, without just compensation." (*Starting to fade as soon as Stewart comes in*)

STEWART

Let's go ahead 150 years from now. Let's rush headlong unstopping, down the corridors of time. Let's go ahead to 1941. The writing dims, the parchment cracks and curls up at the edges . . . The splotch of time is on it.

And now it's in a case in Washington, D.C. It's in a case behind a pane of special glass protecting it from light.

(*Change of tone; confidential*) You see that tourist bending over it? He's trying hard to make the writing out. He's tracing the rights of persons accused of crime . . .

JUDICIAL VOICE

"Amendment Six: In all criminal prosecutions, the accused shall enjoy the right to a speedy and public trial by an impartial jury of the state and district wherein the crime shall have been committed, which district shall have been previously ascertained by law, and to be informed of the nature and cause of the accusation; To be confronted with the witnesses against him; to have compulsory progress for obtaining witnesses in his favor. And to have the assistance of counsel for his defense . . . "

TOURIST.—"Amendment Six: In all criminal prosecutions, the accused shall enjoy the right to a speedy and public trial by an impartial jury of the State and district wherein the crime shall have been committed, which district shall have been previously ascertained by law, and to be informed of the nature and cause of the accusation; to be confronted with the witnesses against him; to have compulsory process for obtaining witnesses in his favor, and to have the assistance of counsel for his defense."

STEWART.—Where does this tourist come from? Maybe from a place undreamed of when the Bill of Rights was born . . . a land as far away from Federal Hall as Europe . . . California. What lies tonight between that place and here? Four dozen states without a yard of fenced-in border. A hundred thirty million people. People working, people resting up to work some more, people working in a mighty unison to prosecute a war.

Let's move along. Let's move among them, let's hear them living lives and thinking thoughts and giving off opinions. Let's see now what they have to say, 150 winters after Richmond. Let's see what happens to the Bill of Rights through their 33 administrations, 77 Congresses, and half a dozen wars.

Has anybody anything to say about the status of men's rights December 15, 1941?

PRISONER.—I have something to say, if you don't mind. I'm in jail tonight, but I'm joining in your celebration and cheering as hard as anybody else.

STEWART.—Er . . . if you don't mind my asking . . . ?

PRISONER.—A trumped-up charge. The old routine in this city. But I'm getting out on bail tomorrow, and when I'm finally tried it'll be by a jury and in public, and none of this Gestapo stuff. Not that they wouldn't try it if they could, but that little 450-word matter you're celebrating tonight stops them short of that.

STEWART.—What did they chuck you in the clink *for?* I mean, what charge?

PRISONER.—Making a speech for the Fusion Party against the mayor. First we hired a hall, but they took away our permit —said the building was unsafe under an old fire ordinance. So then we went down to Garrison Square, where no permit is required to speak in public, and within 10 minutes we were on our way to the police station, on charges of blocking traffic, disturbing the peace, and inciting to riot.

STEWART.—Fine thing.

PRISONER.—Yeah, but listen . . . we'll beat that guy. He's scared of us. He's scared the people will find out the truth . . . and with good reason . . . because when they do, he's finished. That's why he doesn't want us to be heard.

STEWART.—Uhuh.

39

PRISONER: It's only the crooks and the frightened little big shots who need to shut up their opponents. That may work all right in some other countries, but not here.

STEWART.—Well, how are you going to beat him?

PRISONER.—There are such things as rights on our side, and not even the mayor's machine is powerful enough to stop us. We'll fight that fight on every front—carry it to the highest courts if necessary—and we'll win!

STEWART.—(*Change of tone; to listener*) Is this the talk of servile men, of tamed and gutless and obedient men? Is this the kind of talk you hear from slaves and witless followers? Not quite. No, not exactly. This is what they *meant* in Federal Hall, and what they voted for 150 years ago today in Richmond. Those 10 amendments are not dusty statutes loafing in retirement. They are a pep talk to the fighters and a fortress to the undefended; they double-bar the front door of the home against the culprit and the searching party; stand the drinks for everybody toasting freedom. Of all things, they are not a set of legal clauses, dry and dusty . . . although Amendment Seven makes us wonder.

DRY VOICE.—"Amendment Seven: In suits at common law, where the value in controversy shall exceed twenty dollars, the right of trial shall be preserved, and no fact tried by a jury shall be otherwise re-examined in any court of the United States, than according to the rules of the common law."

STEWART.—Except for that, not like a lawyer's brief at all, but mostly like a kind of free-style ode to liberty, 10 verses long.

SECOND VOICE.—"Amendment Eight: Excessive bail shall not be required, nor excessive fines imposed, nor cruel and unusual punishments inflicted."

STEWART.—Treason in most of Europe, a sentiment like that today.

THIRD VOICE.—"Amendment Nine: The enumeration in the Constitution of certain rights shall not be construed to deny or disparage others retained by the people."

STEWART.—Notice how many times it says "the people"? Can it be because it *means* the people? . . . Yes, it can.

40

FOURTH VOICE.—"Amendment Ten: The powers not delegated to the United States by the Constitution, nor prohibited by it to the states, are reserved to the states respectively, or to the people."

STEWART.—Powers reserved to the people in a Bill of Rights? How the mighty and the proud have fallen! Why, King John, who threw a fit when *barons* made him sign the Magna Carta —*barons*, mind you, who were heedless of the common people —John, the tough old monarch, would have died a thousand deaths of apoplexy at the mention of the thought of it! The Pharaohs of old Egypt, masters of the blackest arts of slavery . . . they would have crawled inside a pyramid and shut 147 secret doors behind them in a panic.

MUSIC.—*Theme "Z" in here . . . it backs.*

STEWART.—A promise is a promise.

Has America's been kept? Has it come through peace and war and peace and war untarnished and unbroken? Has it worked, and is it working? For the people, by the people? Is it going anywhere from here?

Are the Rights the right Rights? Are they rolling, do they function, do they click?

Who knows the answer better than the people? Who better can we ask than ask the great custodians themselves, the 100 million keepers of the promise?

We shall ask them. Ask a few of them who stand for many more than few—the high and low among them. Ladies and gentlemen: an office clerk.

CLERK.—Well . . . (*clears throat*) we know what freedom is now. Looked for a while there like a lot of us'd forgot what it really meant and how much we had of it, but the news that kept piling in from the four corners of the earth . . . that reminded us, all right.

STEWART.—Ladies and gentlemen: an editor.

EDITOR.—There have been attacks on the freedom of the press and strangle holds of various sorts, but they've been broken every time; and today a man is free to start a paper, run it as he pleases, differ from the next man all he wants. That would make it seem to me, for one, that our rights have come down undamaged.

41

STEWART.—Ladies and gentlemen: a worshiper.

WOMAN.—I go to the church of my choice. And sometimes when I don't wish to go, I don't go.

STEWART.—Ladies and gentlemen: an auto worker.

WORKER.—We got the right to organize. We got the right to bargain collectively. Those are good rights, and we're proud of them, and we're better workers on account of them.

STEWART.—Ladies and gentlemen: a manufacturer.

MANUFACTURER.—There is nothing in any law which forbids us to forget class differences and work together to strengthen the sinews of our country.

STEWART.—Ladies and gentlemen: an Okie.

OKIE.—I got a right, ef'n I'm hongry an' out of work, which I have been, to go lookin' for work anywhere in my country. The big court says nobody cain't stop me from looking. Dang it, that's my right.

STEWART.—Ladies and gentlemen: A mother.

MOTHER.—I might be afraid to bring a child into the *world*—but not to bring a citizen into the population of the United States.

STEWART.—From men beneath the rocking spars of fishing boats in Gloucester, from the vast tenancy of busy cities, roaring with the million mingled sounds of work, from towns spread thinly through the Appalachians, from the assembly lines, the forges spitting flame, the night shifts in the mines, the great, flat counties of the prairie states, from the grocers and from salesmen and the tugboat pilots and the motor makers —affirmation! Yes! United proudly in a solemn day! Knit more strongly than we were 150 years ago this day!

Can it be *progress*, if our Bill of Rights is stronger *now* than when it was conceived? Is that not what you'd call wearing well? The incubation of invincibility?

Is not our Bill of Rights more cherished now than ever? The blood more zealous to preserve it whole?

Americans shall answer. For they alone, they know the answer. The people of America: from East, from West, from North, from South.

MUSIC.—*Theme "Z" concludes.*

42

An American Crusader*

by ROBERT E. SHERWOOD
From THE FREE COMPANY

ANNOUNCER.—The Columbia Broadcasting System presents The Free Company.

MUSIC.—*Brass choir full . . . strings to back.*

MEREDITH.—"For what avail, the plow or sail,
Or land or life, if freedom fail?"

MUSIC.—*Brass choir . . . strings to back.*

MEREDITH.—This is Burgess Meredith in Hollywood, speaking for The Free Company. Today we hear Franchot Tone and Gail Patrick in a new radio play by Robert E. Sherwood, author of "Abe Lincoln in Illinois" and "There Shall Be No Night." The Free Company is a group of leading writers, actors, and radio workers who have joined together on their own initiative to present a series of dramas illustrating and explaining our basic American liberties. All members contribute their services as a free expression of their faith in American democracy and in the basic civil rights which make that way of living together possible. The list of writers for The Free Company includes some of the most distinguished names in American letters—nine Free Company members have won Pulitzer prize awards.

Today, Robert E. Sherwood's play "An American Crusader" seeks to honor the memory of a man who fought against cruel odds for freedom of speech and for freedom of the press. His name was Elijah Parish Lovejoy. He lived more than a hundred years ago, when our country was in a period of growing uncertainty and fear . . . increasing doubt of the permanence of our institutions. Americans in Lovejoy's time could be heard saying many of the same things that we hear today.

* Copyright 1941 by Robert E. Sherwood.

43

VOICE 1.—People are hollerin' about the need for national unity—but there ain't no such thing.

VOICE 2.—We've got to abolish slavery. There can be no compromise with evil.

VOICE 3.—If we keep on the way we're going . . . we'll be in war —and that'll mean the end of democracy.

VOICE 4.—What this country needs is sound money.

VOICE 5.—This new doctrine of President Monroe's sounds good on paper—but it won't work.

VOICE 6.—The trouble with this country is—we're getting mixed up in the politics of Europe.

BABBLE OF VOICES.—The trouble with this country is . . . The trouble with this country is . . . (*Etc.*)

MUSIC.—*Up and out.*

MEREDITH.—One of the greatest American voices was raised in an expression of faith at the dedication of the Bunker Hill Monument in Boston. It was the voice of Daniel Webster.

WEBSTER.—"If the true spark of religious and civil liberty be kindled, it will burn. Human agency cannot extinguish it. Like the earth's central fire, it may be smothered for a time, the ocean may overwhelm it, mountains may press it down, but its inherent and unconquerable force will heave both the ocean and the land, and at some time or other, in some place or other, the volcano will break out and flame up to heaven."

MEREDITH.—So spoke Daniel Webster, and his words burned into the soul of young Elijah Lovejoy—who had gone from his native Maine to the Theological Seminary in Princeton. The day before his graduation, he is called to the office of Dr. Guthrie, the Dean of the Seminary . . .

DR. GUTHRIE.—Ah, Mr. Lovejoy . . . I'm glad to see you . . . do sit down.

LOVEJOY.—Thank you, sir.

DR. GUTHRIE.—I—I wanted to have a word with you before you leave us. I knew there would be no time in the midst of tomorrow's ceremonies. Of course; like all the others, you'll be glad to be out of this stuffy, scholastic atmosphere.

44

LovEjoy.—I shall never stop being grateful to you, sir . . . for your kindness . . . your understanding . . .

Dr. Guthrie.—(*With a smile in his voice*) I hope you really mean that, Mr. Lovejoy.

LovEjoy.—(*Firmly*) I should not say it if I didn't mean it, Dr. Guthrie.

Dr. Guthrie.—No . . . I'm sure you wouldn't. I've observed that you're one who isn't afraid to speak his mind. I believe you will make a great name for yourself as a minister of the Gospel.

LovEjoy.—Dr. Guthrie . . . I . . . I have a confession to make.

Dr. Guthrie.—I am eager to hear it, Mr. Lovejoy.

LovEjoy.—I am not going to preach the Gospel . . . at least, not from the pulpit.

Dr. Guthrie.—But—tomorrow you will be ordained as a minister. You have been working hard, for years, to reach that goal.

LovEjoy.—I know it. But . . . there is a great battle going on . . . a battle which will decide whether freedom and slavery can continue to exist, side by side, in the same country, in the same world. I want to join in that fight.

Dr. Guthrie.—And how do you propose to fight . . . and where?

LovEjoy.—I have an opportunity to become editor of a newspaper in St. Louis, Missouri. That is where the fight is strongest . . . Do you feel I'm making a mistake?

Dr. Guthrie.—Naturally . . . I'm disappointed. I've been a minister of the Gospel all my life. For the past 30 years, and more, I've been instructing young men like yourself in the word of God . . .

LovEjoy.—And you've taught it well, Dr. Guthrie . . . so well that you've filled me with a desire to preach it . . . not only from the pulpit . . . but in the market place, in the streets, on the farms, and across the great waters. For the word of God is the promise of justice to all men . . . equality for all men . . . freedom for all men . . . by God's will. I know I can say these things in the church to pious people,

45

but I believe I can say them more strongly through the press—the free press—and more people will hear them.

DR. GUTHRIE.—You realize, don't you, that in following this course you will be risking your life. This war you are entering . . . it is a bitter war . . . a war to the death.

LOVEJOY.—I realize that, Dr. Guthrie. But . . . if I am risking my life . . . it could not be in a better cause.

DR. GUTHRIE.—That is no more than the truth, Mr. Lovejoy . . . May God give you strength in the battle that is ahead.

LOVEJOY.—Thank you, sir. (*Music*)

MEREDITH.—Elijah Lovejoy went to St. Louis. He gained recognition as a young man of high promise . . . of courage . . . of intelligence . . . and integrity . . . and there was no one more appreciative of his good qualities than a certain young lady named Celia Ann French. (*Music*)

CLERK.—Good morning, sir. Good morning, miss. What can I do for you?

LOVEJOY.—We . . . want a marriage license.

CLERK.—Well, well . . . I suspected as much . . . seeing as this is the marriage license bureau. Your name?

LOVEJOY.—Elijah Parish Lovejoy.

CLERK.—Date and place of birth.

LOVEJOY.—Albion, Maine, November 9, 1802.

CLERK.—And the lovely bride?

CELIA.—Celia Ann French . . . born right here in St. Louis.

CLERK.—You don't have to say when. Your occupation, Mr. Lovejoy?

LOVEJOY.—I'm a minister of the Gospel—and I'm editor of the *St. Louis Observer*.

CLERK.—Oh. I thought I'd seen your name somewhere. Been having a little mite of trouble, haven't you, Mr. Lovejoy?

LOVEJOY.—Yes—a little.

CLERK.—Well . . . I guess everybody is, these days. Here's your license. I wish you both luck.

46

LOVEJOY.—Thank you.

CELIA.—Thank you.

SOUND.—*Door closes.*

CELIA.—Elijah . . .

LOVEJOY.—Yes, Celia.

CELIA.—What did he mean—trouble?

LOVEJOY.—(*Lightly*) Nothing in particular . . . All newspaper editors have trouble. That's part of our job.

CELIA.—Elijah, don't lie to me. You *have* been having a particular kind of trouble . . . for my father says . . .

LOVEJOY.—(*Laughs*) I know what your father says. He thinks I'm one of those crazy reformers who had better keep their ideas to themselves . . .

CELIA.—And maybe he's right, Elijah, if you endanger yourself by expressing those ideas.

LOVEJOY.—(*Very earnestly*) Celia, listen to me, your father is a dear old gentleman who has a fine big plantation and many slaves. (*Tenderly*) And a beautiful daughter . . . And ideas and beliefs that are not the same as mine . . . He doesn't think anything should ever be changed . . .

CELIA.—And you think . . . everything should be changed?

LOVEJOY.—Not quite everything. But many things. Oh, I don't say your father isn't justified in his convictions, but he doesn't realize that times have changed, that what was true in his time is no longer true in yours and mine. He helped shape and build his world as you and I must shape and build *our* world, Celia . . .

CELIA.—But if it means danger and trouble . . .

LOVEJOY.—There is always danger and trouble when men battle for truth . . . Celia, darling, I love you more than anything in the world except one thing . . .

CELIA.—And that one thing?

LOVEJOY.—Man's liberty . . .

CELIA.—But that's only an idea.

47

LOVEJOY.—Not an idea, Celia. An ideal. An ideal for which men have fought and died since the beginning of history; it's a never-ending battle, for in every generation there is a new threat, a new menace, and it must be met . . . no matter what the cost.

CELIA.—(*Slowly*) I . . . I'm not sure that I understand . . . and I'm a little frightened, too. Oh, Elijah, promise me . . . promise me you'll keep out of danger . . . for my sake . . .

LOVEJOY.—I promise to love you . . . for as long as I shall live . . . be content with that, darling, and right now let's forget everything except the one important fact that we're going to be married.

MUSIC.—*Wedding bells . . . wheezy organ playing the wedding march.*

VOICES.—Good luck to you both. God bless you. I wish you all happiness, both of you.

VOICES OF LOVEJOY AND CELIA.—Thank you . . . thank you. (*Wedding music stops suddenly*)

A MAN.—(*Belligerently*) Stop that music, Mr. Lovejoy.

LOVEJOY.—Yes. What is it?

MAN.—My friends and I here are sorry to break in on your wedding party.

LOVEJOY.—What do you want?

MAN.—We want to wish you happiness, Mrs. Lovejoy.

CELIA.—Why—that's very kind of you.

MAN.—And we want to wish you a peaceful life.

ANOTHER MAN.—Yes . . . Mrs. Lovejoy . . . it'd be too bad to see a nice young bride like you turned all of a sudden into a widow.

LOVEJOY.—What do you mean? Get out of here . . .

MAN.—Now don't start any trouble, Mr. Lovejoy.

ANOTHER MAN.—We mean business.

CELIA.—Let us hear what they have to say, Elijah.

MAN.—That's good advice, Mrs. Lovejoy.

48

LOVEJOY.—Come on, then. What is it you want?

MAN.—We want to tell you that we don't like your newspaper Mr. Lovejoy. And we're telling you . . . in the interests of your health . . . you'd better get out of St. Louis . . . and get out fast. Move to some district where your opinions are more popular.

LOVEJOY.—Have I been printing anything that is false?

MAN.—We're not here to argue that point.

OTHER MAN.—We're telling you to git.

MAN.—We've given you fair warning, Mr. Lovejoy. That's all.

SOUND.—*Retreating footsteps . . . door.*

CELIA.—Oh, Elijah . . .

LOVEJOY.—I'm sorry this happened, darling . . .

CELIA.—Is . . . is this what you meant by . . . by the battle for truth?

LOVEJOY.—Yes, Celia, this is what I meant . . . !

MUSIC.—*Melodramatic.*

MEREDITH.—The country was becoming more seriously divided; one group was shouting, "Slavery must be abolished" . . . and the other group was shouting, "Each state must mind its own business and leave its neighbors alone." Lovejoy was forced to move his printing press across the Mississippi River to Alton, in Illinois. There he and his bride set up housekeeping anew . . . and he started another newspaper.

LOVEJOY.—Look, darling—the first issue of *The Alton Observer.* Aren't you proud? Here . . . read it.

CELIA.—(*Reads*) "Slavery is a crime against God and man. It is poison in the very life blood of human society." But, Elijah, you're saying the very same things that you said in St. Louis.

LOVEJOY.—Of course, I am. They're the *truth* . . .

CELIA.—But people don't want to hear the truth.

LOVEJOY.—Nonsense, Celia. Illinois is a free territory. It was the truth that set us free. It will keep us free . . .

49

CELIA.—It's all very well to fight for the truth, but not at the risk of losing your home and happiness and . . . maybe your own life.

LOVEJOY.—I wish I could make you understand, Celia, that the truth for which I fight is worth all that risk . . . Once you see that . . . once you understand, then you'll not fear any longer . . .

CELIA.—In a way, I understand. But it all seems so hopeless . . . you're only one man against a city . . . What good does it do to raise your voice . . . Who listens?

LOVEJOY.—When I was still in college I heard Daniel Webster . . . I've never forgotten his words . . . They burned into my very soul . . . He said, "If the true spark of religious and civil liberty be kindled, it will burn . . . Like the earth's central fire, it may be smothered for a time . . . the ocean may overwhelm it, mountains may press it down, but its inherent and unconquerable force will heave both the ocean and the land, and at some time or other, in some place or other, the volcano will break out and flame up to heaven . . . " (*Pause*) Those were his words, Celia. I don't want to have it said they were spoken in vain . . . That's why, even though I'm the only voice in all this territory, it must be raised to keep alive that spark of liberty.

CELIA.—But the risk, Elijah!

ELIJAH.—I'm going to fight them to the end, Celia. I'm determined. (*Music*)

A MAN NAMED LEM.—Look at this, Jake.

JAKE.—What is it?

LEM.—The new newspaper. Read that.

JAKE.—"Slavery is a crime against God and man—"

HANK.—Who's printing that disgraceful, inflammatory . . .

LEM.—It's that young preacher that just moved in . . . name of Lovejoy.

JAKE.—Why . . . say . . . he's the feller they threw out of St. Louis.

LEM.—Sure he is.

BILL.—He ain't got no right to print such stuff. That's war talk.

HANK.—That's precisely what it is. Trying to stir up trouble. As Judge Douglas says . . . he's trying to inflame the passions of men.

JAKE.—If you let people like that go on talking . . . and worse . . . *printing* their opinions . . . why . . . we'll end up in war—civil war.

LEM.—Well . . . since we seem to be agreed . . . the next question is . . . what do we do about it?

MUSIC.—*Ominous.*

CELIA.—Elijah, look, there's a mob of men coming up to the house. Men with torches . . . Oh, darling . . . I'm frightened.

ELIJAH.—There's no need to be, Celia.

CELIA.—What are you going to do?

ELIJAH.—I'll go out and talk to them.

CELIA.—Elijah.

LOVEJOY.—I'll be all right, my dear.

SOUND.—*Door opens and closes.*

LOVEJOY.—Well, gentlemen.

LEM.—We just came to call, Mr. Lovejoy . . . to tell you you won't be needing to go down to your newspaper office tomorrow. Because a newspaper ain't any good without a printing press. And your printing press ain't there any longer.

LOVEJOY.—You've stolen it . . . ?

BILL.—Oh, no . . . we ain't stole it. We just heaved it into the Mississippi River.

JAKE.—You'll find it in the mud, Mr. Lovejoy. (*Laughter*)

HANK.—And it won't be in very good condition for printing any more of your firebrand war talk.

LEM.—Have you got anything to say to us before we bid you good night, Mr. Lovejoy?

LOVEJOY.—Just this . . . The Mississippi is a mighty big river . . . but it isn't big enough to drown all the words that are going to be spoken before this issue is settled. Good night.

SOUND.—*Door opens and closes.*

CELIA.—You're all right, Elijah?

LOVEJOY.—(*Wearily*) Yes, dear. I'm all right—but I'm silenced. You should have listened to your father, Celia, and never married a crazy reformer with no gift for anything but antagonizing people.

CELIA.—Will we have to leave Alton now?

LOVEJOY.—I don't know. I don't know where we could go or what we could do. We haven't any money left.

CELIA.—Does it matter, darling?

LOVEJOY.—Yes. It does matter. We can't let them beat us this way.

CELIA.—But what's the use of going on, Elijah. Yours is only one voice crying in the wilderness.

LOVEJOY.—All the more reason why my voice must be heard, then. For surely somewhere, somehow, somebody will hear! (*Almost to himself*) " . . . the ocean may overwhelm it, mountains may press it down, but its inherent and conquerable force will heave both the ocean and the land."

MUSIC.—*Up and fade under.*

MEREDITH.—And there were some who heard. Even in Alton. Some who knew Lovejoy was fighting the good fight. And some, too, who knew that he could not fight alone.

DR. MACKLIN.—Mr. Lovejoy . . .

LOVEJOY.—Yes, Dr. Macklin?

MACKLIN.—I believe you know these gentlemen, Mr. Struther, Mr. Callahan, Mr. Enton.

LOVEJOY.—How do you do, gentlemen?

MACKLIN.—We've come to you on behalf of certain citizens of this town . . . citizens who have come here from all parts of the country, North and South. We represent all sorts of political opinion. But we are united in our devotion to the principles of our construction, including freedom of speech.

LOVEJOY.—(*Bitterly*) I am glad to hear those principles have not been forgotten by all Americans.

STRUTHER.—I am from South Carolina, sir. My family have been slaveholders for generations. But . . . I believe in the words of Voltaire. "I disagree with what you say—but I will defend with my life your right to say it."

LOVEJOY.—Thank you, Mr. Struther. You're a real patriot.

MACKLIN.—As we all are . . . I hope. We have taken up a collection sufficient to buy you a new printing press, Mr. Lovejoy. We wish you to resume publication of your paper.

CALLAHAN.—And if that scalawag mob comes around again . . . call on us . . . and we'll help you fight 'em.

LOVEJOY.—Are you ready to fight for freedom, Mr. Callahan?

CALLAHAN.—I am an American of Irish descent, Mr. Lovejoy. Need I say more?

LOVEJOY.—No . . . you need say no more . . . any of you . . . gentlemen . . . This is an act of great generosity . . . and great faith. I shall do my best to justify it. (*Music*)

MEREDITH.—So once more the *Alton Observer* printed its attacks on slavery . . . intolerance. But the mob was strong, and again the crusader Lovejoy was attacked and his press destroyed. He set up a new press in a warehouse in Alton. An armed guard of volunteers assembled to defend the building. On the night of November 7, 1837 . . .

CELIA.—I suppose it's useless for me to ask you . . . beg you . . . please don't go down there . . .

LOVEJOY.—I have to go, my darling. I've got to get the paper out.

CELIA.—They'll try to kill you. You know that.

LOVEJOY.—Yes, I know it. But I also know that they can't kill what I stand for. All over the country, the friends of freedom are interested in this fight. We can't surrender now.

CELIA.—What satisfaction will there be for me . . . knowing that your ideals live on . . . while you . . .

LOVEJOY.—Darling. There are certain things that are more important than our own lives . . . the things which make our own lives worth living. I'm no hero. I'm just an ordinary person who believes that there's no point in being an American . . . there's no point in being a man . . . unless this country lives in freedom.

If I denied that belief, I wouldn't deserve to be your husband . . . and you know it . . . and there'd be no happiness and no peace for either of us. (*Pause*)

CELIA.—All right, Elijah. If that is what you believe, then I can't change you. But I'm going with you.

LOVEJOY.—No, Celia, you can't.

CELIA.—Wherever you are, I want to be.

LOVEJOY.—I've made this fight against your wishes . . . against your better judgment. Yet you've stood by me . . . no matter what you felt or what you believed. But I can't let you do this . . . the risk is too great, Celia . . .

CELIA.—No matter what the risk . . . no matter what I believe. A wife's place is by her husband's side. And that's where I intend to be . . . I'm going with you, Elijah, and nothing you can say can stop me . . . I'm determined, too, Elijah.

MUSIC.—*At first inspiring, then ominous.*

JAKE.—We've got to stop Lovejoy from printin' that filthy sheet of his. And we've got to stop him now!

VOICES OF MEN.—That's right . . . We can't let him get away with his radical talk any longer . . . Destroy his press . . . Burn his warehouse . . .

JAKE.—(*Silencing men*) But they've got the warehouse guarded

LEM.—Yeh, but there's only 5 or 6 men at most. We got 30.

BILL.—And we got guns, and we can shoot 'em.

LEM.—We got to get that Lovejoy. We've got to prove to him that guns are what talk. They talk louder than words.

HANK.—Guns that'll stop *his* words.

VOICES OF MEN.—Yeh, that's it . . . Kill Lovejoy. That's the only way to stop him . . . Kill him . . .

JAKE.—Then you're with me, men!

BILL.—Sure, we're with you . . .

LEM.—His war talk is being heard all over the country. He's gettin' people inflamed and excited everywhere . . .

HANK.—There's only one way . . . kill him and silence him once and for all . . .

JAKE.—All right. Do we do it now . . . or do we let Lovejoy go on printing his rotten paper?

BILL.—We do it now . . .

CHORUS OF VOICES.—Now . . . now . . . now . . . (*Music*)

LOVEJOY.—Here's the headline, Joe. "Free Men, Arise! Death to Slavery." And the subhead, "Our Forefathers Fought for Liberty, So Must We."

JOE.—If we print that, Mr. Lovejoy, this press will go into the river like all the others.

LOVEJOY.—Just the same . . . go ahead and print it. Where's the rest of that copy. Celia?

CELIA.—Right here, darling.

LOVEJOY.—Thanks. Ready, Joe?

JOE.—Sure, Mr. Lovejoy.

LOVEJOY.—Well, let's get on with the editorial . . . (*Dictating*) The Declaration of Independence said to . . .

SOUND.—*Voices of men . . . marching feet . . . few scattered shots . . .*

CELIA.—Elijah! Listen . . .

CALLAHAN.—(*Coming in*) Lovejoy . . . Lovejoy . . .

LOVEJOY.—Yes, Callahan?

CALLAHAN.—There's a mob of men out there . . . they're armed, and they're surrounding the warehouse. What shall we do?

JAKE.—(*Shouting off-mike*) Lovejoy . . . we want you to come out of there. We're holdin' our fire for one minute . . . and if you ain't out by then . . . we're comin' in!

55

CELIA.—Elijah!

LOVEJOY.—Oh, Celia, I should never have let you come. Now I've no choice but to yield.

CELIA.—Not because of me?

LOVEJOY.—Yes, Celia . . . those men out there are desperate men. They have guns, and they mean to use them . . . your life is in danger here. And it's all my fault. I won't let you take the risk. I'll go out . . .

CELIA.—Elijah, once you said you were not afraid to die. Then neither am I!

LOVEJOY.—Celia!

CELIA.—If those men out there are the ones you're fighting . . . if mob violence and hate and destruction are your enemies, then I understand at last what you've been fighting for. Elijah, go on with your editorial . . .

JAKE.—(*Off-mike*) I'm givin' you a last warnin', Lovejoy! You'd better come out . . .

CELIA.—You're not going out, Elijah. You're going to show them that not even guns can stop you!

LOVEJOY.—Celia! You're wonderful. Callahan, return their fire . . . but shoot over their heads. We don't want any bloodshed . . .

CALLAHAN.—(*Fading*) I'll tell the boys!

SOUND.—*Firing starts . . . and hold under scene.*

LOVEJOY.—All right, Joe . . . once again . . . The Declaration of Independence said to the people of this nation and to the whole world, "We hold these truths to be self-evident, that all men are created equal, that they are endowed by their creator with certain inalienable rights . . . that among these are life, liberty and the pursuit of happiness . . . "

MUSIC.—*Threading through increased sound.*

LEM.—(*Over sound and music*) They can't shoot. They haven't hit one of us yet . . .

JAKE.—(*Further off-mike*) Hey, you and Gus and Bill and Lem . . . get around there behind the warehouse, and heave in some of them flaming fagots. Set it afire . . .

LEM.—You bet, Jake . . .

JAKE.—The rest of you . . . keep shooting . . .

MUSIC.—*Up slightly . . . out.*

LOVEJOY.—. . . and in the final words of that Declaration . . . "with a firm reliance in the protection of Divine Providence we mutually pledge to each other our lives . . . our fortunes . . . and our sacred honor" . . . and where's "our sacred honor" today if we submit meekly and timorously to evil . . . where . . . ?

SOUND.—*Crash of wood and glass and shots.*

CALLAHAN.—(*Coming in*) Lovejoy . . . Macklin's been killed . . .

CELIA.—Oh . . . oh, how terrible . . .

LOVEJOY.—What about the others . . . ?

CALLAHAN.—Two are hurt bad . . . we can't hold out much longer . . .

LOVEJOY.—There's no use going on, Joe.

CELIA.—There's every use in going on. That's just what that mob out there want . . . to stop you. But they can't . . . !

LOVEJOY.—But I'm thinking of you, Celia . . . of your safety . . .

CELIA.—Please . . . please, if you love me, Elijah . . . go on . . . !

LOVEJOY.—You're very brave. All right, Callahan . . . keep firing . . .

CALLAHAN.—All right . . .

LOVEJOY.—Let's go on, Joe . . . ready?

JOE.—Yes . . .

LOVEJOY.—In the preamble to the Constitution of the United States, it is written, "We, the people of the United States, in order to form a more perfect Union, establish justice, insure domestic . . . "

SOUND.—*Crash of building . . . crackle of flames.*

CALLAHAN.—(*Coming in*) It's no use, Lovejoy. We can't go on. They've fired the warehouse.

LOVEJOY.—What!

CALLAHAN.—There's nothing to do but surrender. It's suicide to go on, suicide for all of us.

CELIA.—We've got to fight on.

LOVEJOY.—No, Celia, Callahan's right. There's no use going on . . . they've trapped us. I've got to go out to them . . .

CELIA.—No . . . no! You mustn't.

LOVEJOY.—It's my fight. And I've got to finish it my way . . .

JAKE.—(*Off-mike*) Come on out, Lovejoy. We got you licked. Come on out!

CELIA.—(*Breaking*) Oh, Elijah . . . Elijah . . . I can't bear to have it end this way . . .

JAKE.—(*Off-mike*) Are you comin' out Lovejoy, or ain't you?

LOVEJOY.—You've been very brave, Celia.

CELIA.—It's you that made me brave, darling . . . without you . . . (*Her voice breaks*)

LOVEJOY.—And we've got to go on being brave . . . both of us . . . the fight didn't begin with us . . . it won't end with us.

JAKE.—(*Off-mike*) This is your last chance.

LOVEJOY.—I'm going out to them, darling . . .

CELIA.—Yes . . .

LOVEJOY.—I love you . . . I love you so very much . . . remember that . . . always.

SOUND.—*Footsteps moving slowly off-mike . . . door opening. Voices of men . . . quieting down.*

JAKE.—About time, Lovejoy!

LOVEJOY.—There's no use continuing your useless murder gentlemen. You've succeeded . . .

JAKE.—You bet we've succeeded . . . and that ain't all . . .

58

LOVEJOY.—Once again you've succeeded in suppressing freedom of speech.

JAKE.—We thought you'd learned your lesson, Lovejoy. But I guess you're slow to learn . . .

BILL.—(*Further off-mike*) Takes bullets to learn him.

JAKE.—You've gone on and on with your war talk. And now we're going to put an end to it once and for all.

LOVEJOY.—You believe that guns can suppress freedom of speech.

BILL.—We can certainly suppress you! And that's all we're after.

LOVEJOY.—If you believe that in suppressing me, you suppress the beliefs and the ideals for which I stand . . . then I pity your ignorance . . .

HANK.—What's the use of letting him go on talking . . . why don't we get it over with?

LOVEJOY.—Let me say this one thing . . . if preaching the gospel of freedom is a crime in this land, then I'm a criminal, and I'm ready to die. Other men have died for that same gospel . . . and God willing, there will be men who come after me . . . willing to die!

LEM.—Let him have it, Jake.

JAKE.—As long as you're ready, Mr. Lovejoy . . .

LOVEJOY.—I'm ready.

JAKE.—So be it!

SOUND.—*Shot . . . followed by more shots . . . a scream from Celia. Music.*

MEREDITH.—So dies the Reverend Elijah Parish Lovejoy. And in the halls of Congress, an ex-President of the United States, John Quincy Adams, rises to speak . . .

ADAMS.—"Elijah Lovejoy is the first American martyr to the freedom of the press and the freedom of the slave."

MEREDITH.—And the years went by, and the gospel of freedom that Lovejoy had preached was spread through the land. And in that same state of Illinois, an obscure small-town lawyer arose and spoke. And he was a future President of the

59

United States, and his name was Abraham Lincoln, and he fired the imaginations of men with these immortal words . . . (*Music*)

LINCOLN.—"If we could first know where we are, and whither we are tending, we could better judge what to do, and how to do it. A policy has been initiated with the avowed object and confident promise of putting an end to slavery agitation. Under that policy, that agitation has not only not ceased, but has constantly augmented. In my opinion, it will not cease until a crisis shall have been reached and passed. 'A house divided against itself cannot stand.' I believe this government cannot endure permanently, half slave and half free." (*Music*)

MEREDITH.—Today the freedom Lovejoy fought for—freedom of the press—is increasingly denied as the enemies of all human liberty march to victory after victory. Under the threat of a world half slave, half free, let us renew again the pledge of Lincoln. Let us once more highly resolve that government of the people, by the people, and for the people shall not perish from the earth.

MUSIC.—*Theme up . . . and through.*

MEREDITH.—Franchot Tone and Gail Patrick, as well as the author of today's drama, joined The Free Company, under chairmanship of James Boyd, contributing their services without payment. Leith Stevens composed and conducted an original music score. The Free Company producer is Charles Vanda. To the Screen Actors' Guild, to the American Federation of Radio Artists, and to the Columbia network, all who have combined to make this series possible . . . to all these people, with a word of especial thanks to Irving Reis, who directed . . . this is Burgess Meredith, offering the sincere thanks of The Free Company.

MUSIC.—*Out. Theme . . . full . . . down to back.*

ANNOUNCER.—Next week at this time, The Free Company presents "One More Free Man," by James Boyd, with an all-star cast including Alan Dinehart, Betty Field, Elia Kazan, Margo, Dorothy McGuire, Lionel Stander, and will be directed by Norman Corwin, with music by Bernard Herrmann. This is the Columbia Broadcasting System.

Raymond Gram Swing

May 6, 1941

SWING.—. . . The event of today, not in terms of day-to-day
developments, but in terms of a deeper meaning, was the
entry of Haile Selassie into Addis Ababa. He entered his
capital formally, in the company of the British Commander,
General Cunningham, and was received by his people with
enthusiasm. No one with a sense of underlying propriety will
fail to be stirred by the scene of this dignified and once
abandoned ruler, coming again into his own. He does so as a
by-product of a great war, but he ends his own cycle of
tragedy with a fitting recompense. I must take you back
to the day of June 30, 1936, when Haile Selassie appeared
before the Assembly of the League of Nations, like a figure
out of the Old Testament, addressing men who were sheep-
ishly ashamed to look him in the face. That was the day
when the Italian journalists greeted him with a rowdy outburst of yelling and cat calls, and they had to be cleared
from the gallery by the stupefied Geneva police. Haile
Selassie then made a speech which rang with some of the
soulful poetry of the Old Testament. "I pray to Almighty
God," he began, "that he shall spare the nations the terrible
sufferings that have been inflicted on my people, and of which
the chiefs who accompany me here have been the horrified
witnesses." "It is my duty," he continued, "to inform the
governments assembled at Geneva—responsible as they are
for the lives of men, women and children—of the deadly
peril which threatens them, by describing to them the fate
which has been suffered by Ethiopia." Here was the knell of
prophecy, if ever it has been heard in modern times. And the
so-called Lion of Judah, humbled and wracked by the fate
of his people, was not addressing the League as an outsider.
His country was a full member, and it had been attacked by
another member, Italy, and the League, it is well to repeat
over and over again, did not see the need of bold loyalty
to its principles. "The Ethiopian government," said Haile

61

Selassie that day, "never expected any other government to shed its soldiers' blood to defend the covenant when its own personal interests were not at stake. The Ethiopian warriors asked only means to defend themselves. On many occasions I have asked for financial assistance for the purchase of arms. That assistance has been constantly refused me." Then he raised his final plea. "The problem submitted to the Assembly," he cried, "is much wider today than merely the question of settling the Italian aggression. It is collective security, it is the very existence of the League. It is the confidence which each state places in international treaties. In other words, international morality is at stake. Apart from the Kingdom of the Lord, there is not on this earth any nation that is superior to any other. Should it happen that a strong government finds that it may with impunity destroy a small people, then the hour strikes for the weak people to appeal to the League to give its judgment. God and history will remember your judgment. The aggressor has confronted the states with an accomplished fact. Are they to set up the terrible precedent of bowing before force? What measure do you intend to take? Representatives of the world, I have come to Geneva to discharge in your midst the most painful duty for the head of a state. What reply have I to take back to my people?" The reply was silence; he could take away only the memory of embarrassed statesmen, of averted looks, of supercilious smiles. Ethiopia was not aided or saved. But the wheel of judgment has made a turning. Today there is no League of Nations and today Haile Selassie reentered Addis Ababa. Today France is prostrate, Spain is starving, Holland, Norway, the Balkans are under the heel of the conquerer, and the city ports and industrial centers of Britain are scenes of desolation and grief. The world has chosen to learn the hard way. But Haile Selassie is back, as a witness that the wheel of judgment does make a turning. He is back through the aid that came too late, too expensively late, but it came.

Fred Allen

SOUND.—*Siren and bell.*

MUSIC.—*(Orchestra). Fanfare.*

LARRY.—The Texaco Star Theatre!

MUSIC.—*(Orchestra). Theme up and fade.*

LARRY.—The more than 45,000 Texaco dealers from coast to coast welcome you to an hour of mirth and melody!

MUSIC.—*(Trombone and saxophones). Laughter effect.*

LARRY.—Meet our star comedian—Fred Allen!

MUSIC.—*Orchestra and choir.*

LARRY.—Kenny Baker! Portland Hoffa!

MUSIC.—*(Orchestra). Strong effect.*

LARRY.—Our guest—Mr. Otto Hottendorf—the bologna stuffer!

MUSIC.—*Orchestra.*

LARRY.—The Martin Singers! And Al Goodman's orchestra!

MUSIC.—*(Orchestra) Tympani glissando and flourish.*

LARRY.—It's Texaco time!

MUSIC.—*(Chorus and orchestra). "Manhattan."*

JIMMY.—And now, ladies and gentlemen. Presenting that happy harlequin. That jovial jester. That unique U-know! And here he is—B-r-r! Fred Allen—in person. (*Applause*)

ALLEN.—Thank you. Thank you. And good evening, ladies and gentlemen. Say, what's the matter, Jimmy? What is that shivering? Gosh, you're shaking like the end girl in a Minsky chorus . . .

JIMMY.—It's this cold weather, Fred. It's got me. B-r-r-r!

ALLEN.—Oh! You're one of those thin-blooded guys from California. Why, you'd get frostbitten just playing north in a bridge game.

JIMMY.—Well, at least out in California I can stay warm. B-r-r!

ALLEN.—There are ways of keeping warm here, James.

JIMMY.—I know. I've been sitting on a radiator for so long from certain angles I look like a grilled steak. I'll show you.

ALLEN.—Never mind. Never mind.

KENNY.—Hi, fellas. What's the chatter?

ALLEN.—It's Jimmy's teeth, Kenny. He says he's cold.

KENNY.—He can't take it, eh?

ALLEN.—Say! You're from California, too, Kenny. How is it this cold spell hasn't gotten you down.

KENNY.—I carry a portable smudge pot.

ALLEN.—That keeps you warm, does it?

KENNY.—All but my feet. You know . . . my legs are so blue I don't have to wear stockings.

ALLEN.—Fine. Now, if you'll pick up your blue feet and patter away, Kenny, we'll . . .

KENNY.—Gee, F. A. Why doesn't this show move out to California?

ALLEN.—We're not softies, Kenny. If Gypsy Rose Lee can carry on in this cold, so can we.

KENNY.—But California is great, F. A. Look at this picture Dennis Day just sent me. It's from Palm Springs.

ALLEN.—Which is Dennis?

KENNY.—That's Dennis. Eating the hamburger.

ALLEN.—Ah! What moronic ecstasy. Dennis, lying there in a bathing suit, surrounded by a flock of beautiful Paramount bathing beauties. Girls' arms around him . . . blondes. brunettes . . .

KENNY.—Mmmmmmm!

64

ALLEN.—That gets you, eh?

KENNY.—Boy, I can just taste that hamburger!

ALLEN.—And while Kenny's mind munches his meat mirage, we turn to the Latest News of the Week!

MUSIC.—*Fanfare.*

ALLEN.—The Texaco News presents Your Highlight in the World of News.

MUSIC.—(*Up . . . fade*).

ALLEN.—Des Moines, Iowa. Speakers at the annual convention of the American College Publicity Association stress need for more and better publicity on colleges. Publicity men say cooperation of press and other media is required to let public know what colleges and universities are doing. Texaco News questions little-known educators, old grads, and students to get opinions on college publicity requirements. Professor Eustace Nob, of Wahoo U, advocates roadside advertising for colleges.

JOHN.—Yes, indeed. I'm experimenting, putting little signs along the road with continuity. Like those shaving cream ads.

ALLEN.—What sort of signs, Professor?

JOHN.—Verses like this. "In later life. If you want knowledge. Enroll today. At Wahoo College."

ALLEN.—How far would that stretch?

JOHN.—That verse ran a mile. But I can write jingles for any distance.

ALLEN.—What is the longest jingle you've written so far?

JOHN.—I wrote one last week. It went clean across the state of California.

ALLEN.—How did it go?

JOHN.—I'll recite it for you. "A boy named Rowe. Was pretty slow. A million things. He didn't know. He went to college. Bound to learn. Today he heads. A big concern. Our school can do. The same for you. Usted pablo que sabe tortillas. Buenos noches, señoritas, señores. Si, si, enchillados Wahoo.

65

ALLEN.—What is that finish?

JOHN.—Spanish.

ALLEN.—Spanish in California?

JOHN.—My last three signs ran over into Mexico.

ALLEN.—That explains everything except why you're here. And thank you, Professor Eustace Nob. An ex college girl who was the first student to try stunt advertising for her college . . . You are a graduate of what school, Mrs. Feg?

MIN.—Fumfet Normal, Class of ought 11.

ALLEN.—Fumfet Normal. The hillbilly Bryn Mawr. I often wondered how it became so popular.

MIN.—Why, I put it on the map.

ALLEN.—How did you do it?

MIN.—Goldfish.

ALLEN.—Goldfish?

MIN.—Yes. I started swallowing goldfish.

ALLEN.—Oh, you were the one. I remember now.

MIN.—For 2 years I kept my alma mater in the public eye. I swallowed 20 goldfish a day.

ALLEN.—Phenomenal.

MIN.—I still hold the record . . . 14,600 goldfish. That was 20 years ago.

ALLEN.—And today . . .

MIN.—Today I am happily married and have two lovely sons.

ALLEN.—Congratulations. After swallowing 14,600 goldfish, you felt no ill effects in later life, Mrs. Feg?

MIN.—None whatever. Both of my boys have fins for arms. But that, of course, is no concern of mine.

ALLEN.—Are your sons doing well?

MIN.—Exceptionally. This is their third year with Mr. Ripley.

ALLEN.—Proving that advertising certainly pays. And thank you, Mrs. Nanky Feg. If colleges resort to advertising methods used successfully by moving picture theatres, freak attractions, and burlesque shows, we may soon see barkers outside of colleges. If a barker one day appears in front of Harvard College, he may sound something like this.

Sound.—*Tom-toms beat.*

Ted.—Now gather in a little closer, men. I wanna tell yer what's goin' on in the inside. This is Harvard College, men. The oldest university in the country today. You don't wanno go through life a dope, men. Step inside, Harvard'll smart yer up, men.

Chas.—(*Off*) What's in there, mister?

Ted.—I'll tell yer, son. Enroll and here's whatcha get on the inside. Harvard's got a grand galaxy of multiple intellect. Forty-five red hot professors. I'm showin' yer one of the professors at this free exhibit. Come out, prof.

John.—Yes, Red.

Ted.—Throw 'em some Latin, prof.

John.—De gustibus non est disputandum.

Ted.—That's Latin, folks, and you get it on the inside. Okay. Yer say Latin ain't enough. Yer want more for your tuition. Okay, men. Yer like to sing. On the inside Harvard's got a glee club. Let's go, boys.

Boys.—(*Sing*) Sweet Adeline, my Adeline,
        At night, dear heart . . .

Ted.—Break it up, boys.

Allen.—(*Off*) What happens if you don't like singing?

Ted.—Gentlemen says he don't like singin'. Okay, men. If yer don't want to sing, Harvard gives yer sports. Rattle off them sports, coach.

John.—Baseball, football, basketball, rowing, track, lacrosse, and hockey.

Ted.—And you can play 'em all on the inside. All right. Yer say Latin, singin', and sports ain't enough, men? Here's what I'm gonna do. Spend four years in Harvard and I'm givin' away free! Absolutely free! A beautiful sheepskin diploma. Here's the sheep, men.

CHAS.—Baaa! Baaa!

TED.—Enroll today, and in 1944 any part of this sheep is yours. Move in a little closer men. Let that lady by. Now, before I close this big free exhibit, I'm gonna show yer what Harvard guarantees. This boy here is finishin' his Harvard course this year. Show the folks what you was like four years ago, son.

CHAS.—*Lip business.*

TED.—There y'are, men. That's how this boy was when he came to Harvard. After four years of higher education, show 'em how you are today, son.

CHAS.—*Repeats business much higher.*

TED.—There y' are, folks.

MIN.—(*Off*) He's doin' the same thing.

TED.—Right, lady. But he's doin' it two tones higher. That's what higher education can do. And you can get it on the inside at Harvard. Right this way. Step right in . . .

MUSIC.—*Up to finish.*

ALLEN.—And now the Martins sing "Take Your Girlie to the Movies."

THE MARTINS.—*"Take Your Girlie to the Movies"* . . . . *Applause.* (*First commercial*)

MUSIC.—(*Orchestra*) *Song medley. Applause.*

ALLEN.—Maestro Goodman and his jolly jivers have just played a medley . . . "Three Blind Mice," "Mary Had a Little Lamb," and "In and Out the Window." How come, Mr. Goodman, you're playing three numbers in one this evening?

AL.—Can I help it, the music is stuck together.

ALLEN.—How could your music get stuck together?

AL.—Before the program is starting, I, Goodman, am rehearsing.

ALLEN.—Yes.

AL.—In one hand I am conducting with a baton.

ALLEN.—So?

68

Al.—In the other hand I am holding in my mouth a lollypop.

Allen.—I know, but . . .

Al.—Suddenly, I, Goodman, am getting excited. Why, who knows.

Allen.—What happened?

Al.—My hands I am mistaking. The baton I am sticking in my mouth. With the lollypop I am conducting.

Allen.—I see. When you went to turn over the music your hand was sticky.

Al.—That is my story. And I am stuck with it. Also the music.

Allen.—Fine.

Al.—If you want to lick the music it is peppermint. Delicious!

Allen.—No, thanks. I'm on a diet. Two weeks ago I gained three pounds listening to one chorus of "Sweet Sue." Oh . . . hello, Portland.

Portland.—Hello!

Allen.—You look a little tired tonight.

Portland.—Yes. I haven't been home for two days. I went to see your new picture.

Allen.—And it took you two days?

Portland.—Yes. I got in line Monday afternoon at the corner of 41st Street and Seventh Avenue.

Allen.—But what took you two days?

Portland.—Well, part of the line got pushed into a bus station on 41st Street.

Allen.—No kidding.

Portland.—The next thing I knew I was in Hackensack.

Allen.—Did you finally see "Love Thy Neighbor"?

Portland.—Yes.

Allen.—Well?

Portland.—Jack got the girl at the finish, didn't he?

ALLEN.—Yes. I got paid.

PORTLAND.—Wasn't Jack on the screen longer than you?

ALLEN.—No. It only seemed longer.

PORTLAND.—Do you think you and Jack will ever make another picture?

ALLEN.—Not me. I was hoodwinked into this one.

PORTLAND.—How?

ALLEN.—When I got out to Hollywood, I found out the producer of the picture was Benny's uncle. The director was Benny's cousin. The cameraman was Benny's nephew. When the picture was finished I was informed that Benny's father, who is a tailor, was going to cut the picture. Now, before I get mad, what about our guest?

PORTLAND.—Well, this is Christmas night, and everybody is sitting around the house stuffed with turkey.

ALLEN.—So?

PORTLAND.—So I thought people might like to hear about another kind of stuffing for a change.

ALLEN.—And our guest tonight?

PORTLAND.—He's a sausage stuffer.

ALLEN.—A sausage stuffer?

PORTLAND.—Yes. Mr. Allen, meet Mr. Otto Hottendorf.

ALLEN.—Good evening, Mr. Hottendorf.

MR. HOTTENDORF.—Good evening, Fred.

ALLEN.—You, Mr. Hottendorf, are a bona fide bologna stuffer?

MR. HOTTENDORF.—That's right, Fred. I've been stuffing bologna for 13 years.

ALLEN.—And where do you practice this unique art?

MR. HOTTENDORF.—I work at the Armour Company plant in Jersey City.

ALLEN.—Tell me, Mr. Hottendorf, how did you come to make wurst taxidermy your life's work?

70

MR. HOTTENDORF.—Well, when I was a young fellow I got a job at Armour's. I started off helping around the grinding machines—and finally worked my way up to bologna stuffing.

ALLEN.—Well, after 13 years, I imagine you stuff a beautiful bologna, Mr. Hottendorf. Does the Armour Plant turn out other elongated knickknacks besides bologna?

MR. HOTTENDORF.—Yes. Armour's makes about 5,000 meat items, Fred, including a lot of by-products.

ALLEN.—By-products?

MR. HOTTENDORF.—Yes. They make buttons, combs, violin strings, and many other things.

ALLEN.—You never get confused at your plant, do you, Mr. Hottendorf?

MR. HOTTENDORF.—How do you mean, Fred?

ALLEN.—Well, it would be pretty embarrassing if your deliveries got mixed up. And a delicatessen received 10 pounds of fiddle strings and Heifetz found himself playing "Humoresque" on a salami.

MR. HOTTENDORF.—We don't make mistakes at Armour's, Fred.

ALLEN.—Oh, excuse me. Do you work on these other items, Mr. Hottendorf, or do you just concentrate on bologna?

MR. HOTTENDORF.—Well, there are dozens of different kinds of bologna, Fred. I work on all of them.

ALLEN.—Why, I thought no matter how you sliced bologna, it was still bologna.

MR. HOTTENDORF.—You're wrong, Fred. There's ham bologna, beef bologna, salami, liverwurst, bratwurst, knockwurst, sackwurst, pinkelwurst, gettwurst, brockwurst . . .

ALLEN.—Hold on . . . You win, Mr. Hottendorf. I gave up around pinkelwurst. Tell me, how do you go about conjuring up one of your bloated snacks? What happens before you personally do your stuff?

MR. HOTTENDORF.—Well, before the meat reaches me it's prepared for stuffing by a special grinding and cutting man. It has to be chopped very fine.

71

ALLEN.—Bologna, then, is really just hamburger with a girdle on, isn't it? Tell me, what happens next?

MR. HOTTENDORF.—Well, when the meat comes to me I load up my machine with it.

ALLEN.—Yes.

MR. HOTTENDORF.—I take a casing . . . that's the skin a bologna comes in . . . and put it over a nozzle on top of the machine.

ALLEN.—Yes.

MR. HOTTENDORF.—Then I turn on the machine, and the air pressure forces the meat up into the casing.

ALLEN.—Until it has a skin full. It's practically all machine work, isn't it?

MR. HOTTENDORF.—Not all, Fred. I still have to tie the bologna in the right places. A machine couldn't do it.

ALLEN.—Just how do you apply those delicatessen tourniquets Mr. Hottendorf? Do you employ a sailor's knot or a running noose, or do you use the Dr. Kildare ligature?

MR. HOTTENDORF.—No. There is no fancy work. I just pull the cord good and tight around the bologna.

ALLEN.—I see. As an authority on bologna, Mr. Hottendorf, I wish you would answer one question for me.

MR. HOTTENDORF.—What is that, Fred?

ALLEN.—Is it possible to slice a bologna so as to get the slices evenly between two hunks of bread?

MR. HOTTENDORF.—How do you mean?

ALLEN.—Well, whenever I slice a bologna I either put two slices in side by side, which leaves a gap of bread in the middle, or I cram in three or four slices of bologna and get a lump in the middle of the sandwich that springs my jaw. What can I do about this gastronomic predicament, Mr. Hottendorf?

MR. HOTTENDORF.—The perfect solution for you is the new square bolognas.

ALLEN.—Square bolognas?

72

MR. HOTTENDORF.—Yes. For the past three or four years Armour's has been making a square bologna which fits evenly between two slices of bread.

ALLEN.—A square bologna. Destiny has finally shaped the bologna's end. Well, this has been a very interesting glimpse into the art of meat upholstery and all of its side lines, Mr. Hottendorf. And I think we both deserve to be complimented on a remarkable radio accomplishment.

MR. HOTTENDORF.—What's that, Fred?

ALLEN.—Well, we've been talking about bologna stuffing for 7 minutes, and neither of us once has tried to make a joke out of "that's a lot of bologna." That is a new high in broadcasting restraint, Mr. Hottendorf, and I congratulate you.

MR. HOTTENDORF.—Thanks, Fred.

ALLEN.—Now before you go, I think we ought to sum up the facts on your wurst-inflating career. You say you've been stuffing bolognas for 13 years.

MR. HOTTENDORF.—That's right.

ALLEN.—And about how many bolognas do you stuff a day?

MR. HOTTENDORF.—I average about 14,000 pounds a day. That's around 3,200 bolognas.

ALLEN.—At about a foot and a half each. You stuff 4,800 feet of bologna a day . . . times about 300 working days in a year, times 13 years . . . (*mumbles*) Why, Mr. Hottendorf, do you realize, in your lifetime you have stuffed approximately 18,720,000 feet of bologna.

MR. HOTTENDORF.—That sure is a lotta bologna, Fred.

ALLEN.—Now there you go. You've spoiled our record, Mr. Hottendorf. I guess you just couldn't hold out. But thanks for trying.

MR. HOTTENDORF.—Good night, Fred.

ALLEN.—Thank you, and good night, Mr. Otto Hottendorf. (*Billboard*)

ALLEN.—And now, the Martins. Their song . . . "The Toy Trumpet."

73

MUSIC.—(MARTINS *and orchestra*). *"Toy Trumpet." Applause.*
  (*Second commercial*)

MUSIC.—(*Orchestra*). *"Amapola." Applause.*

ALLEN.—That was "Amapola," played by Al Goodman and his
  "I've Got to Pass Your Horse to Get to My Horse" orchestra. And now, ladies and gentlemen—Oh, hello, Portland.

PORTLAND.—Hello.

ALLEN.—Well, as the schoolteacher said to the little boy who
  spelled snow with an "E," what's snew?

PORTLAND.—This is no place for jokes, Mr. Allen.

ALLEN.—Do you know of a better place for jokes? This is supposed to be a comedy program, isn't it?

PORTLAND.—Yes. But jokes are old-fashioned. Comedy programs today all go in for romance.

ALLEN.—What romance?

PORTLAND.—Well, on Bob Hope's program he's always in love.

ALLEN.—But Bob Hope is a much younger man, Portland.

PORTLAND.—Yes, but you're prettier.

ALLEN.—You don't need your job that badly, do you?

PORTLAND.—And look at Mr. Benny. He's always taking girls
  out.

ALLEN.—Benny with the light brown toupee? The only thing
  Benny ever takes out on a moonlit night is his upper plate.
  What gave you this romance idea, anyway?

PORTLAND.—Well, tomorrow is the first day of spring.

ALLEN.—Again with spring. That's all we've talked about
  tonight. Spring.

PORTLAND.—Yes, but you haven't had any romance.

ALLEN.—But how can you inject romance into a program like
  ours?

PORTLAND.—If somebody would take out a girl we'd have something romantic to talk about.

74

ALLEN.—Do you know of a girl under seventy who would be seen with anyone on this program?

PORTLAND.—I know just the girl.

ALLEN.—Who?

PORTLAND.—Olive Fagelson.

ALLEN.—Olive Fagelson?

PORTLAND.—She'd be crazy about you. She's nearsighted.

ALLEN.—Look, Portland. My scamp days are over. The last girl I took out left town and became a nurse with the Confederate army.

PORTLAND.—How about Mr. Goodman?

ALLEN.—Mr. Goodman?

AL.—Somebody is calling Goodman?

ALLEN.—Yes.

AL.—Then . . . out is popping Goodman . . . like a jerk in the box.

ALLEN.—Jerk in the box is right.

PORTLAND.—Mr. Goodman, would you like to meet a lovely girl? Olive Fagelson.

AL.—No. But positively no! And this I am saying in all reluctance.

PORTLAND.—But why?

AL.—This I can explain briefly in two words.

ALLEN.—What two words?

AL.—Mrs. Goodman.

ALLEN.—You see, Portland. Romance on this program is a dud.

PORTLAND.—But how about Kenny Baker?

ALLEN.—You can't get Kenny to go out with a girl. He thinks billing and cooing is a dance team. Kenny blushes when he passes the Y.W.C.A.

PORTLAND.—Maybe we can talk Kenny into it.

75

ALLEN.—That "we" is singular, Portland. You can talk Kenny into it.

KENNY.—(*Off*) Spring! Spring! Glorious spring! Open the window. And hear the birds sing. Tweet! Tweet! (*On-mike*) Hi, kids.

ALLEN.—Yes, Kenny. There is no season like spring, is there?

KENNY.—Oh, boy!

ALLEN.—The birds twittering.

KENNY.—Yeah.

ALLEN.—The soft, balmy breezes.

KENNY.—Yeah.

ALLEN.—Does something to a man, eh, Kenny?

KENNY.—(*With a sigh*) I know just what you mean, F.A.

ALLEN.—Yes?

KENNY.—Makes you want to get out the old kite and fly the tail off of it!

ALLEN.—(*Sotto*) I told you, Portland. Kenny doesn't even know what romance is.

PORTLAND.—Kenny.

KENNY.—Yes, Porty.

PORTLAND.—Have you ever thought about girls?

KENNY.—Girls? You mean those skinny things that wear dresses and open-toed shoes?

PORTLAND.—Yes.

KENNY.—Yeah. I think about them a lot.

PORTLAND.—What do you think about them?

KENNY.—Don't their toes ever get cold?

ALLEN.—Look, Kenny. You're not *afraid* of girls, are you?

KENNY.—Not unless they're bigger than I am.

ALLEN.—Oh, it's no use.

76

PORTLAND.—Why don't you try talking to a girl, Kenny. You might like it.

KENNY.—I talked to a girl a whole hour yesterday. And I didn't like it.

ALLEN.—Who was the girl?

KENNY.—The cashier at the Paramount Theatre . . . a redhead.

ALLEN.—Why didn't you like it?

KENNY.—I still had to pay to get in.

ALLEN.—But that was a business discussion, a battle of wits.

PORTLAND.—Yes, Kenny, I want you to meet a girl socially.

KENNY.—What for?

ALLEN.—Portland wants you to take out an Olive Fagelson.

KENNY.—What's an Olive Fagelson?

ALLEN.—A girl. She's the girl you're to make a date with.

KENNY.—What's a date?

PORTLAND.—Well, for instance, you buy two tickets for the movies.

KENNY.—Yes.

PORTLAND.—And you take Olive along.

KENNY.—I can't buy her a ticket for the movies. I don't even know her.

ALLEN.—What difference does that make?

KENNY.—She might not pay me back.

PORTLAND.—Here's Olive's number, Kenny. Just try talking to her.

ALLEN.—I'll dial the number for you, Kenny.

SOUND.—*Telephone dial.*

KENNY.—(*Over dial*) But, F.A. . . . I'm liable to get involved.

ALLEN.—(*Over dial*) Don't be such a 'fraidy cat. (*Dial out*)

KENNY.—Something tells me I'm being talked into this.

77

ALLEN.—Here's the phone. They're ringing.

KENNY.—Gosh, F.A., I don't . . .

ALLEN.—Go ahead. Answer the phone.

KENNY.—(*In telephone*) Hello? (*To Allen*) What's her name?

ALLEN.—Fagelson. Olive Fagelson.

KENNY.—Oh, yes. Hello. Is this the residence of Olive Fagelson? What? My name is Kenny Baker. Yes, I'm working, sure! I make around $15 a week. Sure, I plan on settling down.

ALLEN.—Kenny, what kind of talk is that? You just met the girl.

KENNY.—(*To Allen*) This is her father.

ALLEN.—Oh! That's different.

KENNY.—(*In telephone*) Hello . . . What was that? I should say not!

PORTLAND.—What's the matter, Kenny?

KENNY.—(*To Portland*) He says I'll have to bring her home at 11 o'clock.

PORTLAND.—Tell him you will.

KENNY.—(*To Portland*) How can I? *I* gotta be home by 10 myself.

ALLEN.—Look! Ask for Olive, and let's get this romance over with.

KENNY.—(*In telephone*) Hello. Who is this? Oh, you're Olive's mother? I'm Kenny Baker, Mrs. Fagelson. What? Yeah, $15 a week. For Fred Allen. Sure, he pays me every week . . . he's rich. Wait, I'll ask him. (*To Allen*) Mr. Allen!

ALLEN.—What, Kenny?

KENNY.—(*To Allen*) What are *you* doing tomorrow night?

ALLEN.—Never mind. Portland, what kind of people are these Fagelsons!

KENNY.—(*In phone*) Hello, Olive? Well, this is Kenny Baker. Portland asked me to . . . What? Fifteen dollars a week.

PORTLAND.—Tell Olive you want to take her to dinner.

KENNY.—(*To Portland*) But I don't want to take her to dinner. Wait a minute . . . (*in telephone*) What was that, Olive? Oh, I said I didn't want to take you to dinner.

ALLEN.—Kenny! That's no way to talk.

KENNY.—(*To Allen*) It's too late, F.A. She says she'll come anyway. She'll meet me at Lindy's.

ALLEN.—Tell her it's okay.

KENNY.—(*In telephone*) Olive . . . Mr. Allen says it's okay for Lindy's. Hold the wire a minute. (*To Allen*) Mr. Allen.

ALLEN.—Yes?

KENNY.—(*To Allen*) How much is dinner at Lindy's?

ALLEN.—For two. About three dollars.

KENNY.—Three dollars! Good-by, Olive. (*Hangs up*)

ALLEN.—Kenny, you hung up.

KENNY.—You bet! Three dollars is too much money just to stuff an olive.

ALLEN.—You see, Portland. Romance is out. It's no use. Spring or no spring, it's pretty clear that no girl will ever take Kenny away from us.

KENNY.—Yeah, I'm hard to get.

SOUND.—*Telephone rings.*

KENNY.—I'll answer it.

SOUND.—*Up telephone.*

KENNY.—(*In telephone*) Hello? No. Olive! What? Well . . . that's different! (*Intimately*) We'll have dinner at your house at 8 . . . Okay . . . sugar.

ALLEN.—Well, I've heard everything.

KENNY.—(*In telephone*) Okay, Olive . . . Till tomorrow then . . . till we meet again . . . toujours l'amour, Toots!

SOUND.—*Telephone down.*

KENNY.—(*Sighs*) Wow!

79

ALLEN.—Congratulations, Kenny. Spring is here. And today you are a man.

KENNY.—Boy, I'm in for the time of my life. Say, F.A. . . .

ALLEN.—Yes, Kenny.

KENNY.—Can you lend me a quarter?

ALLEN.—For your date tomorrow night?

KENNY.—Yeah. Olive's kid brother Cecil is going to be there.

ALLEN.—I get it. You're going to slip Cecil a quarter and send him out to a movie.

KENNY.—No. I'm gonna slip Olive a quarter and send her out to a movie.

ALLEN.—Kenny!

KENNY.—Cecil's got an electric train with 40 feet of track . . . Yippee!

ALLEN.—Before I give up, I'll take one last chance and try to get Kenny in the mood. I have asked the Martins to dedicate their song to Kenny. And so the Martins sing "A Romantic Guy, I."

MUSIC.—(MARTINS *and orchestra*). *"A Romantic Guy, I." Applause.*

(*Third commercial*)

MUSIC.—(*Orchestra*). *"It's a Hap-hap-happy Day." Applause.*

ALLEN.—Al Goodman, and his Brauhaus Fifteen have just completed "It's a Hap-hap-happy Day." And now, ladies and gentlemen, the Texaco Workshop Players. Tonight these harried harlequins present a swing version of an old masterpiece. It's called "The Hot Old Homestead" . . . or . . . "Let's Make Hay Hay with the F.H.A." Overture, maestro!

MUSIC.—*"Home Sweet Home"* . . . *swing version* . . . *fade.*

SOUND.—*Door slams.*

JOHN.—(*Rube*) Wal, tain't no use, maw. I can't raise that mortgage money. Squire Green'll be here any minute. And out we git! Out we git.

CHARLES.—(*Off*) Go ahead and git. Scram!

80

ALLEN.—Shh. Quiet, please! Go on with the sketch, Ronald.

JOHN.—Squire Green'll be here any minute. And out we git!

CHARLES.—(*Off*) Go ahead, git! Beat it! Hit the road!

ALLEN.—Quiet, please! Who is that heckling in the front row there?

CHARLES.—(*Off*) It's me.

GIRL.—And me, too.

ALLEN.—What's the big idea interrupting our masterpiece "The Hot Old Homestead"?

CHARLES.—Masterpiece. Ha! We know how it's gonna end. Eh, Doris?

GIRL.—Sure, we know it backwards.

ALLEN.—You two know how this novel sketch is going to turn out? Who are you?

GIRL.—Tell him, Luther.

CHARLES.—Tell him, nuthin'. If he kin remember them old jokes, he oughta remember me.

ALLEN.—That's right. You two heckled me last year.

CHARLES.—You got us. This is Doris, and I'm Luther Snell.

ALLEN.—Snell?

CHARLES.—With an "N."

ALLEN.—That's what you think. The last time you were here you came to squawk about your radio peeves.

CHARLES.—And that's why we're here again tonight.

GIRL.—We're gettin bored.

ALLEN.—With radio?

CHARLES.—Yeah. Every week the same old boloney sliced the same old way. Every week the Pot of Platinum givin' away dough. The Hit Parade playin' hits. Gang Busters bustin' gangs.

ALLEN.—Well. That's radio. What do you want?

GIRL.—Can't nuthin' different happen?

CHARLES.—Can't them programs be revoised once in awhile?

ALLEN.—Well, I'm sorry, I've got a 10-minute sketch to do here.

CHARLES.—Okay. Come on, Doris.

GIRL.—I'm comin', Luther. Take my mitten.

ALLEN.—Wait a minute, radio can't afford to lose two fans. I'll tell you what I'll do. Instead of doing our sketch, I'll grant your wish, Luther.

CHARLES.—You'll show us how some of them programs would sound in revoise?

ALLEN.—If I can. Now what particular shows upset you?

CHARLES.—Foist. Them guys that does kid programs.

ALLEN.—You mean those radio uncles?

GIRL.—Yeah. They laugh like their parents was hyenas.

CHARLES.—How can them tomatoes always be so cheerful?

GIRL.—Nobody kin be that happy all the time. It ain't human.

ALLEN.—What you object to is this . . .

MUSIC.—(*Orchestra*). "*School Days*" . . . *fades.*

JOHN.—Ha! Ha! Ha! Good evenin', kiddies. This is old Uncle Humpty saying hello to y'all. Ha! Ha! Ha! Well, have y'all been good kiddies since yesterday? Ha! Ha! Ha! Are you all chewin' Piper's Peppermint Gum tonight? Ha! Ha! Happy birthday, Susie! Little Susie Figsbottle, of Novachord, Michigan, is havin' a birthday party in the family trailer tonight. Ha! Ha! Ha! Susie, if you'll look under the trailer you'll find a present from Uncle Humpty. Ha! Ha! Ha! It's a stick of that delicious Piper's Peppermint Gum. Ha! Ha! Ha! Well, gum-by, kiddies. And when you buy gum, buy Piper's Peppermint. Ha! Ha! Ha!

MUSIC.—(*Orchestra*). *Chord.*

ALLEN.—There you are, folks. This is the type of chap who gets your goat, eh?

GIRL.—Yeah. What's that guy laughin' about?

CHARLES.—Always laughin'. Don't he never feel grouchy . . . ain't he never dull and logy?

GIRL.—Can't he for once come out and say what he's really thinkin'?

ALLEN.—All right. Let's see how Uncle Humpty might sound if he came on someday and said what was on his mind.

MUSIC.—(*Orchestra*). "*School Days*" . . . *fades.*

JOHN.—(*Grouch*) Hello, you little punks. This is Uncle Humpty, you junior rats. Why I keep soft-soapin' you brats for the short dough I'm gettin' beats me. Boy! Have I got a hangover! My mouth tastes like the heel of a motorman's stocking. Little Buster Pincus is having a birthday today. When your mother lights your birthday cake, Buster, step in it. Give yourself a hotfoot. That other runt who wrote in for a free bicycle. I'll give you a bust in yer little mouth. Who do you kids think I am, Sandy Claus? This is Uncle Humpty tellin you little pests off. Boo! And I hope it scares the britches offa you. Good night!

MUSIC.—(*Orchestra*). *Chord.*

ALLEN.—Well, how's that, folks?

CHARLES.—That's more like it.

GIRL.—A pleasure.

ALLEN.—Fine. Now . . . if that's your only peeve . . .

GIRL.—We ain't started yet.

CHARLES.—No. What about them commercials?

ALLEN.—Which commercials?

GIRL.—Where they're always tellin' you the stuff their products contain.

CHARLES.—Yeah. Them names nobody understands.

ALLEN.—You mean this sort of message?

TED.—Folks! Have you ever tried Oato, the new oatmeal mouth wash? The only mouth wash with the genuine oatmeal base. White collar workers! Speed up your breakfasts and morning mouth rinsing with Oato. You simply gargle with Oato. Your mouth is fresh. Enough oatmeal trickles down your throat to serve as breakfast. And you're off! Try Oato. Oato is the only mouth wash that contains . . .

JOHN.—Hydro-whappitate.

CHARLES.—Your druggist knows hydro-whappitate as purified nitro-gimmick.

ALLEN.—Your grocer knows purified nitro-gimmick as undiluted fildil-sulphate.

TED.—Your tailor knows undiluted fildil-sulphate as genuine noxo-strombide.

JOHN.—Your plumber knows genuine noxo-strombide as trenal-delphine.

CHARLES.—And your butcher knows a man who knows that trenal-delphine is in Oato.

TED.—So ask your druggist for Oato tomorrow. He will tell you Oato contains . . .

ALL.—Hydro-whappitate!

TED.—Buy a bottle of Oato tonight!

MUSIC.—(*Orchestra*). *Chord.*

ALLEN.—That is what you had in mind, Mr. Snell?

CHARLES.—Yeah. Who knows Alco-Whappitate, nitro-gimmick, fildil-sulphate?

GIRL.—You gotta go to college to know what yer gettin in a bottle of mouth wash.

ALLEN.—Yes, I . . .

CHARLES.—Why don't they give us commercials we can understand?

ALLEN.—You mean something plain and simple like this?

TED.—Men! Have you tried Slicko, the new hair dress? Slicko keeps your hair in place. Slicko contains nothing you can't pronounce. Men! There is nothing in Slicko but a dash of perfume and pure chicken fat. Slicko won't make hair grow. Slicko just keeps your hair down and makes you smell nice. You simply slop a gob of chicken fat on your forehead. Spread back over your hair with an ordinary butter knife.

Slicko does the rest. The chicken fat gives your hair that greasy gloss. The perfume makes you smell. Men! If you want that greasy gloss! Men! If you want to smell! Try Slicko!

MUSIC.—(*Orchestra*). *Chord.*

ALLEN.—That is what you mean?

GIRL.—Right. With Slicko you know what you're gettin'.

CHARLES.—Yeah. The guy's sellin' chicken fat. He's callin' it chicken fat. He ain't saying it's triple-distilled residue of adipose tissue.

ALLEN.—Well, I guess that . . .

GIRL.—Oh, yeah? What about them crime programs?

CHARLES.—Always crime doesn't pay. Why can't we hear one program where crime does pay?

ALLEN.—You mean, like this?

MUSIC.—(*Orchestra*). *Dramatic . . . fades.*

TED.—Yes. It was a clean getaway. Leaving the Blue Hornet . . . Mr. District Attorney, all the Gang Busters and Superman dead on the sidewalk . . . Mayhem Myer and his mob escaped with $200,000. Tune in next week. Hear these crooks count this money. See how they buy yachts, Florida homes, and high-powered cars. Men like Mayhem Myer prove that—crime does pay!

MUSIC.—(*Orchestra*). *Chord.*

ALLEN.—How was that, folks?

GIRL.—It's impossible.

CHARLES.—Yeah. But it was a pleasure to hear it for a change.

ALLEN.—Well, we've only got a minute left.

CHARLES.—Got time for one more peeve?

ALLEN.—What is it?

CHARLES.—Them programs that's playin' hit songs. The song of the month.

GIRL.—The song of the week.

85

CHARLES.—The song of the day.

ALLEN.—What's wrong with that?

CHARLES.—Do they always have to play good songs?

GIRL.—There's plenty of bad songs written.

CHARLES.—Yeah. How about givin' them dog numbers a break?

ALLEN.—What you'd like to hear is this . . . (*Fanfare*) We present your Flop of the Week! (*Fanfare*)

TED.—The song that rated minus 463 on your Flop Parade.

ALLEN.—And here it is . . . "The Subway Serenade." All right, boys!

JOHN AND CHARLES.—(*Sing*)
Some people like to ride the ferries.
Others rather ride a bus.
Old folks jolly prefer a trolley.
But the subway's good enough for us.
   (*Patter*)
Get on at 72nd.
Packed and jammed.
At 66th yer arm is out.
The door is slammed.
At 59th you start to read
Some guy's *World-Telly*.
At 50th the guy gets off
And slugs you in the—stomach.

At 42nd! All out!
Change for Brooklyn locals.
The guard yells, "Watch them doors."
There go your bifocals.
It's 33rd—a lady's standin'
   On your feet.
A man gets up. You race the lady
   For the seat.
14th Street! The brakes go on.
   Shriek! Squeal!
You fall and hear somebody say,
"You big schlemiel!"

It's push and pull.
Your ribs are broke.
Your clothes are mighty tattery
They give you mayhem
In the Bronx
And assault you at the Battery.

(*Sing*) That's riding in the subway.
It's more fun than a big parade.
It will shatter your illusions.
You'll get black eyes and contusions.
Attendin' the Subway Serenade. Pah!

ALLEN.—There you are. You've never heard anything worse than that, have you?

CHARLES.—That was the Hit Parade in revoise, all right.

ALLEN.—Fine. Now, if you're through . . .

GIRL.—Just one more thing.

CHARLES.—Oh, yeah.

ALLEN.—What is that?

CHARLES.—That mechanical applause radio shows always get at the end. How about some hissin' and booin' for a change?

ALLEN.—From the looks of our audience I think I can get it for you. Ladies and gentlemen. How did you like this little Hassenfetter?

SOUND.—*Boos and hisses.*

ALLEN.—Thank you very much!

MUSIC.—(*Orchestra*). "*Look Out*" . . . *Fade.*

ALLEN.—And now, Larry Elliot.
(*Fourth commercial*)

ALLEN.—Thank you, Larry. And thank you, ladies and gentlemen, for joining us tonight. And make a note. Next Wednesday evening, The Texaco Star Theatre brings you "Advice for Card Players."

TED.—How can I polish up my bridge?

JOHN.—Take it out and rub it with a damp chamois.

MUSIC.—*Chord.*

ALLEN.—Your Song of the Week!

CHARLES.—(*Sings*) I dreamed of Jeanie with the light brown hair.

ALLEN.—Psst! Just a minute, Tito. You're singing that right. You generally have a joke there.

CHARLES.—I'm stuck this week. Me gag writer was drafted.

ALLEN.—Oh!

MUSIC.—*Chord.*

ALLEN.—And our guest will be . . .

JIMMY.—Miss Ruth Hopkins, dance instructress at the famous Arthur Murray School.

MUSIC.—*Chord.*

ALLEN.—And music!

MUSIC.—*Theme up to finish.*

ALLEN.—This is Fred Allen, saying good night for the more than 45,000 Texaco dealers from coast to coast.

MUSIC.—*Siren and bell.*

ANNOUNCER.—This is the Columbia Broadcasting System.

Fibber McGee and Molly

WIL.—The Johnson Wax Program . . . with Fibber McGee and Molly!

MUSIC.—(*Orchestra*). *Theme.*

WIL.—The makers of Johnson's Wax and Johnson's Self-Polishing Glo-Coat present Fibber McGee and Molly . . . written by Don Quinn . . . with music by the King's Men and Billy Mills' orchestra. The show opens with "I Struck a Match on the Moon."

MUSIC.—(*Orchestra*). "*I Struck a Match on the Moon.*"
(*Fade for*)

(*Opening commercial*)

ANNOUNCER.—Ladies, what's the most popular room in your house? Most people say the living room, with the easy chair pulled up alongside the radio, but personally, I want to put my vote down for the kitchen. I spend more time in people's kitchens . . . and in my own . . . than anywhere else. I suppose the icebox has something to do with it . . . but whatever it is, the kitchen *is* a cosy room and deserves to be a cheerful one. You can make it cheerful, too, without spending much money . . . gay curtains at the window, fresh oilcloth . . . and Johnson's Self-Polishing Glo-Coat on the floor. Glo-Coat not only gives linoleum floors sparkling beauty and keeps the colors as bright as new . . . but it protects them against wear, makes them last longer. And it does all this in *addition* to saving you hours of work . . . because Glo-Coat needs no rubbing or buffing. Just apply and let dry . . . Glo-Coat does the rest. May I suggest that you add Johnson's Self-Polishing Glo-Coat to your next shopping list?

MUSIC.—(*Orchestra*). *Swell music to finish . . . Applause.*

WIL.—A man can fool some of the people all the time and all the people some of the time and his wife almost *none* of the time. So when our hero seems unusually gay and light-hearted, laughing at anything, his better half suspects the worst. In other words, when a guy doesn't grouse, his spouse smells a mouse. That's the way it is tonight with . . . Fibber McGee and Molly! (*Applause*)

FIBBER.—(*Laughing like everything*) So when I seen Egghead Vanderveen there in front of Joe's Tavern, I walks up to him . . . (*Laughs*) Hiyah, Egghead, I says, "What's cookin'?" (*Laughs*) . . . and he says, "*I* am! . . . They just gimme the hotfoot!" (*Laughs*) Well, sir, that just about tore my upholstery, because Egghead is the kind of a guy who . . .

MOLLY.—McGee.

FIBBER.— . . . the kind of a guy who . . . er . . . eh?

MOLLY.—What's the matter with you? You're as merry as a grig over nothing. What's on your mind?

FIBBER.—On my mind? Why . . . er . . . why, nothing. But lemme tell you about Egghead. (*Laughs heartily*) So I says to Egghead, I says . . .

MOLLY.—I don't want to hear about Egghead. I want to know about *you*. You always act like this when you're covering up something. Look—did you mail that special delivery letter for me yesterday morning?

FIBBER.—Special deliv . . . oh, that! Don't give it a thought, Molly. But to get back to what I says to Egghead . . .

MOLLY.—*Did you mail that letter?*

FIBBER.—Why, Molly! Am I the kind of a guy who, when you tell him to do something you want done, don't mail it?

MOLLY.—Never mind that. I just asked a simple questi . . .

FIBBER.—Did you ever ask me to do anything that I wasn't only too glad to cooperate into doing it? No, sir!

MOLLY.—McGee! *Did you mail that letter?* (*Pause*)

FIBBER.—No.

MOLLY.—Well, the reason I wanted to know is . . .

FIBBER.— . . . But I'll do it right away. Wait'll I get my coat (*Fade*) *and as soon as* I can run across the street, I'll . . .

90

MOLLY.—But McGee, let me . . .

FIBBER.—No, I'll do it . . . Should o' done it yesterday! . . .
(*Fade in*)

Sorry I forgot, but you can consider the error rectifried!

SOUND.—*Door opens.*

MOLLY.—(*Off-mike*) Wait a minute, McGee, that letter is . . .

FIBBER.—(*Laughs*) I'll just dash across the street to the mailbox,
Molly. Be right back!

SOUND.—*Footsteps on steps . . . sidewalk . . . fast.*

MOLLY.—(*Way off-mike*) McGee!! Wait a minute!! I didn't!!!
Oh, dear . . .

FIBBER.—(*Laughing*) Sometimes I wonder why the government
always puts mailboxes on the corner where somebody else
lives! If I had my way, I'd—hiyah, Gildersleeve!

HAL.—(*Off-mike*) Hello McGee! Hey, don't run across that
pavement!! Can't you see they've just . . .

FIBBER.—Aw . . . go bounce a meatball, you big ape! (*Fade*) I
know what I'm . . .

SOUND.—*Sucking noise, as cow-hoofs-in-mud.*

FIBBER.—Hey, what the . . . What is this? Fresh tar!

HAL.—Get out of there, McGee!! They've just resurfaced that
pavement . . . You'll get stuck!

FIBBER.—Whaddye mean, *get* stuck . . . I *am* stuck! Why didn't
you warn me, you dumbell?

HAL.—(*Off*) I tried to, you little twerp! If you hadn't . . . ah
there, Mrs. McGee!

MOLLY.—Hello, Mr. Gildersleeve. McGee! Come out of that this
minute!

FIBBER.—I can't . . . can't pick up my feet! What *is* this, anyway—tar?

HAL.—No . . . It's a new patent paving material they're trying
out. (*Laughs*) You like it?

FIBBER.—I love it! In fact, I'm stuck on it! Well, dad rat it, *do* something. Get me outa here!

MOLLY.—Can't you pull your feet up, dearie?

FIBBER.—No . . . Wait . . . lemme try again.

SOUND.—*Sucking noise.*

FIBBER.—Nope . . . it's no use . . . harder I try the deeper I get in!

HAL.—You see, Mrs. McGee? (*Laughs*) Confidentially, he sinks!

FIBBER.—Dad rat it, Gildersleeve, if you don't . . .

MOLLY.—Now, now, now . . . let's all keep calm and think this thing out. McGee . . . can you slip out of your shoes?

FIBBER.—Yes, but I ain't gonna. I just had 'em half-soled.

MOLLY.—Come on, McGee . . . don't stand there arguing . . . You're attracting a crowd. Take your shoes off, and start running.

FIBBER.—Okay . . . (*Grunts . . . again*) Okay . . . here I come!

SOUND.—*Sucking noises . . . pause.*

HAL.—Well . . . come on!

FIBBER.—Can't. I'm stuck again!

MOLLY.—Take off your socks, and start over.

FIBBER.—Okay . . . I'll try anything. (*Grunts . . . again*) *Now!*

SOUND.—*Sucking noise . . . pause.*

FIBBER.—Well . . . what do I do now—take off my feet?

MOLLY.—Oh, dear!!!! Who shall I call, dearie? The street commissioner, the fire department . . . the police or the Gallup poll?

FIBBER.—Whaddye mean, the Gallup poll?

MOLLY.—Well, you're the man in the street, all right. What shall we do, Mr. Gildersleeve?

HAL.—(*Laughs heartily*) I don't know what *you're* going to do, Mrs. McGee, but *I'm* going home and get my movie camera.

(*Laughs*) By George, I never saw anything so funny in my life!

FIBBER.—Dad rat it, you stay where you darn are, Gildersleeve, you big heel!

HAL.—Ohhhhhhhh!!

MOLLY.—McGee! You mustn't call Mr. Gildersleeve a heel!

FIBBER.—Wel-l-l . . . maybe not. But I'll bet he could have a lot of fun sliding down a shoe horn! Hey, ain't anybody gonna get me outa here?

MOLLY.—Now, don't get excited, McGee . . . we'll do everything we can to . . .

OLD MAN.—(*Fade in*) Hello there, daughter. H'lo, Gildersleeve. Hiyah, *Johnny* . . . whatcha doin'?

FIBBER.—Whaddye think I'm doin', you old dodo! Tap dancin'?

OLD MAN.—Tap dancing, eh? (*Aside*) You never told me he could tap dance, daughter! Lesee you do a off-to-Buffalo, Johnny!

MOLLY.—For goodness sakes, stop teasing him . . . he's in a terrible predicklement!

OLD MAN.—Hey, what's this all about, kids? What's he doin' out there in the street, daughter?

MOLLY.—He's stuck in that fresh pavement, Mr. Old Timer. Know any way we can get him out?

OLD MAN.—Sure!

HAL.—How?

OLD MAN.—(*Excited*) Look! . . . git a couple shovels! . . . see? Then go down into the basement of your house . . . Dig a tunnel till you're right under him . . . Then dig up till you reach him and pull him down through!

FIBBER.—(*Groans*)

HAL.—Oh, my goodness!

MOLLY.—That's silly!

FIBBER.—It ain't only silly, it's callous and cruel. Everybody makin' wisecracks while I stand here and suffer! Don't you

93

realize this pavin' material is gettin' harder every minute? *Call* somebody. *Do* something!

MOLLY.—But what will we do?

FIBBER.—How should I know!! If you can't think of anything else, throw me a red and green lantern . . . and I'll spend the rest of my life here as a traffic signal!

OLD MAN.—Heh heh heh . . . that's pretty good, Johnny, but that ain't the way I heered it! The way I heered it, one feller says tother feller, "Sayyyyyy," he says—but hey . . . this ain't any time for jokes, is it, with poor little Johnny out there, stuck in the tar!

MOLLY.—It certainly isn't!

HAL.—Of course not!

OLD MAN.—Though, on the other hand, it might cheer him up. The way I heered it, one feller says to tother feller, "Sayyyyy," he says, "I see where Groucho Marx is gonna be a professor of humor at Harvard." "Zat so?" says tother feller. "Where's Harpo goin' . . . to Wellesley?" Hey heh heh . . .

FIBBER.—(*Laughs*) I guess you got somethin' there, Old Timer. That Harpo is a great guy for blondes, but (*Laugh stops abruptly*) Hey, what am I laughin' at? Dad rat it, get me outa here! Do something somebody . . . Don't just stand there . . . Helllp!! Hellp!! (*Etc. Etc. into*)

MUSIC.—(*Orchestra*). "*Poupee Valsante*" or "*Buddy, You Waltz Like a Poop.*" *Applause.*

(*Second spot*)

SOUND.—*Crowd murmur . . . laughter.*

VOICE 1.—What's that guy doing out there in the street? Advertising something?

VOICE 2.—No, they say he got stuck in that fresh pavement.

VOICE 3.—Well, if he saw they were going to pave the street, why didn't he get out of the way? (*Laughter*)

VOICE 4.—They ought to put a rail around him and use him as a statue of a leading citizen!

94

SOUND.—*Laughter . . . murmur of voices.*

FIBBER.—Hey, Molly!! . . . Molly!!!

MOLLY.—Yes, dearie . . . here I am! And here's a little footstool for you to sit on . . . catch!

SOUND.—*Wind whistle . . . thud.*

FIBBER.—Much obliged . . . Is somebody comin' to get me outa this? Whoja call?

MOLLY.—Well, first Mr. Gildersleeve and I called the commissioner of streets. And he referred us to the department of health.

FIBBER.—The department of health!

HAL.—Yes, he said it wasn't healthy to stand there in the street night and day. (*Laughs*)

FIBBER.—Well what did the health department say?

MOLLY.—They referred us to the license commissioner . . . because they said you were making an exhibition of yourself!

FIBBER.—(*Groans*)

HAL.—Yes, and the license commissioner sent us to the board of education.

FIBBER.—Dad rat it, what's the board of education got to do with it?

HAL.—They said *they'd* teach you to stay off of freshly paved streets! (*Laughs*)

MOLLY.—But we finally got to the right people, McGee!! . . . This is a new type of paving, and they're sending the inventor of it out!

FIBBER.—Well, thank goodness . . . at last! When will . . .

VOICE.—Hey, stick-in-the-mud!! . . . Can I have your autograph!

FIBBER.—Why certainly, bud! Throw me your death certificate!

SOUND.—*Laughter . . . crowd murmur.*

MOLLY.—Oh, dear, Mr. Gildersleeve, if that man doesn't get here pretty soon, I don't know . . . Oh, how do you do, Mrs. Uppington?

MRS. UPPINGTON.—How do you do, my deah . . . and Mr. Gildersleeve.

HAL.—Ahhhh, Good-day, Abigail!

MRS. UPPINGTON.—What on earth is the cause of this boisterous crowd, my deah?

MOLLY.—It's McGee, Abigail. He's stuck out there in the middle of the street . . . see?

MRS. UPPINGTON.—Well . . . *reahhly!* How . . . er . . . what did . . . I mean . . . did he step on some chewing gum?

HAL.—(*Laughs*) Oh, no! He just started to trot across a freshly paved street . . . the silly asphalt runner!

MOLLY.—Now, look here, Mr. Gildersleeve . . .

MRS. UPPINGTON.—But Mrs. McGee . . . we simply *cawnt* have your husband making a spectacle of himself . . . He is lowering the tone of the whole neighborhood!

MOLLY.—Don't give me that Vassar vaseline, dearie! Next thing you'll get so exclusive you'll want our fire department to have an unlisted phone number!

MRS. UPPINGTON.—Well, *reahhly*, Mrs. McGee!! I . . .

HAL.—(*Laughs*) Wait a minute, girls . . . Hey, McGee!!! Here's Mrs. Uppington. She wants you to get out of there! (*Laughs*) You're lowering real estate values!

FIBBER.—Oh, I am, eh? Uppy, you mean to stand there, wabbling on your wedgies, and accuse me o' doin' this on purpose?

MRS. UPPINGTON.—I reahhly wouldn't know, Mr. McGee . . . but if you're posing as a personal investigator of paving material . . . I have a suggestion to make.

FIBBER.—Yeah? What's that?

MRS. UPPINGTON.—Did you ever hear of a certain place which is said to be paved with good intentions?

FIBBER.—You mean . . . ?

MRS. UPPINGTON.—Yes! . . . And when you get through heah . . . go *theah!* Good-by!

SOUND.—*Crowd murmur.*

FIBBER.—Hey Molly . . . where's the guy who invented this stuff . . . when's he comin'?

MOLLY.—Just as soon as they can get hold of him, dearie.

FIBBER.—Just wait till *I* get hold of him! I'll . . .
(*Fade in*)

WIL.—Hey, what is all this? . . . Come here a minute, Fibber!

FIBBER.—No, you come here, Wilcox.

WIL.—All right. I'll . . .

MOLLY.—No! No! No! Mr. Wilcox! . . . You'll get stuck, too!

HAL.—McGee is held tight in that new paving material, Harlow. Don't set foot on it!

FIBBER.—Aw, why didn't you let him come? He always claimed he was a guy that would stick by his friends.

WIL.—Say . . . you're in a tough spot, pal! Can't you pull yourself loose?

FIBBER.—Who, me? Why, sure, Wilcox. I'm just standin' here till the steam roller comes by. Then I'll lay down and get my pants pressed.

WIL.—Well, I can really sympathize with you, Fibber. Standing in that tar, you're typical of the stories I hear every day.

FIBBER.—Whaddye mean, *I'm* typical!

WIL.—You're tarred, aren't you?

FIBBER.—Sure, I'm tarred, but . . .

WIL.—Well, so is every housewife in the world! Tarred of the everlasting scrubbing and cleaning and dusting! . . . Tarred of dust and dirt and dampness! . . . Tarred of trying to keep house with old-fashioned, inefficient methods! That's why they all love Johnson's Wax! Because it cuts housework to a minimum and keeps floors and furniture shining and beautiful and protects them against wear and dirt. Get some today . . . Johnson's Wax for that tarred feeling!!!

97

FIBBER.—Wilcox!

WIL.—What?

FIBBER.—You're farred!

WIL.—I am not!! You didn't harr me, and you can't farr . . . and I can prove it.

MOLLY.—How, Mr. Wilcox?
(*Fade out*)

WIL.—I'm going to send the sponsor a warrrr!

FIBBER.—Send the sponsor a warrr! If he'd spend more time listening to Fibber McGee and Molly and less to Lum and Abner . . . Hey, when am I gonna get outa here?

HAL.—Now now now . . . take it easy little chum . . . take it easy! We'll just have to wait till that paving expert gets here . . .

FIBBER.—Don't "little chum" me, you big chump! All you've done since I been stuck here is stand around and crack wise!

HAL.—Is that so! Why, you ungrateful little grunion! You lippy little lizard! You wait till you get out of there, and I'll teach you a few manners.

FIBBER.—Go on . . . you couldn't teach a worm to squirm! You big oaf! By the time I get loose from here I'll be in just the mood to kick you right in the teeth . . . and I don't care if they ain't paid for yet!

MOLLY.—Now, now, now, for goodness sakes, boys! Stop it!

FIBBER.—Let him come out here . . . I'll show him.

MOLLY.—You can't fight here . . . and McGee!

FIBBER.—Eh?

MOLLY.—You owe Mr. Gildersleeve an apology. He's done everything he could to get the city officials to come out here and get you loose.

FIBBER.—Yeah . . . and it's like most of his arrangements. Nothing happens.

HAL.—Is that so!

FIBBER.—Yes, that's so!

98

HAL.—Why, you abbreviated anthropological aberration . . .

FIBBER.—Who's an anthropological aberration?

HAL.—You are!

MOLLY.—He is not!

FIBBER.—I am too!

HAL.—You are not!

MOLLY.—Well, make up your mind! Now, stop this bickering, both of you. Come on, Mr. Gildersleeve . . . let's go call up the street commissioner again.

HAL.—All right. (*Sweetly*) Now don't worry, little chum . . . we'll be right back.

FIBBER.—Okay, Throcky . . . and hurry back, Molly . . .

MOLLY.—All right, dearie . . .

SOUND.—*Crowd murmur.*

VOICES.—Come on, Joe . . . Let's beat it. He ain't gonna do nothin' . . . naw, he just stands there like a dope . . . Come on . . . Charlie.

SOUND.—*Crowd murmur . . . fade out.*

FIBBER.—Hey!! Don't *everybody* leave! Somebody stay and talk to me! Hey! Aw, dad-rat the dad-ratted luck . . . Why does everything have to happen to me! If I'd of only mailed that letter of Molly's when I ought to of, this wouldn't of . . .

TEE.—Hiyah, mister!

FIBBER.—Sorry, sis, I ain't got time to talk to you now. I'm in a hurry.

TEE.—Where you goin'?

FIBBER.—I'm goin' down to the . . . I'm goin' . . . I'm . . . Sayyy, come to think of it, I ain't . . . *Well whaddye want, sis?*

TEE.—Whatcha doin' out there in the street, mister? Hmmmmm? Whatcha doin? Hmmmmmm? Whatcha?

FIBBER.—I'm a scare sparrow.

TEE.—Hmmm?

FIBBER.—I says *I'm a scare sparrow*. That's the same as a scarecrow. Only, I don't scare crows—I scare sparrows.

TEE.—Why?

FIBBER.—Well, they make too much noise. They disturb the frenistans.

TEE.—What's a frenistan?

FIBBER.—That's a kind of a thing that gets disturbed at sparrows.

TEE.—Oh. Well, I betcha you can't scare the widdicums, I betcha.

FIBBER.—What's a widdicum?

TEE.—It's a little girl who doesn't believe that frenistan stuff.

FIBBER.—(*Laughs*) I'm glad you come along sis. You cheer me up.

TEE.—No, you cheer me up.

FIBBER.—You cheer me up first.

TEE.—All righty. Shall I tell you a story?

FIBBER.—Sure, tell me a story.

TEE.—How about Cinderella?

FIBBER.—It ain't riskay, is it?

TEE.—Well, gee, I . . . hmmmm?

FIBBER.—Never mind. Tell me about Cinderella. And take your time, sis. I ain't goin' anywhere for a while.

TEE.—All righty. Once upon a time there was little girl named Cinderella, and she had a nasty old stepmother and she went to a ball and lost her slipper and the prince found it and he married her and they lived happily ever after you wanna hear another one?

FIBBER.—No, thanks. I was gonna ask for the one about Peter Rabbit, but the way you boil 'em down, it'd turn out to be hausenfeffer.

TEE.—I can recite pomes, too.

FIBBER.—You can?

TEE.—Hmmm?

FIBBER.—I says you can?

TEE.—Can what?

FIBBER.—Cherries. And be sure you get all the pits out of 'em.

TEE.—You're silly, mister.

FIBBER.—I guess I am at that, sis. Go ahead and recite somethin'.

TEE.—All righty. This is gonna be a dandy one, I betcha.
        The boy stood on the burning deck
        Mending a pair of socks.
        It roused his ire when the thread caught fire—
        Hot darn! (*Giggles*)

FIBBER.—If you don't mind, sis, I think that ought to conclude your benefit performance. You wanna earn a nickel by running an errand for me?

TEE.—No.

FIBBER.—You don't?

TEE.—No. I wanna earn a dime.

FIBBER.—You're takin' advantage of my desperation, sis. I'm gonna report you to the Labor Board. Okay . . . it's a dime. Now look.

TEE.—All righty.

FIBBER.—Run down to Kramer's drugstore and have 'em throw me a evening paper. Then run over to my house and tell Mrs. McGee I want a little table and a deck of cards. So I can play solitaire. Oh, yes . . . and a portable radio.

TEE.—All righty. Shall I tell her anything else?

FIBBER.—Yes.

TEE.—What?

FIBBER.—*I'm hungry!*

TEE.—Oh, pshaw!

MUSIC.—(*Orchestra*). *"Little Brown Jug"* . . . *King's Men. Applause.*

(*Third spot*)

SOUND.—*Crowd murmur.*

MOLLY.—Have you had enough to eat now, McGee?

FIBBER.—Not quite . . . Toss me one more cookie!

SOUND.—*Short wind whistle.*

FIBBER.—Thanks.

HAL.—How about coffee, McGee . . . Want some more?

FIBBER.—No, thanks, Gildersleeve . . . You can pull in the hose now.

HAL.—Okay!

FIBBER.—Hey, when is that guy gonna get here?

MOLLY.—You mean the man who invented this paving material? He's due any minute, McGee . . . just be patient. Are you terribly tired?

FIBBER.—I ain't as tired as I am disgusted . . . I'm disgusted and humiliated. And my feet are gettin' numb. This stuff is gettin' hard. Hey, did you call the City Hall again?

MOLLY.—Yes, I did, dearie.

FIBBER.—Who'd you get?

MOLLY.—Myrt.

FIBBER.—Myrt! What'd she have to say?

MOLLY.—She said her cousin overturned his canoe yesterday.

FIBBER.—Yeah? Did he get drowned?

MOLLY.—Oh, no. He just got tired of paddling and overturned it to his brother.

FIBBER.—Overturned it to his brother! If that ain't the farthest fetched gag I ever heard, and me standing here helpless.

SOUND.—*Crowd murmur.*

HAL.—By George, here he comes, McGee . . . It won't be long now!

FIBBER.—What? Who?

MOLLY.—It's the inventor of this paving material, McGee . . . He'll know how to get you loose! . . . Make way there, please, folks . . . Let the man through.

SOUND.—*Crowd murmur.*

MOLLY.—McGee! Here's the expert!

FIBBER.—Hiyah, Bud . . . Glad to see you!

WIMPLE.—Hello.

HAL.—Oh, my goodness . . . It's Wallace Wimple!

MOLLY.—Are *you* really the inventor of this pavement, Mr. Wimple?

WIMPLE.—Yes, I am. And I'm *dreadfully* sorry that your husband got stuck, Mrs. McGee . . . It just makes me miserable to think of it.

FIBBER.—Whaddye mean, it makes *you* miserable! Whaddye think of me?

WIMPLE.—I'd rather not say—in front of all these people.

MOLLY.—Well, how do we get him out of there, Mr. Wimple?

WIMPLE.—Well, Mrs. McGee . . . as I see it, the whole thing depends on a chemical analysis of the material. Maybe we can dissolve some of it around his feet.

FIBBER.—That's the first sensible remark that's been made today. What's the chemical formula, Wimple?

WIMPLE.—Oh, that's a secret, Mr. McGee.

MOLLY.—What do you mean, it's a secret?

WIMPLE.—That's what I mean . . . it's a secret.

HAL.—Well, you know what the secret is, don't you?

WIMPLE.—No, but my wife does.

FIBBER.—Your wife! What's she got to do with your invention?

WIMPLE.—Well, she's really the inventor. *I'm* only the one who saw the possibilities in it for paving material.

MOLLY.—What was it in the first place?

WIMPLE.—Her recipe for chocolate pudding. The minute I tasted it. I said to her, I said, "Cornelia," I said, "this would make *wonderful* paving material!"

HAL.—And what did she say?

WIMPLE.—I don't know . . . Everything went black . . . But here's what we better do, Mr. McGee.

FIBBER.—I don't care *what* we better do . . . but let's do it!

WIMPLE.—All righty. I'll go home and analyze this material and see how we can dissolve it around your feet.

MOLLY.—Will your wife give you the formula?

WIMPLE.—If she won't, Mrs. McGee . . . we'll have to use air hammers and chop him loose.

MUSIC.—(*Orchestra*). *Bridge. "William Tell"* . . . *out of music with concrete breaking. Air hammer effect.*

FIBBER.—Hey, go easy, fellas! You're gettin' awful close to my feet.

MOLLY.—Be patient you're nearly free, dearie!

SOUND.—*Hammer sound . . . thuds . . . clanks.*

MAN.—Dere you are, buddy! Sorry you gotta go home wit' a hunk o' pavement on each foot, but dat's de best we could do.

HAL.—I imagine you can soak that off with turpentine, McGee . . .

MOLLY.—Come on, dearie . . . I'll take one arm and Mr. Gildersleeve the other . . .

FIBBER.—Okay . . . Much obliged, fellas . . . All right . . . One side there, everybody.

SOUND.—*Crowd murmur.*

HAL.—Can you walk, little chum?

FIBBER.—I think so . . . lemme try . . .

SOUND.—*Heavy clunks.*

FIBBER.—Yeah . . . I can manage.

SOUND.—*Clunking walk continues . . . then*

FIBBER.—Boy, is this a relief! . . . I thought I'd *never* get outa there. You know what the first thing I'm gonna do is, Molly, after I get these hunks o' pavement offa my feet?

MOLLY.—What, dearie?

FIBBER.—I'm gonna run right out and mail that letter for you!

MOLLY.—Give it here, McGee.

FIBBER.—No, sir . . . I started out to mail it, and by the seven sisters of Maud Kelly, I'm gonna mail it!

SOUND.—*Footsteps out.*

MOLLY.—It's no use dearie. That letter's no good now.

FIBBER.—Whatcha mean? Who was it to?

MOLLY.—The street commissioner.

HAL.—My goodness, Mrs. McGee . . . what did you want him to do?

MOLLY.—Pave the street in front of our house.

FIBBER.—Oh, pshaw!

SOUND.—*Clunking walk into*

MUSIC.—(*Orchestra*). *Selection. Fade for*
      (*Closing commercial*)

ANNOUNCER.—Fibber and Molly will be back in just a moment. Here's a question several people have asked me lately: Is Johnson's Glo-Coat good for other kinds of floors besides linoleum? Yes, it most certainly is. It's good for painted or varnished wood floors . . . and for floors covered with rubber or asphalt tile. Glo-Coat gives all these floors a real coat of protection . . . enhances their beauty . . . makes cleaning easy. And it's just as easy to apply Glo-Coat to these floors as it is to linoleum. When the floor is clean, apply Glo-Coat with a cloth or long-handled Glo-Coat applier, and let it dry for 20 minutes. Glo-Coat polishes itself, without any rubbing or buffing . . . that's why it is called Self-Polishing. Most women find Glo-Coat especially helpful in protecting their kitchen linoleum floors, because these floors get more than average wear. Linoleum manufacturers themselves recommend this easy no-rubbing method for keeping linoleum clean, making it last longer. Try Johnson's Self-Polishing Glo-Coat on *your* floors.

MUSIC.—(*Orchestra*). *Swell music . . . fade on cue.*
 (*Tag gag*)

FIBBER.—(Mutters) Of all the dad-ratted . . . if that wasn't the darndest . . .

MOLLY.—Who you talkin' about, McGee? . . . Egghead Vanderveen?

FIBBER.—No. Egghead McGee. I'm disgusted. Makin' a spectacle of myself, everybody jeerin', pointin' at me . . . and me squawkin' and hollerin' there like a . . .

MOLLY.—Oh, stop fussin' about it. It wasn't that bad. And anyway, I'll give you credit for one thing!

FIBBER.—What's that?

MOLLY.—It's the first time you ever put your foot in it and *then* opened your mouth!

FIBBER.—Eh? Oh. Good night!

MOLLY.—Goodnight, all!

MUSIC.—(*Orchestra*). *Closing signature . . . Fade on cue.* (*Closing tag*)

MOLLY.—"Good night, all." (*Cue*)

WILCOX.—This is Harlow Wilcox . . . speaking for the makers of Johnson's Wax and Johnson's Self-Polishing Glo-Coat . . . inviting you to be with us again next Tuesday night. Good night.

WOMAN.—Mr. Jones, do you have that new kind of enamel that contains wax?

DEALER.—Yes, indeed, I have, and lots of my customers are buying it. Here it is . . . Johnson's Wax-O-Namel, and a wonderful enamel it is! See those 19 stunning colors . . . all selected by prominent decorators. Wax-O-Namel gives a smoother finish and a more beautiful luster than any enamel I've ever handled . . . not a harsh glare at all. And the wax in Wax-O-Namel gives it added protection against wear and makes it easier to clean. Here's a free color chart for you . . . just try Wax-O-Namel on old furniture or on your bathroom or kitchen walls.

The Quiz Kids

CARPENTER.—Here they are—The Quiz Kids!—presented by the makers of Alka-Seltzer. We're on the air with the School Kids' Questionnaire!

MUSIC.—*(Organ). Theme.*

CARPENTER.—The Quiz Kids! Five bright, lovable youngsters, ready for another difficult examination in the Alka-Seltzer Schoolroom of the Air. The examination tonight will be conducted in exactly the same manner as all our regular Wednesday night Quiz Kid programs, and, as usual, none of the children have seen or heard any of the questions in advance.

BENNY.—I'll say we haven't. Let's get going.

CARPENTER.—All questions were sent in by you listeners and were selected by Sidney L. James, of the editorial staffs of *Time* and *Life* magazines.

BENNY.—I don't care who sent them in. Let's get going. I can answer them, you know.

CARPENTER.—A new Zenith portable radio will be awarded the sender of each question used on this program tonight. And now our chief quizzer himself . . . Joe Kelly!

SOUND.—*Applause.*

KELLY.—Thank you, Ken Carpenter, and good evening, ladies and gentlemen. Well, we'll proceed directly to the roll call. Richard . . .

RICHARD.—I'm Richard Williams. I'm eleven years old, and I'm in the sixth grade at Harrison School, East Chicago, Indiana.

KELLY.—Jack Lucal . . .

JACK.—I'm Jack Lucal. I'm fourteen years old, and I'm a freshman at the Oak Park and River Forest Township High School.

107

KELLY.—Joan . . .

JOAN.—I'm Joan Bishop. I'm fourteen years old, and I go to the Chicago School for Adults.

KELLY.—Claude . . .

CLAUDE.—I'm Claude Brenner. I'm twelve years old, and I am a sophomore at Senn High School in Chicago.

KELLY.—Gerard . . .

GERARD.—I'm Gerard Darrow. I'm eight years, and I go to the Bradwell School on Burnham.

KELLY.—And, Jackie . . .

BENNY.—I am Jackie Benny. I'm six years old . . . ah—I didn't have a chance to go to school at all.

SOUND.—*Laughter.*

BENNY.—I was just a poor boy, and I used to stand on the corner selling papers (*laughter*), barefooted in the winter, and I used to say, "Extra . . . extra . . . paper here . . . get your paper . . .

KELLY.—Quiet, please.

BENNY.—Hmn . . . Fine chance I'm going to have here, I can see that . . . You know . . .

KELLY.—Now, Jackie, please.

BENNY.—I know just as much as the kids, you know. You just ask the questions, that's all.

KELLY.—Jackie, please. And incidentally, where are your curls?

BENNY.—What?

KELLY.—Where are your curls?

BENNY.—On my lap. They got hot.

SOUND.—*Laughter.*

KELLY.—Well, while we're getting ready for our first question, just a word or two from Ken Carpenter.

CARPENTER.—Here's a word of friendly advice to all you parents and older folks. Alkalize with Alka-Seltzer. Yes, the next time you eat too much or too fast or eat while under stress and strain alkalize with Alka-Seltzer. Alka-Seltzer's just the thing to relieve the misery of acid indigestion and distress after meals. It helps to neutralize excess stomach acids, so often the immediate cause of the distress of an upset stomach. But that isn't all. You see, Alka-Seltzer is a pain reliever, also, and if you have a sickish headache along with the stomach upset. Alka-Seltzer can bring you mighty comforting relief in both of these disturbances. Be wise—take Alka-Seltzer. You'll feel better—*fast!*

BENNY.—You said it.

KELLY.—Quiet, please. We'll now start with the questions. All right, Quiz Kids . . .

R. S. Hart, of Seattle, Washington, says he was in the desert and after making an analysis of the only water available showed that it was 100 per cent aqua fontis. Would you drink such water? Joan . . .

JOAN.—Yes, I would.

KELLY.—Well, can you give us anything further?

JOAN.—Well, aqua fontis is fountain water.—

KELLY.—That's right . . . Well . . . it's really spring water, Joan.

JOAN.—Oh.

BENNY.—Yeah, it's *spring* water, Joan.

SOUND.—*Laughter.*

BENNY.—That's right, Mr. Kelly, it's spring water.

KELLY.—Yes, I know. It says so on my card.

BENNY.—Oh, that's where I saw it before.

SOUND.—*Laughter.*

KELLY.—All right, the next question.

Pete McDonald, of Veronia, Oregon, a schoolboy, who says that he never enjoyed anything in school but recess until he began listening to The Quiz Kids, sends in this one. Incidentally, he adds that his grades are improving. Here it is— if you had something that contained a prothorax, a meso-thorax . . .

BENNY.—A what? . . . a mess o' what? . . . What did you say
. . . a mess o' what . . .

KELLY.—A mesothorax.

BENNY.—Oh, a mesothorax.

KELLY.—And a metathorax, what would you have? Gerard . . .

BENNY.—Gerard, you answer. You had your hand up first.

GERARD.—Now, Mr. Benny, don't butt in, *please*.

BENNY.—Well, that's something . . . I can see I'm certainly
going to have a fine chance here today.

KELLY.—All right, Gerard.

GERARD.—The metathorax, the mesothorax, and prothorax are
all part of the thorax, which is part of an insect on the . . .
the thorax is the part between the abdomen and the head on
an insect.

KELLY.—Well, good for you, Gerard. That was marvelous.

SOUND.—*Applause.*

KELLY.—That's very good.

BENNY.—I used to know that when I went to school .   . You
know, when you get older you forget those things. You can't
remember everything . . .

KELLY.—Now, our next question.

BENNY.—I used to know algebra, too, when I went to school.

KELLY.—Quiet, please.

BENNY.—Oh . . .

KELLY.—Mrs. Burdett E. Truedson, of New York City, says you
can prove you have a good background by naming at least
three persons whose names will live forever because their
names have been used to identify their chief contributions to
humanity. For example, the name of Roentgen is perpetuated
in the word "roentgenology" . . . Claude . . .

CLAUDE.—Nobel . . . he was a Swiss scientist who discovered
dynamite and . . . he . . . people . . . he gives out prizes
to people who do something great for the world.

KELLY.—That's fine, Claude. Let's see what Joan has to offer.

JOAN.—Well, there's Calvinism . . . That's the doctrine as to the downfall of man . . . and Darwinism . . . ah . . . the theory of anthropology.

KELLY.—Very good, Joan. Jack Lucal.

JACK.—There's Alessandro Volta . . . his name is perpetuated in the volt, by which we measure electricity. And James Watt . . . they use his name, too, for the watt.

SOUND.—*Applause.*

KELLY.—Nice going, Jack Lucal. Let's see . . . Richard.

RICHARD.—Well, Martin Luther in the word "Lutheran," which is a church, and Dr. Roentgen who discovered the Roentgen rays.

SOUND.—*Applause.*

KELLY.—That's very good, Richard. Jackie has his hand up. What . . .

BENNY.—Well, there's a fellow named Max . . . he had something to do with the Maxwell . . . the Maxwell . . .

SOUND.—*Laughter.*

KELLY.—Now, wait a minute, Jackie . . . there's no connection there.

BENNY.—There is, too, a fellow named Max . . . sold me my car . . .

SOUND.—*Laughter.*

BENNY.—Max . . . Maxwell . . . his name was Max Miller . . . I've certainly got a fine chance on this program . . . I should have stayed on my own Jello show.

KELLY.—Well, it's beside the point, but we'll accept it as half right. Claude . . .

BENNY.—Oh, well. It's about time.

CLAUDE.—Also there's Jean François Ampère* . . . He had something to do with electricity, and his name lives in the ampere.

BENNY.—Oh, the ampere, the ampere . . .

* Actually Ampère's baptismal names were André Marie.

III

SOUND.—*Laughter.*

KELLY.—That's right, Claude. Jack Lucal.

JACK.—Well, Cadillac and La Salle were French explorers, and their names are names of automobiles.

SOUND.—*Laughter.*

KELLY.—Very good, Jack Lucal . . . I guess that will hold Jackie for a while. All right, our next question.

BENNY.—If everybody is going to get laughs on this program, I'm going home.

SOUND.—*Laughter.*

KELLY.—Gerard . . .

GERARD.—Well, there is also De Soto, whose name is a car . . .

SOUND.—*Laughter.*

GERARD.—He was the Spanish explorer that found the Mississippi.

KELLY.—That's right, Gerard. I am glad you brought that up.

BENNY.—What about Johnny Chev that made the Chevrolet . . .

SOUND.—*Laughter.*

BENNY.—For heaven's sake, if you're going into that kind of stuff . . . you know . . . Johnny Chev . . . What about Harry Stu . . .

SOUND.—*Laughter.*

BENNY.—With that stuff I can answer a million of them . . . you know . . . just ask some questions, that's all.

KELLY.—We'll all withdraw from the garage right now . . . and get into our next question.

SOUND.—*Laughter.*

KELLY.—Miss Margaret Faith, of Camden, New Jersey, poses this mountain climbing and mathematics problem.

BENNY.—(*Mumbling*)

KELLY.—A mountain climber was making his way along a mountain-side ledge . . .

BENNY.—Wait. Pardon me, who was it asked the question, please?

KELLY.—Miss Margaret Faith, of Camden, New Jersey . . .

BENNY.—Oh . . . Camden . . . yes . . . yes, I see.

KELLY.—Let's see, where are we? Oh, yeah.

SOUND.—*Laughter.*

KELLY.—A mountain climber was making his way along a mountain-side ledge at an altitude of 6,440 feet. While edging his way, he accidentally kicked a rock which went flying toward the bottom of the mountain at some animals who had to scurry for shelter. Ignoring the friction of the air, how long did the animals have to reach safety before the rock hit? Now, you have to do this in your head, kids. No pencil and paper.

BENNY.—What is the last question again, please? How many . . . how long did it take what?

KELLY.—Well, that's the question . . . how long did it take?

BENNY.—One minute and 43 seconds.

KELLY.—That's wrong . . . Richard.

BENNY.—I've certainly got a fine chance here.

KELLY.—Richard.

RICHARD.—Twenty seconds.

KELLY.—Twenty seconds is correct.

SOUND.—(*Applause*)

BENNY.—Well!

SOUND.—*Bell.*

BENNY.—No wonder. He *squared* the root. I tripled it.

SOUND.—*Laughter.*

KELLY.—Well, nice going, kids, and though I don't think you need it, you can rest a while. It's recess time.

CARPENTER.—We've been telling you over and over again about Alka-Seltzer. We've told you how good it is, how convenient and economical, and how fast it can bring relief in the distress of so many common ailments. And now . . . suppose we let Alka-Seltzer speak for itself. All right . . . first of all we take two Alka-Seltzer tablets from the package and drop them into a glass of water. Listen! (*Sound of Alka-Seltzer dropped into water . . . 3 seconds of fizz*) Hear that fizzing, sparkling sound? Sounds good, doesn't it? Well . . . it *is* good! It looks good, tastes good, and is *so* good for relief in so many common ailments. That's Alka-Seltzer, all right . . . the two-in-one remedy . . . two kinds of relief in one glass. First, Alka-Seltzer is a pain-reliever . . . just what you *want* for relief of headache or sore, aching muscles. And second, Alka-Seltzer is an alkalizer . . . just what you need when excess acid upsets your stomach and causes distress. Be sure to try a sparkling glass of Alka-Seltzer the next time any of these annoying ailments cause you trouble. See for yourself how good it is . . . how fast it can make you feel better! Ask your druggist for Alka-Seltzer!

MUSIC.—(*Organ*). *Theme . . . final eight bars to ending.*

CARPENTER.—Ladies and gentlemen, you are listening to The Quiz Kids, presented every Wednesday night at this time by the makers of Alka-Seltzer. Now, just a word about the questions. You can win a new Zenith portable radio with patented, built-in wave magnet if you send us a question which our question editor finds suitable for use on the air. Yes, Alka-Seltzer awards a famous Zenith portable radio for each question used on this program. Just mail your questions by post card or letter to Quiz Kids, National Broadcasting Company, Chicago. We reserve the right to reword questions, and if like questions are submitted, the first received will be used. All questions become the property of Quiz Kids. So send in your question, and win a radio.

BENNY.—You better see that I get that $100 bond, too . . . that's all I'm worried about.

CARPENTER.—All right, Joe, are you ready with the scores at the halfway point?

KELLY.—Yes, Ken, but in deference to our guest contestant, I hesitate to read them. I think I'll just let them go until after the second question session. Maybe a miracle will happen. By the way, Richard, that last question we had before the bell, can you tell us how you worked that out?

RICHARD.—Well, Mr. Kelly . . . any body falling through space, disregarding the friction of the air, accelerates at the rate of 32.2 miles . . . uh . . . feet per second, and so the rule is, the distance equals the time in seconds squared times half of the acceleration per second, and in this case it was 6,440 feet equals 16.1 times the time squared, so I divided 6,440 by 16.1 and got 400, which is the square of the time in seconds, and I extracted the square root, and that gave me 20, and so the answer is 20 seconds.

KELLY.—Good for you, Richard, my boy.

SOUND.—*Applause.*

KELLY.—Now let's see . . .

BENNY.—Where I made *my* mistake there, see . . . I took the least common multiple . . .

SOUND.—*Laughter.*

BENNY.—*That's* where I got wrong. That's where I got the minute 43 seconds.

SOUND.—*Laughter.*

KELLY.—You sort of squared it there.

BENNY.—That's what I said.

KELLY.—Well, let's get along here now. Here's a question from Mrs. Daniel Stormont, of Evanston, Illinois.

BENNY.—5,280 feet is 1 mile.

KELLY.—What? What did you say?

BENNY.—I said 5,280 feet is 1 mile.

KELLY.—Well, nobody asked that one.

BENNY.—Well, if they *do*, I'm ready, Watch out.

SOUND.—*Laughter.*

KELLY.—All right, we'll continue.
If you told the election board you were a mugwump, would you be listed as a Republican, Democrat, Socialist, or Independent?

BENNY.—I wouldn't tell *anybody* I was a *mugwump*.

SOUND.—*Laughter*.

KELLY.—Well, Claude.

CLAUDE.—I'll take a guess. I'd say an Independent.

KELLY.—That's right, but how did you guess it?

CLAUDE.—I just guessed.

KELLY.—Oh, you just guessed, that's right. You see the political name of mugwump . . . well, let's see what Joan has to say.

JOAN.—Well, I rather thought it was Independent too, because there's a column in one of our Chicago papers called "Mugwump."

KELLY.—That's true . . .

JOAN.—On politics.

KELLY.—You see, the political name of "mugwump" started in 1884, when it was applied to the political supporters of James G. Blaine, who switched to Cleveland because of his civil service views. Blaine was Republican candidate for President . . . Jackie . . .

BENNY.—I know what a mugwump is.

JOAN.—Oh, oh.

KELLY.—You do? All right.

BENNY.—A mugwump is a bird that sits on a fence with his mug on one end and his wump on the other.

SOUND.—*Laughter and applause*.

GERARD.—Mr. Benny, I'm afraid you're wrong.

KELLY.—Well, let's have a little more discipline, please. Getting back to the political situation, Jackie Benny, who was President of the United States in 1901?

BENNY.—Grover Cleveland.

KELLY.—That's wrong.

BENNY.—Well, I ought to know. I voted for him.

SOUND.—*Applause*.

BENNY.—It was Grover Cleveland.

KELLY.—You're wrong. It was William McKinley.

BENNY.—I just wish I had a history book, brother, that's all.

KELLY.—I've got one.

BENNY.—Well, give it to me, I've got a low chair here . . . It was Grover Cleveland, that's who it was.

KELLY.—Let's continue with the next question. Pauline Salzman, of Grand Rapids, Michigan . . .

BENNY.—It was Grover Cleveland. I know Grover Cleveland . . .

KELLY.—Quiet, please. I'd like to present this question. Pauline Salzman, of Grand Rapids, Michigan, found these ads in the paper. She would like you to tell her just what is advertised. Here is the first item: "For rent. Colonial estate near Charlottesville, Virginia. Designed by owner. Adjoining buildings make estate virtually a community. Write owner— T. J., Charlottesville, Virginia."
Jackie Benny you're holding your hand up.

BENNY.—I'm waving at some friends in the audience. I can have friends in the audience, can't I? Hello, Mamie!

SOUND.—*Laughter.*

KELLY.—Well, let's complete this question. Richard.

RICHARD.—Monticello.

KELLY.—Monticello, the home of . . .

RICHARD.—Thomas Jefferson.

KELLY.—That's right. Good for you.

BENNY.—That's right.

SOUND.—*Applause.*

KELLY.—Here's the next item: "For sale . . . "

BENNY.—You can have friends in the audience you know . . . good heavens . . . otherwise, there's no use in being here . . .

KELLY.—Quiet, quiet, please. Here's the second part of this question . . . "For sale. Sacrifice. Ten million dollar marble home in Land of Veda. Stands on 313-foot-square marble

117

terrace. Absolutely unique as architects' eyes poked out after construction completed " . . . Claude.

CLAUDE.—That's the Taj Mahal.

KELLY.—The Taj Mahal in India. Good for you.

BENNY.—It took 22,000 men 22 years to build it.

SOUND.—*Laughter.*

BENNY.—And I'm right about Grover Cleveland, too . . . I guess I know about Grover Cleveland . . . you know.

KELLY.—Well, we'll continue . . . Frank O. Estes, of Towson, Maryland, sends in this one. Last Christmas his wife went shopping to get her girl friends gifts. She bought Grace a green umbrella for $2.95, Ellen a blue scarf for $2.50, Jo Anne a brown leather pocketbook for $2.99, and Priscilla a yellow sport skirt for $3. What was the color of the scarf for Ellen? . . . Joan.

JOAN.—Blue.

KELLY.—Blue. That's right. Good for you.

BENNY.—1901 *was* Grover Cleveland . . .

SOUND.—*Laughter.*

BENNY.—I know, because I won a pair of cloth-topped shoes on the election . . . I remember that . . .

KELLY.—We'll forget about Grover Cleveland.

BENNY.—I won't forget about him.

SOUND.—*Laughter.*

KELLY.—Well, this next question here . . .

BENNY.—It burns me up. Come over here and you . . .

KELLY.—Quiet, please. Connie Haitomt . . .

BENNY.—Connie Haitomt . . . Connie Haitomt . . .

SOUND.—*Laughter.*

KELLY.—Now, Jackie, I'm reading a name . . .

BENNY.—All right, read the name.

KELLY.—All right, quiet. Connie Haitomt . . .

BENNY.—I'm not getting paid for this, you know . . .

SOUND.—*Laughter.*

BENNY.—I just came over . . . I'm just a guest . . . that's what burns me up . . . you know.

KELLY.—Connie Haitomt . . . Listen, Jackie, I'm beginning to think you're getting into what little hair I've got left.

BENNY.—I can always tell you where to get a toupee, you know.

SOUND.—*Laughter.*

KELLY.—Quiet. Connie Haitomt of Minneapolis, Minnesota, wants you to sing or hum these notes as I give them to you, and stop me as soon as you recognize the scales you are singing. All right, here is the first one: C, D, E♭, F, G, A♭, B, C.

JOAN.—(*Sings*)

KELLY.—All right, Joan, do you recognize the scale?

JOAN.—That's the harmonic minor.

KELLY.—That's very good. Two: C, C♯, D, D♯, E, F . . .

BENNY.—If I had my violin here I'd have gotten it.

KELLY.—I'll tell you what we're going to do. We've got some other hands up. I'm going to give this one . . . to Claude.

CLAUDE.—That's the chromatic.

KELLY.—Chromatic is correct. Good for you Claude.
And here is the last one: C, D, E♭, F, G, A, B, C, B♭ . . . Richard.

RICHARD.—That's the melodic.

KELLY.—Melodic is good. Good for you kids.

SOUND.—*Applause.*

BENNY.—It's one of the *silliest* questions I've ever heard.

SOUND.—*Laughter.*

BENNY.—(*Mumbling*) Once in a while . . .

KELLY.—Now, Quiz Kids, you'll need mythology . . .

BENNY.—I raise my hand all the time, and nobody even calls on me . . .

SOUND.—*Laughter.*

KELLY.—You'll need mythology as well as ornithology to answer this one. Ethel Baker, of St. Louis, Missouri, wants to know why peacock feathers are spotted.

BENNY.—Is that Paul Baker's sister?

SOUND.—*Laughter.*

KELLY.—What?

BENNY.—It isn't Paul Baker's sister, is it?

KELLY.—When you want to talk, Jackie, will you please hold up your hand?

BENNY.— . . . because I *know* a Ethel Baker, you know . . .

KELLY.—Well, remember to hold up your hand when you want to say something.

BENNY.—All right, I'll hold up my hand. For heaven's sake what does he think he is . . . the boss or something?

KELLY.—Quiet, please.

BENNY.—It's the last time I'll come on this show . . .

KELLY.—*You're telling us!*

SOUND.—*Laughter.*

KELLY.—Now, let's see, where am I? . . . Ethel Baker, of St. Louis, Missouri, wants to know why peacock feathers are spotted. Gerard.

GERARD.—The peacock has eyes in its tail feathers because . . . ah . . . it's a mere myth . . . you see when . . . a long time ago when Jupiter married Juno, after a few years he became jealous of her and turned her into a calf, and he sent Argus to watch, but Juno turned herself right back into her regular form, and Argus was the one that had a hundred eyes in . . . his head, and Juno killed Argus and put the eyes in the peacock's tail.*

KELLY.—Well, thank you very much, Gerard.

* Gerard was partly wrong on this, but it wasn't caught on this program.

120

SOUND.—*Applause.*

KELLY.—That was a very fine description . . . Jackie, I see you've got your hand up.

BENNY.—I'm wiping my forehead. It's hot in here. You can't even raise your hand. Most ridiculous questions I ever heard.

KELLY.—We'll continue. James Wilson, Jr., of Toledo, Ohio, wants you to compose a second line to his one-line verse. Here it is—"Fred Allen has a funny show . . . "

BENNY.—*I'm going home.*

SOUND.—*Laughter.*

KELLY.—You keep your seat . . . All right . . . "Fred Allen has a funny show" . . . Let's hear a second line to that . . . Joan.

JOAN.—Fred Allen has a funny show
But there's not a thing he doesn't know . . . Hum!

KELLY.—Very good, Joan. All right, let's have another one.

BENNY.—What's funny about that?

KELLY.—Gerard.

GERARD.—When Mr. Benny hears that he'll surely blow.

SOUND.—*Laughter.*

KELLY.—All right, Jackie, what do you have to offer?

BENNY.—Fred Allen has a funny show.
How he does it, I don't know.
His jokes are old, his gags ain't funny.
He ought to be paid in Confederate money.
The end.

SOUND.—*Laughter.*

KELLY.—Now, then, here is really one for you, Jackie Benny.

BENNY.—Fine, my father is listening in.

KELLY.—All right, Jackie, how many strings on a violin?

BENNY.—Five, I mean four.

121

KELLY.—Very good . . . How do you spell rosin?

BENNY.—R-O-S-O-N.

KELLY.—That's wrong. It's R-O-S-I-N.

BENNY.—I can't understand it. I've been using it for years.

SOUND.—*Laughter. Bell.*

KELLY.—Well, there's the bell, kids. I'll have your scores in just a moment.

CARPENTER.—Have you had your vitamins today? Well, here's the answer to your daily vitamin A and D problem: Take One-A-Day Brand vitamin A and D tablets, now offered and guaranteed by the makers of Alka-Seltzer. Each One-A-Day tablet is equal in vitamin A and D content to 2 whole teaspoonfuls of cod-liver oil, meeting minimum United States Pharmacopoeia standards. One a day is all you take—one a day is all you need—and a penny a day is all it costs. Listen to these low prices: 30 tablets, 35 cents; 90 tablets, only 85 cents; and 180 tablets, only $1.50. One a day is all you take; 1 penny a day is all it costs. Remember, One-A-Day brand vitamin A and D tablets have been developed and are guaranteed by the makers of Alka-Seltzer, tested and approved by Good Housekeeping Bureau, and commended by Consumer Service Bureau of *Parents' Magazine*. Every member of your family should take One-A-Day tablets—every day. Ask your druggist for One-A-Day tablets. That's the name . . . One-A-Day tablets. Ask your druggist for One-A-Day Tablets. Look for the big "One" on the package.

MUSIC.—*(Organ). Theme . . . final eight bars to ending.*

KELLY.—Well, kids, as a group you missed only one question tonight, and the individual winners are Richard—first, Joan—second, and Claude—third.

I congratulate all you Quiz Kids and take pleasure in presenting to each of you, in behalf of the makers of Alka-Seltzer, a $100 denomination United States savings bond. Jackie Benny, I don't have one for you. You see, these bonds are to help the children pay for their future education, and we didn't think you'd spend your money in going to college. But here's a Zenith portable radio. Maybe you can learn something listening to the Quiz Kids every Wednesday night.

BENNY.—Well, at least I can hock the radio.

KELLY.—Well, we'll be back in Chicago next week, and we'll resume competition with only the three highest scorers remaining for the succeeding examination. The three winners on our last competitive program were Claude, Richard, and Jack. Completing the board will be Gerard and Joan, the same children on the program tonight. Meanwhile, this is Joe Kelly dismissing the Quiz Kids class until next Wednesday at the same time. Good night, kids!

KIDS.—Good night, Mr. Kelly.

BENNY.—Come on, ask some more questions. Let's get going here! Come on . . .

MUSIC.—(*Organ*). *Theme.*

CARPENTER.—Listen again next Wednesday night to The Quiz Kids. The makers of Alka-Seltzer present three programs each week . . . all of them on NBC networks. On Friday night, Alec Templeton Time; on Saturday night, the famous Alka-Seltzer National Barn Dance; and next Wednesday night again, The Quiz Kids. For interesting variety and entertainment, listen to the Alka-Seltzer shows. Ken Carpenter speaking.

ANNOUNCER.—This is the National Broadcasting Company.

Rudy Vallee Program

MUSIC.—(*Orchestra*). *Theme.*

BILL.—The Sealtest System of Laboratory Protection presents . . . Rudy Vallee, with John Barrymore, Susan Miller, and our special guest, Virginia Bruce.

MUSIC.—(*Rudy, glee club, and orchestra*). *Theme.*
I'll give you a smile for a smile,
A song for a song for a while.
I'll give you a heart for a moment sublime.
Right from the start, we'll have a grand time . . .

MUSIC.—*Up and under.*

RUDY.—Good evening, ladies and gentlemen. This is Rudy Vallee, welcoming you to another Sealtest program. Tonight we're blazing a trail to the frozen north, the Klondike, where we present a hot icicle entitled "Yukon, If You Think You-kon." So we hitch up our dog sleds, and off we go. Mush! Mush!

JOHN.—Sounds like a lotta mush to me, Vallee . . . but go ahead. If you mush, you mush.

MUSIC.—(*Rudy, glee club, and orchestra*). *"Come to the Yukon."* (*Original*).
Come on
To the Yukon,
Where life's full of chills and thrills.
There is drama—in this white panorama,
And there's gold in "them thar" hills.
Every reindeer
Drinks champagne here,
And you never will grow old.
So come on
To the Yukon,
And you'll find your pot of gold.

SOUND.—*Wind effect up and under.*

124

BILL.—In the wind-swept reaches of Alaska, in the rough, tough mining town of Bonanza-Split, there flourishes that ratty rendezvous of the riffraff, "Club Frostbite."

SOUND.—*Crowd noises up and fade.*

BILL.—Here mingle prospectors, adventurers, gamblers, and . . .

SUSAN AND PIANO.—(*Off-mike*) All my life I've had a plan
That someday there'd be a man . . .

BILL.—Oh, yes, and the lady known as Bruce!

SUSAN AND PIANO.—(*Slow fade*) He'd find me . . . waiting around.

BILL.—It is here we meet the sinister character who owns this unsavory den . . . dangerous John McBarrymore!

JOHN.—(*Sinister laugh*) *I'm bad* . . .

HAL.—(*Chinese . . . calling*) Missy Ballymore! Missy Bally-more!

JOHN.—O, so it's you, is it, One Low Punch?

HAL.—Yeah. Haw haw. Thatsie me! Haw! Haw!

JOHN.—How many times have I told you not to slink in here this way?

HAL.—Me can't help it. Me always walk this way!

JOHN.—You do?

HAL.—Yeah. Confidentially, I slink!

JOHN.—I agree with you perfectly—now, what do you want, my meanderin' mandarin?

HAL.—Aw say—me glot blig news . . . Man just come into bar. Name is Ludy Vallee! Haw! Haw!

JOHN.—Rudy Vallee?

HAL.—Yeah. He got gold! Muchee gold!

JOHN.—How much has Vallee got?

HAL.—Vallee much! Haw! Haw!

John.—Hmm! A prospector with gold, eh? That gives me an idea. I think I'll pinch his poke.

Sound.—*Door opens . . . crowd noises . . . piano tinkle . . . fade for*

John.—Howdy, stranger!

Rudy.—Howdy, friend.

John.—Allow me to introduce myself! Barrymore's my name, better, known as "Dangerous John."

Rudy.—Be you the feller the northern gals call "Sweet Smellin' John, the Yukon Don Juan"?

John.—The same. And be'n't you the feller they call "Lucky Rudy, the Klondike Patootie"?

Rudy.—The same.

John.—They tell me you found a heap of gold, son.

Rudy.—Yep. But I had a heap of trouble, too. Had to find the vein, dig the shaft, scrape out the ore, melt down the gold . . . been so busy I haven't seen a woman in 6 years. Yes, sir, a heap of trouble.

John.—Such trouble I should have! . . . But speakin' of mines, son, just where is yours located?

Rudy.—I ain't a-sayin', stranger. Suffice it to say, it's out *ch*onder!

John.—Out *ch*onder?

Rudy.—Yep. *Way* out chonder . . . and git away from that well.

John.—What do you mean, git away from that well?

Rudy.—Stop pumping me!

John.—No offense meant, son! Just what brings you through this blizzard all the way into town?

Rudy.—Wal, sir, it's this-a-way! I got my gold, and I got my gold mine, and now I come to get me a helpmate.

John.—Oh, lookin' for a gal to marry up with, eh?

Rudy.—Yep—I'm fixin to go mixin' with a vixen.

126

JOHN.—Oh, you are, eh? Well would you like to meet Virginia, the lady known as Bruce!

RUDY.—(*Clicks tongue*) Sure would.

JOHN.—You just wait here, son! I'll speak to her, and possibly I can arrange it! . . . Possibly! (*Dirty laugh*)

RUDY.—Gosh, he sure laughs dirty like.

MUSIC.—*Bridge.*

JOHN.—Now that is the story, Virginia! All you got to do is make a play for this Vallee, find out the location of his gold mine, and leave the rest to me!

BRUCE.—As you say, tall, dark, and double cross.

JOHN.—Good . . . Now all you gotta do is to find out where his mine is, and then I'll go up there and grab it off alone!

BRUCE.—Grab it off alone! (*Laughs*) Do you think you could mush through the snow, tramp through the wilderness, grab off a gold mine, and run it all by yourself? At your age?

JOHN.—Of course I could!

BRUCE.—My . . . my . . . they must have upped your octane again!

JOHN.—Just leave it to me! Now you wait here, and I'll bring Vallee over! And be on your best behavior!

BRUCE.—You mean you want me to be a lady?

JOHN.—Well, I don't ask miracles! Wait here! (*Calls*) Oh, Rudy, me boy!

RUDY.—Yes, McBarrymore!

JOHN.—Rudy, my boy, meet Virginia, the lady known as B-ruce. Pretty pretty, ain't she?

RUDY.—Say, she's mighty beautiful! I could do a lot worse!

JOHN.—You have! (*Calls*) Oh, Ginny, dee-ar. This is Rudy Vallee from way out chonder!

BRUCE.—(*Very cordial*) Oh, how do you do, Mr. Vallee! I've always wanted to meet a *great, big* outchonder man.

RUDY.—Well, gal, I ain't really much.

127

JOHN.—Before I'm forced to agree, I will scram.

BRUCE.—Mr. Vallee, let's sit over here on top of this piano, where we can be alone and talk!

RUDY.—Say, I'm proud to meet you, Miss Virginia. Mighty proud.

BRUCE.—Me too, Mr. Vallee.

RUDY.—Gee, you're about the sweetest, most innocent-lookin' little gal I ever seed. Could I buy you a drink?

BRUCE.—Good gracious, no! I never drink!

RUDY.—Cigarette?

BRUCE.—Oh, no—I never smoke!

RUDY.—Have a chaw?

BRUCE.—Well—just a little one.

RUDY.—Little gal—I don't know if I ought to say this, but . . .

BRUCE.—Go ahead.

RUDY.—Well, little gal, I been up in the wilderness all alone, living by myself for 6 long years, and . . . (*dramatic*) and all those years one thing's been on my mind more than anything else.

BRUCE.—Yes . . . Yes . . .

RUDY.—I know I shouldn't ask you, gal . . . but I *got to* . . . I been away so long I got to ask you!

BRUCE.—What?

RUDY.—Whatever happened to Dick Tracy?

BRUCE.—I'll tell you, if first you tell me why you came to town.

RUDY.—Well, I came because I want to pick me out a partner, a bride.

BRUCE.—Oh, a bride, eh? Are you proposing that . . . well, are you proposing?

RUDY.—Well, I know this is all kind of impulsive and sudden like, but—Miss Virginia—will you marry me and come to my mine with me?

128

BRUCE.—Listen, my major little minor, don't you realize I'm working with Mr. Barrymore?

RUDY.—Oh, yes, Barrymore! . . . Wonderful man, Barrymore. So rough and so tough. Wonder *how* he keeps going.

BRUCE.—Me, too. And *where*.

RUDY.—Tell me, Miss Virginia, is there a chance for me?

BRUCE.—Maybe. But first tell me . . . Just where *is* your mine?

RUDY.—Gal—get away from that pump!

BRUCE.—What?

RUDY.—Never mind, I'll tell you later. In the meantime, would you agree to kiss me? You know, I been away so long . . .

BRUCE.—Why, Rudy! A kiss!

RUDY.—Yep, you know. Sorta like this . . .

SOUND.—*Big kiss*.

BRUCE.—My . . . you *have* been away, haven't you? Gee, that was heavenly!

RUDY.—Did you say heavenly, gal?

BRUCE.—Yes, why?

RUDY.—Why! Why! Why, that's my song cue, that's why!

MUSIC.—(*Rudy and orchestra*). "*I Touched a Star*" . . . (*Chorus and a half*).

RUDY.—(*Solo*) I touched a star
    When first your lips touched mine
    And brought it down to earth for you.
    I touched a star
    As soft as candle shine,
    A lover's lantern in the blue.
    And then I pinned it in your hair . . .
    It looked so lovely there.
    And as I breathed a prayer,
    Those golden beams brought starlight dreams.
    The night was still,
    And our love grew until
    My heart flew up so far
    I touched a star.

GLEE CLUB.— And when I pinned it by your side
It looked so lovely there . . .
And as I breathed a prayer,
Those golden beams brought starlight dreams . . .

RUDY.—(*Solo*) The night was still,
And our love grew until
My heart flew up so far—I touched

ALL.—   A star.

BRUCE.—And that, too, was heavenly, Rudy. Heavenly! (*Kraft cue*)

MUSIC.—(*Orchestra*). *Music bridge . . . reprise . . . "Touched a Star" . . . fade for*
(*Network commercial*)

BILL.—Yukon! The Klondike! Yes, those were magic words not long ago . . . drawing men to incredible hardships in their search for gold.

But let me tell you about a *richer* gold mine . . . one that stretches over the length and breadth of the nation.

It is *America's great dairy industry!*

RUDY.—You're right, Bill. Dairy products are a gold mine of *wealth* for our nation . . . and a gold mine of health for our people.

Just think. Dairy products furnish *one-quarter of all the food we eat!*

The Sealtest System of Laboratory Protection plays an important part in helping to protect this vital food supply . . . in helping to keep it pure, fresh, and wholesome.

Sealtest maintains scores of laboratories in local Sealtest milk and ice-cream plants over a good part of America. In these laboratories, Sealtest "men in white" are constantly testing, checking, and supervising the purity of Sealtest milk, ice cream, and other dairy products.

BILL.—Yes, in millions of homes, today, the name "Sealtest" has come to mean *added care, extra precautions, complete laboratory control* over quality and purity.

Now here's a suggestion: Sunday is Easter . . . and it's a day of feasting. So be sure to order plenty of rich, golden Sealtest cream. It will add so much to your day's enjoyment . . . in steaming coffee . . . with fresh fruits and crispy cereals . . . in appetizing soups, sauces, and gravies. And you housewives know a dozen luscious desserts that you can make with real cream and top with whipped cream.

We'll tell you in a few minutes where Sealtest products are sold in your community.

MUSIC.—*(Orchestra)*. *Bridge* . . . *"Come to the Yukon."*

BILL.—Back in the cold and crew-el Klondike, we find Dangerous John McBarrymore in *sneer*ious conversation with Virginia— the lady known as Baruce!

JOHN.—Well, you did a great job, me blonde beauty. I saw Vallee hand you the map of his mine and now his mine is my mine and what's my mine is your mine. In short, we've struck a bonanza.

BRUCE.—Not so fast, Jake. I tore up that map.

JOHN.—Tore up the map! You mean . . .

BRUCE.—Yes, we have no bonanza!

JOHN.—What? No bonanza to split?

BRUCE.—No, and I don't care. I love this clean-cut, curly-haired, Klondike cutie, Rudy Vallee . . . and I'm going to marry him!

JOHN.—*(Menacy)* Now wait a minute . . . do you think I'm going to let you walk out of here with Vallee, that nasal nugget? Oh, no! First you'll have me to reckon with! And remember, it's not for naught they call me Yukon Jake, the Slithery Snake.

BRUCE.—Oh, what a plight! What a plight! What to do. What to do.

JOHN.—Give me the map. Give me the map.

BRUCE.—Never! Never!

JOHN.—Do we have to double-talk our way out of this? Gimme that map by the time I count three, or I'll reveal everything to your green little Vallee . . . One . . . two . . . two and a half . . . two and seven-eighths . . . Stop me. I'm running out of fractions.

BRUCE.—Stop! Don't tell Rudy! Here's the map! Take it! Take it! *(Sobs)* You vile viper. *(Sobs)*

JOHN.—I knew I'd get it! So long, me frost-bitten canary. (*Laughs*)

SOUND.—*Door closes.*

RUDY.—Oh, there you are, Dangerous John.

JOHN.—Out of me way, Vallee! I'm on me way to steal a gold mine.

RUDY.—Steal a gold mine! Is that cricket?

JOHN.—No . . . It's crooked. (*Laughs*) I have to laugh when I think how easy it was. The fellow who owns it is such a simple boob to bamboozle.

RUDY.—He must be.

JOHN.—He is . . . so long, sucker.

RUDY.—So long. Now to see my sweet gal, Virginia . . .

SOUND.—*Knock on door.*

BRUCE.—(*Off-mike*) Who is it?

RUDY.—It's the man who kissed you last night!

BRUCE.—Answer my question—who is it?

SOUND.—*Door opens.*

BRUCE.—(*Crying*) Oh, Rudy! It's choo!

RUDY.—Yes, it's schme! Why, you've been crying, gal.

BRUCE.—Oh, Rudy! I'm so unhappy . . . I'm so *ashamed!*

RUDY.—What have you to be ashamed of, gal? Ain't you the sweetheart of Rudy Vallee?

BRUCE.—Please don't make it worse.

RUDY.—Gal, are you hiding something from me?

BRUCE.—Yes, Rudy, I am! I've been hiding my past from you!

RUDY.—Your past?

BRUCE.—Yes, my lurid past! Rudy . . . I am not . . . I am not a happy hearth and home girl.

RUDY.—Good gracious to Betsy, gal. You might have spared me this. But tell me more. (It's hot stuff.)

132

BRUCE.—If I do, you'll never find it in your heart to forgive and forget me.

RUDY.—Forgive, ay. Forget, nay. I still love you, hay, hay.

BRUCE.—Oh, you're so kind and so sweet and so handsome . . . well, anyhow, you're kind. And wherever you lead me I shall follow.

RUDY.—Then come along. I'll lead you into a song. (*Music in*) This way to the down beat, gal.

MUSIC.—(*Susan Miller and orchestra*). *"Waiting Around."* (*Original*).

SUSAN.—All my life I've had a plan
    That someday there'd be a man
    Who'd find me—waitin' around.
    In his dreams if he could place
    Lonely me in his embrace,
    He'd find me—waitin' around.
    Have you ever spent your nights so lonely,
    Hoping that you'll meet your one and only?
    If you feel the way I do
    And want to make my dreams come true,
    You'll find me—waitin' around . . .
    Waitin' around.

RUDY.—Your waitin' is over, gal. I'm stakin' my claim to your heart right now.

BRUCE.—Oh, but Rudy, I forgot to tell you something else.

RUDY.—Else! You mean there's more? Good gracious to Betsy.

BRUCE.—Yes. I told Dangerous John where your gold mine is.

RUDY.—Oh, that's all right. I don't mind. As a matter of fact, I saw him just awhile ago, and he told me he was on his way to bamboozle some boo . . . *what?!!*

BRUCE.—Yes, my trusting lover, Barrymore is on his way to steal *your mine.*

RUDY.—Come, gal. We must foil the pernicious profile's putrid plan. We're off—to the mine! (*Kraft cue*)

MUSIC.—(*Orchestra*). *Music bridge . . . 8 seconds . . . then down for*

133

BILL.—Now a brief pause for Sealtest identification. Here we go to all of those communities where Sealtest milk and ice cream are sold. Ready?

(*Local commercial . . . 1 minute*)

MUSIC.—(*Orchestra*). *Bridge . . . Sleigh-bell stuff.*

BILL.—Across the frozen wastelands of the North, on the road to Vallee's mine, speeds a dog sled, driven by Dangerous John's Chinese henchman. And low down in that dog sled is that low-down dog, John Barrymore. Sssssssss.

SOUND.—*Windh owling . . . dogs yapping . . . fade down under.*

MUSIC.—(*Glee club and orchestra*). *"Mush, Mush, Mush."* (*Original*).

GLEE CLUB.—Mush, mush, mush, through the ice and slush
 Goes Barrymore—to the mine.
 Through the snow and cold, seeking Vallee's gold,
 Goes Barrymore—to the mine.
 He's the claim-jumping wizard of the regions polar.
 He'd brave a blizzard to steal gold from your molar.
 Some folks say when his ears are frostbitten
 And his hand turns blue beneath his mitten,
 That he'll repent and be conscience-smitten,
 But that's a lot of mush, mush, mush—to the mine!

SOUND.—*Wind howling . . . dogs yapping . . . fade down under*

JOHN.—Mush! . . . Hey, One Low Punch, aren't we ever going to reach Vallee's gold mine?

HAL.—Oh, ho . . . as honorable ancestor say, quote . . . keep honorable shirtee on. Honorable unquote.

JOHN.—Honorable this and honorable that. Why don't you ever call *me* honorable?

HAL.—(*Laugh*) Answer pletty obvlious!

JOHN.—Well, make those dogs go faster!

HAL.—(*Ad libs Chinese*) Al light.

JOHN.—A fine kettle of chow mein! We're hardly moving! I can't wait to jump Rudy Vallee's claim . . . Why, it'll make me the richest clook in the Krondike, One Low Punch.

134

HAL.—Thank youee, but Mr. Blarrymore, please . . . don't call me One Punch Low. My name Fuey-on.

JOHN.—Fuey-on? Fuey-on who?

HAL.—(*Laughs*) Answer pletty obvlious! Mr. Blarrymore, look! I see sign in snow!

JOHN.—This must be Vallee's claim! Yes, it is! The sign says "Sealtest Gold Mine."

HAL.—Sealtest Gold Mine. Ho-ho. Plug pletty obvlious. Say, Mr. Blarrymore, this mine looks pletty deep. How you get gold out?

JOHN.—I'll hire gold diggers.

HAL.—Aw, Mr. Blarrymore . . . you know where to find gold diggers?

JOHN.—Haw haw . . . Answer pletty obvlious! . . . But don't you worry, Fuey . . . We'll get the gold out of this mine if we have to dig right down to China!

HAL.—Oh, ho, ho . . . Chinese people get gleat big shock if they see John Blarrymore.

JOHN.—The Chinese people would be shocked to see me? Why?

HAL.—Up to now they think Confucius oldest man!

RUDY.—(*Off-mike . . . calls*) Barrymore! Stop! Halt in the name of Yukon jus-tyce.

JOHN.—Curses! Caught by that curly Klondike crooner!

RUDY.—(*Fade-in*) Barrymore, I should beat you within a quarter inch of your life!

BRUCE.—Rudy . . . you mean within an *inch* of his life.

RUDY.—No . . . on him you have to figure closer!

JOHN.—Do what you will! The gold mine belongs to me! I've jumped your claim!

RUDY.—Barrymore, I'll get this mine back if I have to drag you through every court in the country.

JOHN.—Better let me drag you . . . I know the way!

RUDY.—Gal o'mine, denounce this cur, McBarrymore. Tell him what you think of him! Tell him to his face!

BRUCE.—There must be an easier way!

JOHN.—So! You mock me, me proud beauty! I'll teach you to trifle with Dangerous John . . .

BRUCE.—(*Slight scream*)

RUDY.—Unhand her, you cowardly cad!

JOHN.—You call me a cowardly cad, egad!

RUDY.—Yes, you are not only a cad but also the following! Loafer, villain, scoundrel, gambler, blackguard, cheat, viper, and crook.

JOHN.—You should see the 1942 model.

RUDY.—Barrymore, you have wrong-ed me, and we shall settle this—man to man!

BRUCE.—Oh! I'll step outside . . . I can't stand the sight of men fighting!

JOHN.—I can't either . . . I'll step out *with* you!

RUDY.—Not so fast, Yukon Jake! The time has come for you to *pay* for all your evil doings! To *pay* for all your wicked deeds!

JOHN.—Couldn't I just get them refinanced!?

RUDY.—You can't get out of it this time! The code of the North demands that we fight bare-fisted . . . like cavemen fought in prehistoric days.

BRUCE.—That gives Barrymore the advantage . . . he was there!

RUDY.—But I shall triumph, for I am all that is good and clean and wholesome!

JOHN.—Fiddle faddle.

RUDY.—I have trained rigorously, and you have not! I have abstained from harmful habits, and you have not! I have learned the science of boxing, and you have not!

SOUND.—*Loud smack of fist . . . body falls.*

JOHN.—But I have a pair of brass knuckles, and you have not!

BRUCE.—You've knocked Rudy down, you big bully! . . . Rudy, speak to me. Speak, Rudy . . . speak . . . speak!

RUDY.—Arf . . . arf . . . arf!

BRUCE.—Oh, I'm so glad you're normal again! . . . Come on, Rudy, let's get out of this evil old gold mine and go back to . . .

SOUND.—*Rumbling noise.*

RUDY.—Shhhh—listen! Do you hear something?

BRUCE.—I don't hear anything.

JOHN.—I don't hear anything.

SOUND.—*Terrific crash and rumble of snow slide.*

RUDY.—That's strange . . . I could have sworn I heard something.

BRUCE.—Look! It was a snow slide! We're trapped by tons and tons of ice!

RUDY.—Oh, this is terrible! I can see my whole life unfolding before my eyes!

BRUCE.—I can see *my* whole life unfolding before *my* eyes!

JOHN.—(*Screams*)

RUDY.—What's the matter?

JOHN.—Me, too!

BRUCE.—Rudy—Rudy, the ice is making it terribly cold in here. I'm so chilly! Can't you do something?

RUDY.—Well, if I build a fire it will use up our oxygen.

BRUCE.—(*Coyly*) Well, Rudy . . . isn't there some other way you could keep me warm . . . hmmmmm?

RUDY.—(*Dopey*) You could stamp your feet!

JOHN.—Here stands a forest fire, and she plays with matches!

RUDY.—Come, gal, we must find a way out of here. The air will only last another minute or so with Barrymore breathing here!

BRUCE.—All right, Rudy . . . (*Fading*) We must hurry . . . we *must* find a way out.

JOHN.—(*To self*) Only enough air for another minute or so! No! This can't happen to me, John Barrymore. I'm too young to go like this . . . cut down in the full bloom of my tender youth! . . . No! I haven't lived! There are too many things I haven't done!

HANS.—(*Echo chamber*) Name one.

JOHN.—Who said that? Who are you?

HANS.—(*Echo*) I am your conscience, John.

JOHN.—Conscience? What's that?

HANS.—(*Echo*) Your conscience is something that keeps you from doing wrong . . . keeps you on the straight and narrow . . . keeps you out of trouble.

JOHN.—A conscience does that?

HANS.—(*Echo*) Yes.

JOHN.—*Now* he tells me!

HANS.—(*Echo*) John . . . there's not much time left. Don't you think you'd better reform? You've been a very naughty boy, John.

JOHN.—Me? John Barrymore? (*Snort*) Naughty?

HANS.—(*Echo*) Yes, you . . . John Barrymore . . . (*Snort*) Naughty! Reform, John, reform.

JOHN.—Say, conscience . . . you sound a little younger than I do.

HANS.—(*Echo*) Why not . . . I haven't been active since you were twelve! Hurry, John, before it's too late . . . reform! Give this gold mine back to its rightful owner. Give it back!

JOHN.—(*Imitating conscience*) Well . . . All right . . . (*Normal voice*) That guy's got me doing it . . . I'll do it. I'll give the gold mine back to Rudy Vallee!

RUDY.—(*Fade in yelling excitedly*) John! John! We're saved! Saved!

BRUCE.—Yes, John . . . your Chinese servant saved our lives . . . Fuey-on cleared out the entrance to the mine!

JOHN.—But how?

RUDY.—He *ayte* his way through it!

JOHN.—(*Incredulous*) *Ayte* his way through 3 tons of ice?

HAL.—Ice?! (*Cries*) Jimily clickets! I thought you say *rice!*

JOHN.—Vallee, my boy, I'm giving up my claim to your mine. And to your girl, too. Marry him, Virginia, and may you live sappily ever after.

RUDY.—Barrymore, you're a pal. But Virginia, my gal, now that I've got my mine back and am worth 10 million dollars . . . will you marry me?

BRUCE.—(*Imitates Chinaman*) Oh, ho, ho . . . answer pletty, obvlious!

MUSIC.—(*Orchestra*). *Tag . . . applause . . .* (*Rudy and orchestra*). *Theme.*

RUDY.—Next Thursday, John and I shall don our silk and satin sarongs to welcome that glittering and gorgeous glamour gal, Dorothy Lamour. Together we shall ambulate through a satire of the silver screen entitled "Seeing Hollywood with Gun and Camera" . . . so plan to be with us.

Until next Thursday, then, this is Rudy Vallee, reminding you to look for the red-and-white Sealtest symbol when you buy milk, ice cream, and other dairy products. Au revoir and good night.

SOUND.—*Applause to fill.*

BILL.—Sealtest, Inc., and its member companies are subsidiaries of the National Dairy Products Corporation. This is the National Broadcasting Company.

Jack Benny

WILSON.—The Jell-O program . . . starring Jack Benny . . . with Mary Livingstone, Phil Harris, Dennis Day, and "Yours truly" Don Wilson.

The orchestra opens the program with "Honolulu Lulu, How Are You?"

(Segue into number)

MUSIC.—*(Phil Harris and orchestra). Cue* 5.
(Opening commercial)

WILSON.—When it comes to gay, colorful beauty, ladies and gentlemen . . . "the flowers that bloom in the spring" certainly have a real rival in Jell-O! Jell-O is one of the most attractive, most inviting desserts you can possibly serve! It fairly glistens with goodness, shining and shimmering with a rich, lustrous look all its own! And Jell-O's bright, glowing colors are a joy just to behold! As for flavor . . . well, Jell-O's flavor is simply irresistible! . . . as delightful and refreshing as the juicy-ripe fruit itself! And Jell-O is pleasantly inexpensive . . . pleasantly *easy to make!* So enjoy this swell treat real *soon,* folks . . . in all of Jell-O's six delicious flavors . . . strawberry, raspberry, cherry, orange, lemon, and lime! Be especially sure to try strawberry, raspberry, and cherry Jell-O. Because each has a new improved flavor, obtained by using a natural flavor base, artificially enhanced. And that means a new, distinctive goodness! . . . something really fine! Make up a luscious mold of *rich, radiant* Jell-O . . . tomorrow!

WILSON.—That was "Honolulu Lulu, How Are You?" . . . played by the orchestra . . . and now, ladies and gentlemen, once again I bring you our master of ceremonies . . . a man who last Sunday night refereed that famous battle of wits between the Quiz Kids of Chicago and the Jell-O Kids of . . .

PHIL.—Hold it, Don, hold it . . . Mary just called up and said that Jackson can't be here tonight.

WILSON.—Why not?

PHIL.—Well, he's worried to death about his appearance on The Quiz Kids' show next Wednesday night . . . He's home studying, so he'll be as smart as they are.

DENNIS.—He should live so long.

PHIL.—You said it, Dennis . . . Them kids is mental giants . . . Why even *I'd* be afraid to go on their program . . . No kiddin'.

WILSON.—Well, Jack *is* taking this pretty seriously. I understand he's even had Mary over to his house all day yesterday, asking him questions (*Start to fade*) That's all that's on his mind . . . The Quiz Kids . . . Questions, answers . . . questions, answers . . . You'd think it was the most important thing that . . .
(*Cross-fade to*)

JACK.—What a mess . . . I can't get over it . . . If my father told me once, he told me a thousand times . . . go to college, learn something . . . But no! I had to get into vaudeville.

MARY.—Jack, concentrate . . . have you got the answer to this question yet?

JACK.—Hm! . . . I can name you every vaudeville threatre in the country . . . I even know the first name of every one of Fink's mules . . . from Bessie to Jerome . . . But will they ask me that next Wednesday? . . . No!

MARY.—Oh, quit beefin' . . . Do you know the answer to this question or not!

JACK.—No, what is it?

MARY.—1492.

JACK.—Holy smoke, was it that long ago? . . . All right, Mary, ask me another one.

MARY.—Okay . . . Here's an easy one . . . What's the Taj Mahal?

JACK.—An auto court on Ventura Boulevard.

MARY.—Oh, for heaven's sake! . . . The Taj Mahal is in India; and it's one of the Seven Wonders of the World.

141

JACK.—Oh . . . gee, I'm dumb. I guess I don't know anything, do I?

MARY.—Well, let's keep on, anyway . . . Here's another question . . . Name the President of the United States whose likeness appears on a $20 bill.

JACK.—A $20 bill? . . . I don't know.

MARY.—Well, go up and look in your mattress.

JACK.—Oh, stop, will yuh? Say, I wonder if The Quiz Kids know anything about the Taj Mahal. I'll have to ask them after dinner.

MARY.—After dinner?

JACK.—Oh, didn't I tell you, Mary? You know I'm so nuts about those kids, I invited three of 'em to stay here at my house. I just couldn't let them go to a hotel . . . Oh, Rochester!

ROCHESTER.—Yes, boss.

JACK.—Where are The Quiz Kids?

ROCHESTER.—Well . . . Richard and Gerard are in the backyard, discussin' anthropology.

JACK.—Anthropology, eh? . . . Well, did you hide in the bushes and make notes of what they said . . . like I told you to?

ROCHESTER.—Yes, sir . . . And say, boss.

JACK.—What.

ROCHESTER.—Did you know I'm not a Caucasian?

JACK.—No . . . but if they say so, it's right . . . Now, where's the other boy . . . Claude?

ROCHESTER.—He's in the library, readin' Shakespeare.

JACK.—Shakespeare? Well I'm going to have it tough enough Wednesday night without him pulling that on me . . . Go in the library and see if you can mix him up.

ROCHESTER.—Mix him up?

JACK.—Yes.

ROCHESTER.—I tried to, and he said "Othello, don't mess around!"

142

JACK.—*Gazooks, I'm cooked!* . . . Well, at least find out what he's reading, and I'll read the same thing . . . See you later.

ROCHESTER.—Okay, boss . . . Parting is such sweet sorrow.

JACK.—Get outta here!

SOUND.—*Door slams.*

JACK.—Hm!

MARY.—Say, Jack, here's a question in American history they might ask you.

JACK.—A lot of good that'll do . . . All I know is show business and vaudeville theatres . . . Go ahead anyway.

MARY.—Here's a question in American history they might ask you . . . What city is on an island that was purchased from the Indians for $24?

JACK.—What city . . . is on an island . . . that was . . . Let's see.

MARY.—I'll give you a clue . . . Where's the Roxy Theatre?

JACK.—*New York* . . . New York is the answer . . . I got that one right . . . You know, Mary, I might do pretty well against those Quiz Kids Wednesday night.

MARY.—Oh, sure.

JACK.—All I need is a little hint now and then.

MARY.—A big hint would throw you.

JACK.—Oh, I don't know about that . . . Well, that's enough for now, Mary. I'm going into the library and talk to Claude . . . See you later.

SOUND.—*Door opens . . . a few footsteps.*

JACK.—Now, let's see . . . the Taj Mahal is in New York, and it was built in 1492 . . . I must remember that . . . And then if I . . . *Whoops!* (*Footsteps stop*) Rochester, what are you doing at that keyhole?

ROCHESTER.—Bend down here, boss, and take a look at Claude.

JACK.—What's he doing?

ROCHESTER.—That boy's got Shakespeare in one hand, H. G. Wells in the other, and his forehead ain't even wrinkled.

JACK.—Well, I'm going in there and talk to him . . . Meanwhile, Rochester, why don't you get Richard and Gerard and take 'em down in the basement to see Carmichael.

ROCHESTER.—I better not, boss . . . That bear's been in a mean mood ever since he came out of hibernation last week.

JACK.—Oh, nonsense . . . Carmichael's as gentle as a lamb.

ROCHESTER.—Then what happened to the gas man?

JACK.—Will you stop worrying about the gas man . . . He probably went downstairs, read the meter, and walked out the basement door.

ROCHESTER.—Well, we *know* he went downstairs . . . and we *know* he read the meter . . .

JACK.—A-huh.

ROCHESTER.—But walkin' out that basement door oughta pay fantastic odds.

JACK.—Oh, don't be so pessimistic . . . Now take Richard and Gerard down to see Carmichael . . . I'm going in and talk to Claude.

SOUND.—*Door opens.*

JACK.—*Well* . . . how's my little man this evening?

CLAUDE.—Fine, thank you, Mr. Benny.

JACK.—Good, good . . . I see you're studying up on the immortal bard . . . That's Shakespeare you know . . . hm, ha, ha, ha, ha, ha! . . . How are you coming along?

CLAUDE.—Very well. I'm memorizing "Hamlet."

JACK.—Memor . . . memorizing it? . . . Well, look, Claude, I want to ask a little favor of you. It's nothing much, but it might help me out.

CLAUDE.—What is it, Mr. Benny?

JACK.—Well . . . when I appear on your program, I wish you and the rest of the kids would kinda take it easy and miss on a few questions . . .

144

CLAUDE.—Miss?

JACK.—Yes . . . (*Then pathetically*) Now, I wouldn't ask you any favors, Claude . . . but you see, when I was a child back in Waukegan, I was kind of a poor kid . . . and I didn't have any books or much of an opportunity to learn anything.

CLAUDE.—Well, didn't they have a library in Waukegan?

JACK.—Yes, Claude, but you had to walk up three flights of steps to get there . . . and I was such a weak, sickly child, I didn't have the strength to climb those steps . . .

CLAUDE.—Well, didn't you have any friends who could go to the library and get a book for you?

JACK.—No, Claude, everybody hated me . . . They used to call me Mouse Face . . . So you see . . . if you'll just give your Uncle Jackie a break Wednesday night, you'll be doing me a great favor.

CLAUDE.—Well, I'd like to, Mr. Benny . . . but I'm afraid it wouldn't be ethical.

JACK.—Oh.

CLAUDE.—We *must* answer the questions if we know them . . .

JACK.—Hm! . . . *All right, kid, if it's a battle you want, let's go!* What's the Taj Mahal?

CLAUDE.—The Taj Mahal is a white marble mausoleum, which was built at Agra, India, by the Shah-Jehan in the seventeenth century as a monument for his favorite wife, Mumtaz Mahal.

JACK.—Oh, yes . . . Mumtaz.

CLAUDE.—It took 20,000 men 22 years to construct this edifice . . . and it is believed that . . .

JACK.—That's enough, Claude. You know it all right . . . And let me tell you something . . . As long as you're so ethical, I'm going back and study *my* books, too.

CLAUDE.—But Mr. Benny, I didn't mean to hurt your feelings.

JACK.—You didn't, eh? Well, before I go, kid . . . here's one that'll stump *you* . . . Answer this . . . Who is the

145

manager of the Penn Theatre in Wilkes Barre, Pennsylvania *Come on, what's his name?*

CLAUDE.—I'm sure I don't know.

JACK.—*Johnny Galvin, that's who!* . . . Think it over, kid.

SOUND.—*Door slams . . . footsteps.*

JACK.—That burns me up . . . I invite him to the house, and he can't do me one little favor . . . He has to be ethical.

SOUND.—*Door opens.*

JACK.—And what kills *me*, at dinner tonight that kid'll probably have four helpings of mashed potatoes . . . He eats like a horse.

MARY.—*Who* eats like a horse!

JACK.—Claude . . . He won't even cooperate with me.

MARY.—Did you pull that Mouse Face on him?

JACK.—Not only that, I had tears in my eyes . . . Oh, well . . . Ask me some more questions, Mary.

MARY.—Okay.

JACK.—I got him on that Johnny Galvin, though . . . You should have seen his face, Mary.

MARY.—I'll bet . . . Here's a good one, Jack . . . Name the states that border the Mississippi River.

JACK.—The Mississippi? . . . Let's see . . . There's Missouri . . . Tennessee . . . Louisiana . . .

MUSIC.—*Start the number.*

JACK.—. . . And then there's Idaho . . . No, that's wrong . . . I know! Alabama . . . You know, Mary, one time I played Mobile, Alabama, and I . . .

MUSIC.—*(Orchestra). Cue 2.*

JACK.—. . . And then there's Louisiana, and . . .

MARY.—You named that one.

JACK.—Well it's on the Mississippi, I know *that* . . . I guess that's about all . . . Ask me another question.

MARY.—Okay . . . Here's one in spelling . . . How do you spell physiotherapy?

JACK.—What?

MARY.—Physiotherapy.

JACK.—Physiotherapy? Let's see . . . capital F . . . I . . . Z . . .

MARY.—Never mind. Spell cat.

JACK.—Wait a minute, I'm not through with physiotherapy yet.

MARY.—I am, and I'm sick of you too!

JACK.—That's a fine attitude . . . *Well*, I've got a headache again . . . Come on, Mary, let's go out in the yard and see what Richard and Gerard are doing.

MARY.—Okay.

SOUND.—*Door opens . . . footsteps.*

JACK.—That burns me up . . . Why did I ever accept that invitation to go on their program . . . I wouldn't mind being stupid, but I've got gray hair . . . Oh, well, this is only Saturday . . . I've still got four days to study.

MARY.—Yeah, why worry? You might get run over before Wednesday.

JACK.—With *my* luck, they'd broadcast from the hospital . . . Where are you going, Rochester?

ROCHESTER.—I'm goin' out in the kitchen and fix dinner.

JACK.—Well, did you take the children downstairs to see Carmichael?

ROCHESTER.—Boss, I don't think I oughta take those kids near that polar bear.

JACK.—Now listen, Rochester . . . if you're so worried about what happened to the gas man, for goodness' sake, call up the gas company!

ROCHESTER.—I *did* call the gas company.

JACK.—What did they say?

ROCHESTER.—*Where's the man?*

147

JACK.—Oh, you're as crazy as Mr. Billingsley . . . Now, call us as soon as dinner is ready . . . I'll be with Gerard and Richard.

SOUND.—*Door opens.*

JACK.—Physiotherapy . . . I hope I can . . . Oh, there they are!

MARY.—Gee those kids are cute.

JACK.—Yeah . . . Let's sneak over and hear what they're talking about. Every little bit helps. (*Short pause*)

GERARD.—Say, Richard, hasn't Mr. Benny got a nice house?

RICHARD.—He certainly has . . . But you know, Gerard, I think we're paying as much here as we would at a hotel.

JACK.—Hm.

MARY.—Why, Jack Benny! So that's why you put that sign out front . . . "Beverly Hills Tourist Haven."

JACK.—I just did that for a gag . . . *Well* . . . hello, Gerard . . . Richard.

RICHARD.—Hello, Mr. Benny.

GERARD.—Are you still worrying about next Wednesday?

JACK.—No, no, I've been studying like a little demon, and I except to be very good on your program.

RICHARD.—I hope so, Mr. Benny . . . We like you.

GERARD.—We sure do.

JACK.—Well, that's good . . . You know, kids, I didn't intend to bring this up, but . . .

MARY.—Oh-oh, here comes Mouse Face again!

JACK.—*Mary* . . . Now, kids, I was wondering if you'd sort of cooperate with Uncle Jackie and help me out Wednesday night.

RICHARD.—What do you mean, Mr. Benny?

GERARD.—Are you trying to pull a fast one?

JACK.—No, no, that's not it at all . . . But you see, boys, when I was a child about your age . . . I had to stand on the street corner, selling newspapers when I should have been in school. What chance did I have to study?

RICHARD.—Well, why didn't you read the newspapers?

JACK.—My eyes were bad . . . I tell you kids, I used to stand there on the street corner, barefooted . . . "Get your paper here," I'd say . . . "Extra, extra!"

MARY.—*Dewey takes Manila.*

JACK.—Oh, stop! Anyway, kids, if I miss on some of the questions Wednesday night, *you* miss some of them, too . . . will you?

RICHARD.—But, Mr. Benny, we don't know what the questions *are* until they ask us.

JACK.—I know . . . but whatever they *do* ask you . . . miss a few . . . Just as a favor to me.

GERARD.—Well, that wouldn't be ethical.

JACK.—Ethical shmethical, that's all I hear . . . How would you kids like it if I raised your rent . . . Now look, fellows, I don't like to get tough, but . . .

MARY.—Hey, Jack, look who's coming.

JACK.—Oh, yeah . . . Pardon me, kids . . . Good evening, Mr. Billingsley.

BELOIN.—Good evening, Mr. Benny . . . playing with the kiddies I see?

JACK.—Yes, yes, we're having a lot of fun . . . They're adorable little rascals . . . very brilliant, too.

BELOIN.—Yes, I know . . . I asked one of them to look at my watch this morning, and he told me the exact time.

JACK.—Your watch? Well, what's so difficult about that?

BELOIN.—The hands have mittens on 'em.

JACK.—Oh . . . Oh, I see . . . Well, look, Mr. Billingsley, if the hands on your watch are covered, how do *you* tell time?

BELOIN.—Oh, I always go by the stars . . . you *can't* miss that way.

149

JACK.—The stars? . . . Well, that's a good system at night . . . but what do you do during the day?

BELOIN.—I'm a bus boy at the Brown Derby.

JACK.—Oh . . . hm! . . . Well, I can see we're not getting anyplace, so let's discuss this later, shall we, Mr. Billingsley?

BELOIN.—Yes . . . Good-by, Mr. Benny.

JACK.—Good-by.

BELOIN.—Ohh . . . I wouldn't dare!

JACK.—Hm! I can't understand that guy.

MARY.—Say, Jack, why is he wearing that candle on his head?

JACK.—Just for sentiment, I guess . . . he's been living here one year today . . . Now, kids, getting back to the little discussion we were having . . . I think that . . .

ROCHESTER.—Hey, boss, dinner's ready!

JACK.—Okay, Rochester, go get Claude . . . Come on, Mary . . . come on, Richard . . . Gerard.

RICHARD.—Oh, boy, food!

GERARD.—Gee, I'm hungry.

JACK.—Well we've got a nice dinner prepared for you . . . roast duck and everything. You know, kids, there was another thing I forgot to tell you about my childhood . . . There was a public library in my home town,

MUSIC.—*Start band number.*

JACK.—But you had to climb three flights of steps to get there . . . and I was so weak and frail that as much as I wanted an education . . .

MUSIC.—*Number up . . . "Ciribiribin."*

SOUND.—*Rattle of silverware . . . dishes, etc.*

JACK.—Gee, I'm full . . . Well, kids, didn't Uncle Jackie give you a nice dinner tonight?

CLAUDE.—Yes, Mr. Benny.

JACK.—I'm glad you liked it.

GERARD.—I certainly enjoyed the marila collaris.

JACK.—Oh, it was simp . . . I beg your pardon? . . . marila collaris? What's *that*, Gerard?

GERARD.—That's the Latin word for "duck."

JACK.—Oh . . . Oh, the roast duck . . . Yes, it was delicious.

MARY.—I thought the mashus potatus were a little too lumpus.

JACK.—Mary, don't be funny . . . Well, kids, Uncle Jackie is pretty tired from studying all day . . . so if you don't mind, I think I'll go up to bed . . . See you in the morning, everybody.

RICHARD.—Oh, Mr. Benny, do you want me to tell you a story again tonight?

JACK.—No, thank you, I'll fall asleep all right . . . Well, good night kids.

RICHARD, GERARD, and CLAUDE.—Good night, Mr. Benny.

JACK.—Good night, Mary.

MARY.—Good night Jack, and for heaven's sake stop worrying!

JACK.—I'm not worried.

SOUND.—*Door opens.*

JACK.—Say, Rochester, go upstairs and turn down my bed, will you?

ROCHESTER.—Okay, boss.

SOUND.—*Door buzzer.*

JACK.—I'll answer the door.

SOUND.—*A few footsteps.*

JACK.—Marila collaris! . . . Amazing how that little child knew that.

SOUND.—*Door opens.*

JACK.—Good evening.

BLANCHE.—Good evening.

MORROW.—Say, mister, my wife and I would like to rent a room.

JACK.—A room?

MORROW.—Yes, we were driving by and saw your sign . . . We're on our honeymoon.

JACK.—Oh, that sign . . . Beverly Hills Tourist Haven . . . Well, I just put that up for a gag. I really have no rooms for rent.

BLANCHE.—*Show him the license, Homer!*

JACK.—No, no, I really haven't any vacancies . . . I'm sorry.

MORROW.—Okay . . . Come on, Goldie.

SOUND.—*Door slams.*

JACK.—Hm! . . . I must tell Rochester to take that sign down.

SOUND.—*A few more footsteps.*

JACK.—Well . . . I might as well hit the hay.

SOUND.—*Jack climbing the steps.*

JACK.—Now, let's see . . . Physiotherapy is the Latin word for "duck" . . . No, that's not it . . . What was that long word he had for duck? . . . Oh, well, I'll probably think of it in the morning.

SOUND.—*Door opens . . . footsteps stop.*

JACK.—Well, good night Rochester . . . Tomorrow is Sunday, and it's my busy day . . . so wake me up early.

ROCHESTER.—Yes, sir.

JACK.—Boy, am I tired.

SOUND.—*Bed creaks.*

JACK.—It's been a tough day for me, all right. (*Yawns*) Gee, this bed feels good. I wonder if I oughta look now and see whose picture is on the $20 bill. No, I'll wait till morning.

ROCHESTER.—You better take your clothes off, boss . . . you're liable to fall asleep that way.

JACK.—I'll just rest for a minute and take 'em off later.

SOUND.—*Door opens.*

JACK.—Good night, Rochester.

152

ROCHESTER.—Good night, boss . . . I left your chin strap on the dresser.

JACK.—Thanks.

SOUND.—*Door closes.*

JACK.—(*Yawns*) Boy, am I all in! (*Mumbling*) Questions, answers . . . (*Yawning*) I don't know why I ever got into this mess . . . Taj Mahal . . . Imagine, it took 22 men (*yawns*) 20,000 years to build it . . . No, that can't be it . . . It must have been 20,000 men . . . (*snores*) I can't get over that little kid knowing all about . . . (*two snores*)

MUSIC.—*Start.*

JACK.—Physiotherapy . . . I never saw kids with so much . . . (*three snores*)

MUSIC.—*Weird dream music . . . finish with Chinese cymbal.*

ELLIOTT.—Here they are, The Quiz Kids . . . presented every Wednesday night by the makers of Alka-Seltzer!

SOUND.—*Applause record up and down.*

JACK.—Gee, look at all those people . . . Well . . . I'll just have to do the best I can.

ELLIOTT.—I will now call the roll . . . *Jackie.*

JACK.—I am Jackie Benny. I am nine years old, and I attend the Taj Mahal School in Wilkes Barre, Pennsylvania . . . I'm ready, sir.

ELLIOTT.—*William.*

NELSON.—I am William Shakespeare. I am seven years old, and I go to the King Lear School in Hamlet, Indiana.

JACK.—Shakespeare? . . . Gee, he ought to know all about Shakespeare . . . What chance have *I* got?

ELLIOTT.—*Isaac.*

PHIL.—I am Sir Isaac Newton. I am four years old, and I discovered the law of gravy.

JACK.—That's gravity . . . Hey, mister, Phil got that wrong, I mean Sir Isaac . . . Gee, he looks like Phil . . .

ELLIOTT.—And now *lady!*

153

KELLY.—I am Lady Godiva.

JACK.—Lady Godiva?

KELLY.—I am twelve years old, and I'm riding at Bay Meadows.

JACK.—Oh, boy, I pity the horse . . . Well, let's get going with the questions . . . Did Uncle Jackie give you a nice dinner tonight?

CLAUDE.—Yes, Mr. Benny.

PHIL.—Yes, Mr. Benny.

NELSON.—Yes, Mr. Benny.

KELLY.—Yes, Mr. Benny.

ALL VOICES.—Yes, Mr. Benny, Yes, Mr. Benny. (*Blend into*)

MUSIC.—*Theme . . . "Yes, Mr. Benny" . . . Finish with cymbal.*

ELLIOTT.—The score is now . . . Quiz Kids, 1,492 . . . Benny, nothing.

JACK.—Gee, I better get going here.

ELLIOTT.—Now . . . William Shakespeare!

NELSON.—Yes, sir.

ELLIOTT.—Finish the quotation . . . "To be or not to be . . . "

JACK.—Hey, I know that one . . . but I haven't any vacant rooms.

BLANCHE.—Show him the license, Homer.

JACK.—To be or not to be . . .

NELSON.—To be or not to be, that is the question.

WILSON.—And the answer is Jell-O, America's favorite gelatine dessert.

JACK.—That's Don . . . Don Wilson.

WILSON.—It is not only economical and easy to make but comes in six delicious flavors . . . strawberry, raspberry, cherry, orange, lemon, and marila collaris.

JACK.—Gee, that must be the Latin word for lime.

WILSON.—So look for the big red letters on the duck.

154

JACK.—Darn it, that's another question I missed . . . Hey mister, ask *me* something . . . I know lots of answers.

ELLIOTT.—(*Weird voice*) All right, Jack Benny, here's a question for you . . . (*And does the weird laugh*)

JACK.—Gee!

ELLIOTT.—If you had a farm of 22,000 acres and on this farm you planted library steps . . .

JACK.—Library steps?

ELLIOTT.—Yes . . . And each of these farmers had three sons . . . but the *fifth* son could only work every *eighth* day . . . and the *seventh* son . . .

JACK.—Wait a minute, wait a minute!

ELLIOTT.—Now, here is the question . . . How wide is the river?

JACK.—*What* river!

ELLIOTT.—The Taj Mahal.

JACK.—What are you talking about? . . . Are you crazy? Who are you!

ELLIOTT.—I am the gas man . . . I am thirty-two years old, and I'm wearing a white fur coat.

JACK.—*Oh, my goodness, he's inside of Carmichael!*

ROCHESTER.—Correct. One point for Rochester Van Jones!

JACK.—You keep out of this.

ELLIOTT.—(*Weird voice*) Come on, Jackie, are you going to answer the question or not? *How wide is the river?* (*Does the weird laugh again*)

MUSIC.—*Start weird music.*

JACK.—Let's see . . . 22,000 acres of library steps . . . I've got to find the prime factor and the least common multiple . . . Well . . .

ELLIOTT.—*Do you know the answer or not?*

JACK.—Give me a chance, will yuh?

PHIL.—Let him have it, chief . . . We'll *beat* it out of him.

JACK.—I'll get it, I'll get it.

NELSON.—You better get it, or you'll get the electric chair.

JACK.—The electric chair? No, no, I didn't do it, I tell you, I didn't do it.

MARY.—The electric chair? (*Starts to laugh*)

JACK.—Mary, what are you laughing at?

MARY.—Who discovered electricity?

JACK.—Benjamin Franklin, but I'm sorry . . . Hey, mister, I've got the answer . . . *the river is* . . .

BLANCHE.—(*Gives a loud scream*)

JACK.—Take it easy, Goldie . . . I know the width of that river . . . The river is . . .

GANG.—He doesn't know, he doesn't know, he doesn't know, *he doesn't know* . . . Mouse Face, Mouse Face, Mouse Face, *Mouse Face!*

MUSIC.—*Weird music.*

JACK.—Please, fellows, give me a chance.

ELLIOTT.—Strap him down, men!

NELSON.—Off with his head.

JACK.—Let me out of here, let me out of this chair . . . I know the answer . . . *The river is* . . .

ROCHESTER.—*Boss, boss . . . wake up.*

JACK.—The river is 350 . . .

ROCHESTER.—Boss, what's the matter with you? *Wake up.*

JACK.—Rochester, get away from me, I've got the answer.

ROCHESTER.—Boss, wake up . . . You've been dreamin'.

JACK.—The river is . . . (*Music out*) *What?*

ROCHESTER.—You've had a nightmare, boss . . . *Wake up.*

JACK.—A nightmare? Ohhhh . . . Well, gee whiz . . . Wow! what I've just been through . . . You know, Rochester, I just dreamt I was on The Quiz Kids' program and didn't know the answers.

ROCHESTER.—Did you have to *dream* that?

JACK.—Well, thank heaven, it *was* only a dream . . . Hand me that chin strap Rochester. I want to look nice for my new picture.

ROCHESTER.—Here you are . . . Good night, boss.

JACK.—Good night, Rochester.

SOUND.—*Door slams . . . Segue into*

MUSIC.—*(Orchestra). "We Go Together."*
(Closing commercial)

WILSON.—Folks, when you receive your copy of General Foods new dessert recipe book, I'll bet that the first thing you'll say is, "What a beautiful book!" Because it's certainly one of the most attractive books you ever saw. Just take the cover itself! Front and back, it's one big beautiful picture! . . . showing almost two dozen different luscious desserts in a vivid pattern of reds, blues, yellow, pinks, and every other color you can think of! And when you look inside this lovely book, you'll be practically *dazzled* by the sight of so many rich, glowing color photographs and paintings! And then you'll see that the whole book is crowded with what strikes you as the world's cleverest, most enticing recipes! . . . recipes for every dessert under the sun! . . . pies, cakes, cookies, bavarians, ice creams, and . . . well, simply *everything!* Three hundred sixty-five different dessert recipes and suggestions of all kinds! . . . a brand new dessert for every day in the year! So, friends, be sure to write in for *your* copy! All you have to do is mail 10 cents in coin or stamps to Don Wilson, care of General Foods, Battle Creek, Michigan! That's all . . . just 10 cents! And remember the address . . . Don Wilson, care of General Foods, Battle Creek, Michigan! Send for *your* copy *today!*

MUSIC.—*Orchestra up.*

BINGHAM.—*(Loud barker style)* Hurry! . . . Hurry! . . . Hurry! . . . Hurry! . . .

WILSON—*(Trying to interrupt)* Say . . . wait a minute, John!

BINGHAM.—*(Still calling)* Hurry! . . . Hurry! . . . Hurry! . . .

157

WILSON.—Frank Bingham! What's all this "hurry" about? Is there a circus in town?

BINGHAM.—Well, it *is* circus time, Don! But what I'm telling folks to hurry about is to hurry and try Jell-O puddings . . . those new, creamy, ready-prepared puddings that bear the Jell-O name! Like Jell-O, Jell-O puddings are tops for quality! . . . and unsurpassed for rich, delightful flavor! And like Jell-O, Jell-O *puddings* are easy to make!

To prepare them, you simply add milk, cook until thickened, and then cool! And what a grand, mellow flavor! Jell-O puddings sell for the same low cost as Jell-O, too. And you can have your choice of three flavors . . . chocolate, vanilla, and butterscotch! Start in tomorrow to enjoy the tempting goodness of smooth, creamy Jell-O puddings! Remember, when you go to your grocer's for Jell-O, be sure to get Jell-O puddings! (*Fade*) Hurry . . . hurry . . . hurry . . .

MUSIC.—*Chord in G.*

JACK.—This is the last number of the twenty-eighth program in the current Jello series, and we will be with you again next Sunday night at the same time . . . And now I want to take this opportunity of thanking the makers of Alka-Seltzer, Louis Cowan, and The Quiz Kids for their splendid cooperation on tonight's program . . . And, folks, if you think I had a nightmare tonight, listen in Wednesday . . . those kids'll *murder* me . . . Good night, folks.

MUSIC.—*Jell-O signature.*

Maudie's Diary

MILLET.—Maudie's Diary . . . brought to you by the Happy Wonder Bakers!

SOUND.—*Clang bell in rhythm with orchestra.*

MUSIC.—*(Trio and orchestra).* "Yo-ho" theme.

MILLET.—The bakers of fresh Wonder Bread . . . the bread that is slow-baked for lasting freshness . . . bring you Maudie's Diary, the personal history of a girl in her teens.

MUSIC.—*Diary theme . . . fade under.*

MAUDIE.—Well, diary dear, my vacation is over, and another chapter of my intense life is definitely completed. Looking back over the summer, I'd say that my vacation was neither a dog nor a four-star dinger. I guess it could be classed as adequate plus, which is halfway between super-peachy and riotously undistinguished . . . But why am I writing about plain me, when my best woman friend, Pauline Howard, is being tortured by unrequited love?

It is ever woman's lot to suffer, and poor Pauly is suffering in spades with the deuces wild. She feels that she has forever lost Bill Brandt, whom she considered her mate. Bill and Pauly are supposed to be just right for each other, on account of he's Scorpio and she's Gemini or something . . . Anyway, let me start at the beginning, which was this morning, when two carfuls of us rolled into our driveway, having driven up from the shore. The family were first in the legitimate job, and Davy and I were right behind them in the Fallen Arch, which is what Davy has christened that one-cylinder pencil sharpener of his . . .

SOUND.—*Fade in jalopy motor . . . slows down and shivers to a stop . . . car door opens.*

DAVY.—Okay, woman. Hit the gravel.

MAUDIE.—Thanks for not helping me out.

SOUND.—*Clatter of loose metal automobile step.*

DAVY.—Hey! Don't put your whole weight on that step. It's only hung on with picture wire.

MAUDIE.—Quiet, Muffin-mouth . . . Well, family, here we are, and Davy and I are all in one piece.

FATHER.—(*Coming in*) Yes, Maudie, I see you are . . . Hm . . . we made excellent time.

SYLVIA.—I thought father was going to lose you back there around Vineland.

DAVY.—Not a chance, Sylvia. Maudie and I were right on your tail like a tin can.

MOTHER.—How long did it take us to make the trip, Wilfred?

FATHER.—Exactly 2 hours . . . and . . . 23 minutes. Twenty-*one* minutes, if you subtract the delay when the collector at the bridge dropped our quarter.

SYLVIA.—Why is it that whenever we pay toll anywhere the man always drops our money?

MOTHER.—That's because your father will never come to a complete stop, Sylvia. He's always trying to break some kind of a record.

FATHER.—It isn't that at all, Kate. It's simply a matter of economy. Each time you start a car from a dead stop, it eats up . . .

MOTHER.—Oh, good heavens!

| MAUDIE. | FATHER. |
| What is it, mother? | What's the matter? |

MOTHER.—I just remembered! I forgot to turn off the electric toaster!

FATHER.—Don't worry, Kate. You turned it off, all right. I saw you do it.

MOTHER.—When, dear?

FATHER.—When we got up from the breakfast table this morning.

MOTHER.—Oh, I know I turned off the toaster at the seashore this morning.

FATHER.—Then what are you worried about?

MOTHER.—I meant the toaster here at this house last June.

ALL.—(*Laugh*)

MOTHER.—Hurry up, Wilfred . . . open the door, and let's see.

FATHER.—(*Good-humoredly*) There's no hurry, Kate. If the toaster was left on last June, I think it's too late to do anything about it now.

MOTHER.—Yes, I imagine it must weaken a toaster to be left on for 3 months.

SYLVIA.—Mother, how in the world could you have forgotten to turn it off?

FATHER.—That's your mother's only weakness, Sylvia—a poor memory for details . . . Well, let's open up and see if the old house still looks the same. (*Pause*) Hm.

SOUND.—*Patting on pockets.*

MAUDIE.—What are you looking for, father?

FATHER.—The key to the front door. Don't seem to have it.

MOTHER.—That's your father's only weakness, girls. A poor memory for details.

ALL.—(*Laugh*)

DAVY.—That's one round for you, Mrs. Mason.

FATHER.—Nothing of the kind. I never forget a thing. I've got that key right here somewhere.

MOTHER.—Is this it, Wilfred?

FATHER.—Let's see . . . Why, yes. Where did you get it?

MOTHER.—You forgot and left it on the bureau this morning.

FATHER.—Oh. Must have been thinking of something else.

SOUND.—*Key turns in Yale lock . . . door opens.*

FATHER.—Well, here we are. Step inside. David, I'm grateful to you for getting Maudie here without any serious injury.

DAVY.—Oh, that's all right, Mr. Mason. I didn't mind.

SYLVIA.—(*Going out*) I hope they'll connect the phone this afternoon. Jerry said he'd give me a ring from the office.

PAULY.—(*Off*) Maudie! Davy! Wait a minute.

MAUDIE.—It's Pauly! (*Calling*) Hello, Pauly, dear.

DAVY.—Hi, Ravenlocks. What're you featuring?

PAULY.—Absolutely nothing.

FATHER.—(*Off*) Coming in, Maudie?

MAUDIE.—(*Calling*) Not right now, father.

FATHER.—(*Off*) All right.

SOUND.—*Door closes.*

MAUDIE.—Pauly, dear, it's sublime to see you again! How are you?

PAULY.—Perfectly stark. I feel like the crawling dead.

DAVY.—Maybe you need vitamin pills.

PAULY.—No, it isn't my health that's shattered. It's Bill.

MAUDIE.—Bill Brandt? What's he done?

DAVY.—Maybe *he* needs vitamin pills.

MAUDIE.—Oh, file it away, Davy. Can't you see Pauly's absolutely devastated?

DAVY.—My error. I was just trying to be mama's little helper.

MAUDIE.—Well, give it up, you don't jell . . . Now, Pauly, drop the back hair. What about Bill Brandt?

PAULY.—Maudie, it's the most tragic thing you've ever heard.

MAUDIE.—Well, what is it? Is Bill sick, or was he run over or something?

PAULY.—Oh, no, I wish it were as simple as that . . . Maudie, he's learning to play the trombone!

MAUDIE.—Oh, how ill-making!

DAVY.—Wait a sec. What's criminal about playing a trombone?

MAUDIE.—Oh, quiet, duckfeet. You wouldn't understand.

DAVY.—Gosh, I seem to be wrong straight across the board.

PAULY.—It's terrifying. I could just crawl away and quietly die.

MAUDIE.—You mean Bill doesn't play the trombone very well?

PAULY.—Oh, it isn't how he plays it—it's when he plays it.

DAVY.—You mean he turns it on at 3 A.M. or something?

PAULY.—Not exactly. But take last night, for instance. Bill wanted to drive me up to Willow Grove. There was an oversized moon and everything, so when Bill parked on a side road somewhere, I didn't complain in as loud a voice as usual.

MAUDIE.—Bill's very persuasive in the moonlight.

DAVY.—Yeah . . . Hey! How do you know?

MAUDIE.—Davy, will you kindly tie your tongue somewhere and let Pauly talk!

DAVY.—Talk, Pauline.

MAUDIE.—Go on, Pauly. After you parked in the moonlight, then what?

PAULY.—Bill reached out his arm, got his trombone from the back seat, and began playing it!

MAUDIE.—Oh, disgust!

DAVY.—The guy's a raisin brain.

PAULY.—Anyway, that's what he did—and I just can't cope with it.

MAUDIE.—Of course, you can't. It's perfectly loathsome.

DAVY.—Is Bill any good on the slip horn? I mean, can he really play it?

PAULY.—He can play do, re, mi, but that's about all.

DAVY.—With a trombone what else is there?

PAULY.— . . . Anyway, I feel as though I've failed as a woman. I've protected Bill against blondes, brunettes, and redheads, but there's no defense against a slide trombone. I feel as though my life is over.

163

MAUDIE.—Oh, no, it isn't, Pauly. Davy and I will go right down and have a serious talk with Bill Brandt.

DAVY.—Yeah, he needs a boot. Where is this meatball—home?

PAULY.—Oh, no. His family won't let the trombone in the house. So Bill practices under the grandstand at the football field. He's down there now.

DAVY.—Well, come on, hop into the Arch. We'll crab on down to the field and throw a butterfly net over that trombone player.

SOUND.—*Starter . . . jalopy motor wheezes and catches.*

PAULY.—Oh, I do hope you can bring Bill back to life.

MAUDIE.—Don't worry, Pauly. I specialize in bringing men back to life.

DAVY.—Come on, females, get in.

SOUND.—*Clatter of foot on loose metal automobile step as before.*

DAVY.—Will you *please* not put your whole weight on that step? It's only hung together with picture wire!

MAUDIE.—Oh, so are you! Come on, let's hurry.

SOUND.—*Motor accelerates . . . blow klaxon.*

MUSIC.—*Bridqe . . . segue into trombone playing a sad, sad scale . . . off-mike . . . hold.*

SOUND.—*Fade in jalopy motor . . . brakes . . . motor out.*

PAULY.—(*Small voice*) Look. There's Bill now. Isn't it awful?

MAUDIE.—Poisonous.

DAVY.—Phew! Slightly on the limburger side.

SOUND.—*Door opens.*

PAULY.—Oh, Bill.

MUSIC.—*Trombone out.*

BILL.—Huh? . . . Oh—hi, Pauly, Hi, gang.

MAUDIE.—Hi, Bill.

DAVY.—Hi, tall, noisy, and offensive.

164

BILL.—Some sense of humor, eh, keed? When did you get back?

MAUDIE.—This morning.

DAVY.—Where'd you get that groaning drainpipe, Bill?

BILL.—My trombone? I got it from Dexter Bell. Swapped my typewriter for it. Listen to this.

MUSIC.—*Notes on trombone.*

BILL.—(*Proudly*) Ever hear a tone like that?

DAVY.—Yeah. When I drove over my uncle's foot.

BILL.—Say, Davy, you must have kept 'em laughin all the time down there at the shore.

DAVY.—Sure. They were holding their stomachs night and day.

PAULY.—(*Pleadingly*) Bill.

BILL.—What, Pauly?

PAULY.—Have you almost finished practicing?

BILL.—Nup. I'll be another hour at least. You know what, Pauly?

PAULY.—What?

BILL.—My lip's getting tougher every day.

PAULY.—That's nice.

MAUDIE.—Nice? What good is a man with a tough lip?

BILL.—You don't understand, Maudie. When you play the trombone, the lip is very important.

MAUDIE.—Maybe so. But there's another important use for lips, too.

BILL.—Yeah? What?

PAULY.—(*Almost in tears*) Oh, Bill!

MAUDIE.—Look, Bill, let's celebrate our homecoming. Let's all go over to the Marble Slab and eat something slithery. What say?

BILL.—Sorry, but I can't.

MAUDIE.—It's Davy's treat.

DAVY.—Who, me?

PAULY.—Oh, Davy, how generous of you! Come on, Bill. Won't you go?

BILL.—Uh-uh. Gotta stay here and practice my trombone.

MUSIC.—*Trombone plays . . . hold and fade to background during following.*

DAVY.—Well, gals, Gabriel's off again. Come on over here where we can talk . . . I think this calls for diplomacy.

MAUDIE.—I think it calls for an ax murder.

DAVY.—Look, why don't you two fade and let me handle this buzzard?

PAULY.—But Davy, what can you do?

DAVY.—I don't know, Pauly, but let me stay here and try. Now go ahead . . . put the show on the road.

MAUDIE.—But when will I see you?

DAVY.—Tonight. I'll stop around for you at 8 bells. We'll go for a ride somewhere.

MAUDIE.—Well . . . all right. But do something really constructive, Davy, for Pauly's sake.

PAULY.—Yes, Davy, please do. I'm practically a stretcher case.

DAVY.—Leave it to me. Now scatter, will you? I've got a big job to do here. Almost a government project.

MAUDIE.—(*Going out*) All right. Don't forget—tonight at 8.

DAVY.—(*Calling*) I'll be there with a high fever and ready for romance.

MUSIC.—*Trombone fades in.*

DAVY.—Hey, Bill! *Bill!*

MUSIC.—*Trombone out.*

DAVY.—Let up on that thing, will you?

BILL.—Okay, Davy. I'll take five. That's a musical term.

DAVY.—Yeah? Look, lad, what say we chew the fatta about thisa and thatta?

BILL.—Why not? . . . Say, where are the girls going?

DAVY.—Who ever knows where girls are going? Look, fella, are you really serious about this horn of yours?

BILL.—Why not? Lotta guys are doing all right with their trombones. Paying the rent and putting a little aside for an overcast morning.

DAVY.—Mind if I take a small gander?

BILL.—No. Here . . . help yourself.

DAVY.—Hey, it's a lot lighter than I thought it would be.

BILL.—Yeah. Most trombones are made out of brass. This is a special job. Hey, what's the matter? Don't you even know how to hold it?

DAVY.—Why should I? I never played one.

BILL.—Well, the left hand goes here, and the right hand goes there, like that.

DAVY.—Then what?

BILL.—You blow through the mouthpiece.

DAVY.—Oh.

SOUND.—*Wind blown through horn . . . no tone produced.*

BILL.—Not like that. Like this. (*Makes sound with pursed lips*)

DAVY.—Fine thing! I get the razzberry before I even start.

BILL.—Go ahead, try it.

DAVY.—Oke.

SOUND.—*Weak tone on horn.*

BILL.—That's it! You got it! Now move the slide in and out.

SOUND.—*Trombone heard on steady tone, up and down, up and down.*

BILL.—Hey, that's good! Now stop on each note and play the scales.

DAVY.—I'll give it a try.

MUSIC.—*Trombone plays up the scale hesitantly.*

167

DAVY.—Phew! How was that, Bill?

BILL.—The payoff! You're terrific on that trombone, Davy! This guy Tommy Dorsey better look out!

MUSIC.—*Bridge.*

SOUND.—*Fade in jalopy motor . . . hold in background.*

DAVY.—Well, honeycomb, how do you feel . . . cold?

MAUDIE.—Uh-uh. Just right. (*Deep breath*) Mm! Just smell that wonderful smell! You know, Davy, that's what I missed down at the shore. That woodsy smell.

DAVY.—Yeah. Kind of good to be back in old Philly again. Look, you can see the lights around Billy Penn, all the way out here.

SOUND.—*Brakes . . . car shudders to stop . . . motor out.*

MAUDIE.—What are we stopping for?

DAVY.—Didn't you ever hear of parking in the moonlight?

MAUDIE.—Oh, yes. I read about it somewhere. They say it's a popular pastime. What happens next?

DAVY.—Well, this is where lip meets lip. C'm'ere, armload.

MAUDIE.—Davy . . . behavey!

DAVY.—Hey, that reminds me. Remember, this morning you told Bill about the other important use for lips?

MAUDIE.—(*Dreamily*) Yes, Davy.

DAVY.—Well, shut your eyes and get a surprise.

MAUDIE.—They're shut. What's the surprise?

DAVY.—This.

MUSIC.—*Trombone on sustained note, up and down, up and down.*

MAUDIE.—Davy! Where did you get that?

DAVY.—Out of the back seat.

MAUDIE.—It's Bill's trombone!

DAVY.—Uh-uh. I swapped my portable radio for it this afternoon! It's mine!

168

MAUDIE.—Yours? . . . Oh, nausea!

MUSIC.—*Up to finish, possibly with laughing trombone.*

MILLET.—(*Dramatically*) And across that lovely scene of moonlight and romance we shall momentarily draw a veil. (*Chuckling and speaking normally*) More about Maudie in a jiffy . . .
(*Middle commercial*)

MUSIC.—*Main theme.*

MILLET.—And now back to Maudie's Diary.

MUSIC.—*Diary theme in and fade under.*

MAUDIE.—Do you know, diary, when a woman can't hold a man's undivided attention in broad moonlight, she is hitchhiking on the road to oblivion. After my ghastly failure with Davy last night, I think I might as well buy a brown dress with a high neck and start tatting in a rocking chair. I'll probably end my days in a little gray cottage somewhere, living on a small pension left to me by a dead uncle. I should be weeping, I guess, but even my tear ducts are too stunned to give. Imagine—my romance with Davy shattered by a mess of portable plumbing! There seems to be no end to Davy's callousness. They're holding tryouts for football this morning, so before Davy went down to the field he brought his odious trombone here and actually asked me to *mind* it for him! It's like Adam asking Eve to hold the snake till he gets back. Anyway, here I am on our front porch, nursing a slide trombone that apparently has more sex appeal than I. What strange tricks fate plays on . . .

SIMMONS.—Good morning, Maudie.

MAUDIE.—Oh! Hello, Mr. Simmons.

SIMMONS.—Writing the great American novel?

MAUDIE.—Not exactly. Just . . . uh . . . some letters. Won't you come up on the porch and sit down?

SIMMONS.—Believe I will for a minute.

SOUND.—*Feet climbing porch stairs.*

SIMMONS.—I get kind of tired doing my own leg work . . . Ah!

MAUDIE.—What happened to that nice young reporter you used to send around?

169

SIMMONS.—Ray Duncan? Oh, he got called. He's over at Fort Dix. So I'm getting out our little newspaper all by myself.

MAUDIE.—Well, doesn't that keep you awfully busy?

SIMMONS.—Oh, I don't mind. We've all got to do our part these days. When did you get back from the shore?

MAUDIE.—Yesterday morning.

SIMMONS.—I see. Think I'll run a little item about that in the *Courier*. By the way, Maudie, did you receive your copies of the paper all right down at the shore?

MAUDIE.—Yes, Mr. Simmons. Our family wouldn't miss reading the *Suburban Courier* for anything. We love it.

SIMMONS.—Well, I think it's a pretty nice little sheet. What I'm looking for now are some good human interest items. That's what people like to read. Takes their minds off the war. Got anything like that for me?

MAUDIE.—Well, I'm not sure, Mr. Simmons. Just what do you mean by human interest?

SIMMONS.—Well . . . stories about people in particular. Things they do out of the ordinary. Sacrifices they make.

MOTHER.—(*Off*) Oh, Maudie!

MAUDIE.—(*Calling*) On the front porch, mother. Mr. Simmons is here.

SOUND.—*Screen door opens.*

MOTHER.—(*Coming in*) Oh . . . good morning, Mr. Simmons. How are you?

SIMMONS.—Still covered with printers' ink, Mrs. Mason . . . Say, I read about the U.S.O. fair you ran down at Beach Harbor. You did a fine job.

MOTHER.—Thank you, but it was Mr. Mason who really managed it.

MAUDIE.—I helped, didn't I, mother?

MOTHER.—You certainly did, dear. Maudie ran a little gambling game that made even more money than the cake booth.

170

SIMMONS.—(*Laughing*) I read about that, too. That's what I mean about human interest items, Maudie.

MAUDIE.—Oh, I see.

SIMMONS.—By the way, Mrs. Mason, you weren't here during July, when we had the big aluminum drive. You should have seen the *Courier* office. I had to wade through aluminum pots and pans to get to my linotype machine.

MOTHER.—That's wonderful, Mr. Simmons . . . Oh, now that you mention it, is the President still collecting aluminum? Or has he gone back to stamps?

SIMMONS.—Oh, the government can use all the aluminum it can get. It's for the defense of our shores.

MOTHER.—I shouldn't think an aluminum battleship would be very safe. Aluminum dents so easily. However, Mr. Simmons, if you're still collecting, I might have a few things in the kitchen that I could part with. What sort of things will you take?

SIMMONS.—Anything at all that's aluminum.

SOUND.—*Screen door opens.*

MOTHER.—Well, come right inside and let's have a look.

SIMMONS.—Glad to. By the way, Maudie, did you read the human interest story I ran in July about Jascha Heifetz?

MAUDIE.—No, I think I must have missed it. What did he do?

SIMMONS.—He donated his aluminum violin to the drive.

MAUDIE.—That was nice. (*Take*) His violin. Do they make musical instruments out of aluminum?

SIMMONS.—I guess they do.

MOTHER.—(*Off*) Better come in and close the screen door, Mr. Simmons. The flies are pretty bad.

SIMMONS.—All right, Mrs. Mason. Excuse me, Maudie.

SOUND.—*Screen door closes.*

MAUDIE.—Jeepers-weepers! I wonder! . . . No—that's too much to hope for! . . . But suppose it's *really* . . . no, it couldn't possibly be.

171

SOUND.—*Motor of big car purrs in, running slowly . . . motor idles . . . hold under.*

FATHER.—(*Off*) Oh, Maudie.

MAUDIE.—Yes, father?

FATHER.—I'm going to the office now. Can I drive you down-town?

MAUDIE.—No, thanks.

FATHER.—All right. Good-by.

MAUDIE.—Good-by . . . Oh, father, wait a minute.

FATHER.—Yes, dear?

MAUDIE.—I want to ask your advice about something.

FATHER.—Oh? What is it?

MAUDIE.—It's something you have to look at. Wait. It's right here on the porch swing. I'll bring it down to you. (*Pause*)

SOUND.—*Feet down porch steps.*

MAUDIE.—This is it, father.

FATHER.—Good gracious—where did you get that?

MAUDIE.—It belongs to Davy.

FATHER.—So that's the banshee I heard wailing last night.

MAUDIE.—Yes . . . Here, father, lean out of the car and take it. I want you to look at it and tell me something.

FATHER.—Hm. Much lighter than you'd expect. What did you want me to tell you?

MAUDIE.—Father—is that made out of aluminum . . . Oh, be very sure, father dear, before you tell me. My whole future depends on your answer . . . Is it?

FATHER.—Why—uh—yes, Maudie, I believe it is.

MAUDIE.—But I want you to be absolutely sure.

FATHER.—Well, let me examine it a little more closely. Certainly looks like aluminum and feels like it, too . . . Wait a minute! What's this?

MAUDIE.—What?

FATHER.—Some lettering here inside . . . M—A— . . . yes, I was right. It says "Made of Aluminum." See? Right here.

MAUDIE.—Oh, father! You wonderful, brilliant, wise father!

FATHER.—(*Modestly*) Oh, I wouldn't say that, Maudie. They weren't very long words.

MAUDIE.—Now I have one more question, and then you can go.

FATHER.—Well?

MAUDIE.—Do you think it's all right to tell a lie . . . I mean just once . . . if it's for a very fine, noble cause?

FATHER.—Well, Maudie, I—I can't answer that until you tell me what the cause is.

MAUDIE.—National defense!

FATHER.—How's that again?

MAUDIE.—Mr. Simmons is in the house right now, collecting aluminum for the government . . . Father, do you see what I mean?

FATHER.—*Do* I? . . . My dear Maudie, what are you waiting for? This is *really* part of the defense program. Defense of my nerves in particular. Give that thing to Mr. Simmons immediately! And if he won't accept it, I'll take it down to Washington myself!

SOUND.—*Motor speeds up . . . car drives away.*

MAUDIE.—(*Calling*) Oh, thank you, father, thank you. You're divine!

SOUND.—*Feet running up steps . . . screen door opens and slams.*

MAUDIE.—Oh, Mr. Simmons! Mr. Simmons!

SIMMONS.—(*Off*) Yes, Maudie?

MAUDIE.—I have the most marvelous human interest story you can possibly imagine.

SIMMONS.—(*Fading on*) Really? About whom?

MAUDIE.—Davy Dillon! He wants to make a great personal sacrifice!

Music.—*Bridge.*

Maudie.—Now, Davy . . . will you please stop jumping up and down and tearing your hair!

Davy.—Look, woman . . . you've been talking for 10 minutes, and I still can't savvy why you gave away my brand new trombone.

Maudie.—But look what it's done for you . . . your picture here on the front page of the *Courier* . . . and this wonderful story under it!

Davy.—The whole thing's crazy!

Maudie.—It is not, Davy! You were simply marvelous to do it!

Davy.—What're you talking about? You know doggone well I didn't do it! You did it yourself while my back was turned.

Maudie.—But you *would* have done it—if you'd thought of it.

Davy.—I would not! I swapped a swell radio to get that trombone!

Maudie.—Oh, Davy dear, I know you better than you know yourself. You're the sweetest, thoughtfulest, most unselfish boy in the whole world . . . the kind that would make a great personal sacrifice for a noble cause.

Davy.—(*Falling for it*) I am?

Maudie.—Why certainly, Davy. And it's right here in black and white for the whole town to read. And at this very moment everybody in town *is* reading it. Why, you'll be one of the greatest heroes we've ever had.

Davy.—Gosh! You really think so?

Maudie.—I know so.

Bill.—(*Off*) Hey! There he is!

Maudie.—Look . . . it's Bill Brandt and Pauly.

Pauly.—(*Coming in*) Oh, Davy, that was the most prodigious thing!

Bill.—Davy, I never knew you had it in you! Here, slip me the skin, and let me shake it.

Davy.—Well . . . thanks.

PAULY.—You're absolutely famous! It was a beautiful gesture.

DAVY.—Aw, gosh, Pauly, I wouldn't say that.

MAUDIE.—Did you read the whole story?

BILL.—Read it? We lapped it up. Listen to this: "In making this magnificent sacrifice, our local son David Dillon, has proven that in his veins courses the rich, red blood that inspired our noble forefathers," et cetera, et cetera, et cetera. "David Dillon is a typical American boy. Raised in our . . . " well, so on and so on. Brother, you're practically Superman!

DAVY.—Wait a second, Bill. I only did what I . . .

SOUND.—*Screen door opens and closes.*

SYLVIA.—(*Coming in*) Here he is now, mother.

MOTHER.—Oh, David—congratulations!

DAVY.—Thanks, Mrs. Mason.

SYLVIA.—Davy, my little sister can be mighty proud of you this afternoon.

DAVY.—Aw, now, Sylvia, anybody would have done the same thing.

SOUND.—*Automobile motor in.*

MAUDIE.—Here comes father!

SOUND.—*Brakes . . . motor out . . . car door opens.*

FATHER.—(*Coming in*) Ah, there, David, I've just seen the *Courier*. How does it feel to be the town hero?

DAVY.—Aw, now, Mr. Mason, wait a minute.

MOTHER.—Wilfred, don't you think David was magnificent?

FATHER.—Indeed I do, Kate.

ALL.—(*Talk excitedly in background*)

FATHER.—And Maudie . . .

MAUDIE.—Yes, father?

FATHER.—(*Low*) You were rather magnificent yourself!

MAUDIE.—(*Giggles*)

MUSIC.—*Bridge.*

SOUND.—*Fade in jalopy motor . . . fade under.*

DAVY.—*(Fade in)* And when I walked into the grocery store to get the tapioca, everybody congratulated me and shook my hand.

MAUDIE.—Yes, Davy, and imagine that old miser Mr. Scott giving you a free lemon coke.

DAVY.—Yeah, that was practically a historic occasion.

MAUDIE.—You'll have to wear dark glasses like a movie star so you can walk around without being mobbed by admirers.

DAVY.—Say, where'd Simmons get that picture of me, anyway?

MAUDIE.—I loaned it to him. That's the one I keep on my dressing table.

DAVY.—Holy bazoo! I didn't know you kept my photo up in your room.

MAUDIE.—Certainly. That's what gives women the reputation of being mysterious. There's always something men don't know about them.

DAVY.—Well, sugarpan, you're mysterious all right.

MAUDIE.—How do you mean, Davy?

DAVY.—Well . . . what you did for me today for instance.

MAUDIE.—Oh, poo. I told you it was only what you would have done, if you'd thought of it.

SOUND.—*Brakes . . . motor slows down and stops.*

MAUDIE.—What are we stopping for?

DAVY.—Well, I'd like to say I was out of gas, 'cause since that law was passed I wouldn't be able to get more till 7 o'clock tomorrow morning.

MAUDIE.—Davy! What a fascinating idea!

DAVY.—Yeah . . . I thought it was kind of ripe . . . Now look, Mason.

MAUDIE.—What is it, Dillon?

DAVY.—I haven't had a chance to really thank you for what you did for me today.

MAUDIE.—Oh, Davy—why should you?

DAVY.—Well, in the first place, I don't deserve all that publicity. It was you that did it. You ought to share the spotlight with me somehow.

MAUDIE.—But don't you see, I do share the spotlight with you.

DAVY.—How?

MAUDIE.—Well . . . it reflects off you onto me and lights up my happy smile. Look. See it?

DAVY.—Uh-huh. Now I really need dark glasses.

MAUDIE.—Tell me more of the same. I'm beginning to care for it.

DAVY.—Say, did I tell you how happy mother and dad were when they read that stuff in the paper?

MAUDIE.—No, but I bet they were proud.

DAVY.—Proud? Dad's chest was sticking out like a bullfrog's. Mother read it first and phoned him about it while he was still downtown at the office.

MAUDIE.—Sh . . . listen.

DAVY.—What is it?

MAUDIE.—You can almost hear the stillness. Oh, Davy, isn't this the clearest, stillest night you've ever seen?

DAVY.—Yeah. It's just like last night. You can almost read the time on the clock way down there under Billy Penn . . . Say—are you asleep?

MAUDIE.—No. Why?

DAVY.—You've got your eyes shut.

MAUDIE.—Yes, Davy. This is where we came in. Remember? I'm still waiting for that surprise.

DAVY.—Huh? . . . Oh . . . I almost forgot . . . Are your eyes still shut?

MAUDIE.—Yes.

177

Davy.—Okay. Here's the surprise.

Sound.—*Blare of trombone.*

Maudie.—Davy Dillon! Where did you get that trombone?

Davy.—It's a present from dad. He brought it home with him tonight. It's solid brass!

Maudie.—Oh-h-h-h . . .

Music.—*Up to finish.*

Millet.—Poor, devastated Maudie has one more entry to make in her diary tonight. But while she's brushing aside her tears, a word with you.
(*Closing commercial*)

Millet.—Here's Maudie Mason again.

Music.—*Diary theme . . . fade . . .*

Maudie.—I once went out to Robin Hood Dell to hear the Philadelphia Orchestra. It was a beautiful moonlight night, and Stokowski's hands never looked lovelier. The violins and all those wooden cornets and trombones were sweet and mellow. Now, diary, a slide trombone with a lot of other instruments is one thing, but a slide trombone all by itself can make you start thinking of a career of crime. If it had been any other man but Davy who's whipped out a trombone at a romantic moment, I would have stomped out of his life in two stomps. But I don't *dare* walk out on Davy! . . . He needs me! . . . He's nuts!

Music.—*Closing theme in and down.*

Millet.—A week from tonight the bakers of Wonder Bread bring you another chapter of Maudie's Diary, a chapter in which trombones are not even mentioned. The title . . . "I Thought I'd Dye." Won't you join us then?

Music.—*Up and down.*

Millet.—The characters and incidents depicted in Maudie's Diary are based on stories and written for radio by Albert G. Miller. This is Art Millet speaking.

Music.—*"Yo-ho" theme song.*

Millet.—This is the Columbia Broadcasting System.

Honest Abe

MUSIC.—*Theme up and out.*

LINCOLN.—My name is Abraham Lincoln, usually shortened to just Abe Lincoln. (*Sneak music*) Josh Billings once said that contentment and peace of the soul were born in men with Adam but that they both took instantaneous flight when Eve arrived in all her pristine glory. How well do the sons of Adam, in general, know this! They tell me there is a time in every man's life when he feels that he'd give a little very fine gold for a snatch of the gay and innocent contentment of the times before he met his own personal Eve, named Sarah or Lulu or Mary!

MUSIC.—*Up and out.*

ANNOUNCER.—The Columbia Broadcasting System presents Honest Abe. This is the thirty-fifth program in an extensive series featuring Ray Middleton in the role of Abe Lincoln, of the Illinois river country, and Muriel Kirkland in the role of Mary Todd, the same role she originated in the Broadway production of "Abe Lincoln in Illinois" by Robert Sherwood.

MUSIC.—*Full and down behind.*

LINCOLN.—After the long and very real storms and stresses of love, you'll remember Mary Todd and I finally got together happily around Joshua Speed's organ. That same night we set a date for our wedding, and it wasn't long in coming around. The whole affair has always been so unclear in my mind that I have never been sure just what happened, except that I know many things did happen! Speed had gone on an errand. Miss Todd was over at her sister's house getting ready. It was an hour . . . perhaps half an hour . . . till time to go to the church.
(*Fade into*)

SOUND.—(*Distant roll of thunder . . . then sound of door slamming . . . Mary's laughter.*

LIZZIE.—You'll get wet, Mary! Listen . . . it's going to let down and rain any minute!

MARY.—Let it, let it!

LIZZIE.—Come back in the house, now! Ma-ry . . . !

MARY.—I tell you I'm going to run over to the church and see that they've not put the lilac sprigs where the groom is to stand! I certainly don't intend to be married to a lilac sprig!

LIZZIE.—(*Farther off*) But the ceremony's to take place in less than an hour, and we've got to get your clothes on you and your hair done and . . . (*remonstrating, provoked*) Mary! Ma-ry!

MARY.—I'll be back directly, and if I'm late . . . let the guests wait! And if I'm wet . . . let 'em set! This's *my* wedding today, isn't it?

LIZZIE.—(*Far off now . . . dismally, worried*) Oh, my; oh, mercy . . . oh, Mary!

MARY.—(*Near by*) Oh . . . hello, Speed. You can't walk with me unless you come along on the wings of Pegasus apace, Speed!

SPEED.—Where're you "wings of Pegasus a-pacing'" *to*, Mary?

SOUND.—*Thunder.*

MARY.—Oh, my! Speed up, Speed! I'm "wings of Pegasus a-pacing" over to the church by the back alley to see that things are *just so!* You know they have to be *just so* to suit me!

SPEED.—Yeh! And I only hope Abe'll prove to be just *that* . . . *just* so! I been prayin' all night and up to noon today that he'll wear well, prove worthy, and suit you to a T-X-Y-Z, by golly!

MARY.—(*Obviously walking fast . . . a bit breathless*) How is the young groom-to-be on his wedding day? Hurry up . . .

SPEED.—I ain't seen him in a couple of hours . . . I been over to Colonel Brown's to borry a diamond-studded, gold-plated extry collar button for Abe . . . and I'm on m' way back to Abe's office now.

MARY.—I suppose he was reasonably happy and getting his Sunday bib and tucker on, wasn't he?

SPEED.—When I left him, he was polishin' up his shoes and tryin' his level best to sing "Work, For the Night Is Coming" . . . or mebby it was "Will There Be Any Stars in My Crown?" You never can tell just what Abe's tryin' to sing . . . he can't carry a tune in a jug even with a corncob stopper in it, though he *is* good on th' *bass* end of a bar simple singin' with a leetle *toccato con brio!*

MARY.—Well . . . you see that he wears the new cambric shirt and tie Major Stuart bought him and that he puts on his gold chain and the fob with my picture in it I gave him!

SPEED.—Ye-eh.

MARY.—And help him get all his things into the new portmanteau he got from Ninian. And not to forget the change of . . . (*hesitant*) . . . well, underwear.

SPEED.—Yes, sir-e-e-e! I'll see to all them little items th' which I took two pairs out of my store of which for a weddin' present!

MARY.—And tell him not to forget to come past the livery stable and have the team and their best Studebaker surrey at the house at 4 to carry us down to the depot.

SPEED.—Yes, sirree, ma'am . . . and I've already done bought the sleeping-car reservations to Danville. Can you think of any other thing?

MARY.—Be sure to have him at the church at two o'clock sharp and for heavenly days not to forget the ring!

SPEED.—I've seed to that m'self, too! I got two here m'self in case th' need arose for 'em, and I've planted three more over Abe's various person in th' places where he's apt to look when th' parson says, "Do you?" and Abe says, "Yes, sir, do *you?*" or whatever it is!

MARY.—(*Laughing*) Well, I'd think that ought to . . . to *do you* two!

SPEED.—So would I; but you don't know me and Abe! We're just as likely t' git nervous and fumble about and mislay *all five* b'fore th' "Do you" comes; so . . . for safety, I slipped one in that crack under th' chancel rail, by golly! (*He laughs*) That ort t' cover th' sityation, as th' old lady said as she set on the sofa!

SOUND.—*Thunder again.*

MARY.—Here's the church. You come inside a minute. I . . . may need you.

SPEED.—(*Forewarning*) Y'know, I ain't any good at carryin' or movin' heavy things no more, like church benches or pianos!

SOUND.—*Footsteps on steps.*

SPEED.—Y'know, Mary . . . they're buryin' old Uncle Kelso from here this afternoon after . . . th' wedding!

MARY.—I know. But I've too many other things to think of. Well, they got the lilac sprigs all right, didn't they? Let's see about . . .

SPEED.—Yes, sir; yes, sir! (*Overawed*) Th' old church looks mighty, mighty perty with all these-here posies and paper ribbons and things around. But I guess it don't look as perty as th' bride's goin' t' look as she comes down th' aisle here!

MARY.—(*Off . . . busying about things*) I'll put these candles over here. Let's see . . . the rug isn't up far enough . . . umm.

SPEED.—(*Near by . . . still overawed and daydreaming*) Y'know, I don't know anything pertier than a bride a-sailin' down th' aisle . . . not even a three-masted windjammer comin' around th' headlands back in Vineyard Sound! It's a mighty perty sight, and you're a mighty lucky gal to git a feller like Abe! Now . . . you just *take* Abe. (*Musing*) I never knew a big feller that thought of his own self so little as Abe. I never knew any man that was so eternally poorly in material things and cared so little for his personal looks . . . and yet was so rich in thinkin' materials and clothes hisself so rich in the coat and pants of natural dignity! I don't know *no* man, and few women, I'd druther be with, and none that raises in me so much good cheer, and eternal seriosity, and downright human respect as this poor bean pole of humanity you're a-marryin' today . . . this feller Lincoln!

182

MARY.—(*Matter of fact*) You go on and see to him, Speed! And remember all I told you!

SPEED.—(*A bit let down by her failure to enter into his enthusiasm*) Yeh . . . yeh . . . I'm a-goin'.

SOUND.—*Door opening and closing at distance.*

MARY.—(*In prayer*) Oh, Lord, be with me in this dear ordeal today, and give me the light and strength to be a good wife. Forgive me my bad temper, and help me to control it, and bless my friends for being so generous with me. Bless Mr. Lincoln, and bring us both . . .

LIZZIE.—(*Yelling, far off*) Mary! Ma-ry!

MARY.— . . . worldly happiness and great peace of mind and soul.

LIZZIE.—(*Louder, off*) Oh, Mary!

MARY.— . . . A-men. (*Then rather petulantly*) Oh, well! For heaven's sakes!
(*Fade into*)

MUSIC.—*Bridge tune . . . fade out of music into*

ABE.—(*Talking to himself, greatly upset*) Lawdy-mercy! Oh, Lawdy mercy, Abe, you poor durned benighted old fool, don't you go and do something you feel in your heart, and soul, and gizzard, and bootstraps is th' dead wrong thing to do, if you come to feel finally it *is* the dead wrong thing! No matter what, don't you go do it now; and th' Lord protect you if you do! Yet . . . (*hesitant*) if you feel you *ought* to go ahead and marry her, Abe, and *want to*, then don't go make a fool of yourself that way and *not* marry her . . . *no matter what!* (*Pause*) Oh, tarnal mercy, deliver me from this splitting headache if from nothing else!

SOUND.—*Door opens.*

SPEED.—What you doin', Abe?

ABE.—Just talkin' to myself, Speed.

SPEED.—What about?

ABE.—About . . . myself!

SPEED.—Abe . . . you ain't got no business settin' here *talkin'* to *nobody* about *nothin'!* Don't you know it ain't but half an hour till you're gettin' spliced for better or worse, if not the worst!

ABE.—(*A bit of a groan and shudder*) Don't *tell* me, Speed!

SPEED.—I *got* to, Abe! You ain't lifted your little finger since I left, includin' your big toe! You get to work and finish slickin up them clodhoppers while I dump your truck into th' portmanteau. You ain't got th' gumption of a tortoise today, Abe, let alone a comin' bride-to-be-*groom!* Get busy, now, Abe!

ABE.—I . . . I . . . well, all right.

SPEED.—Abe, I got th' tickets on th' cars and th' extry collar button I went for, and th' rings are all properly planted. I . . . Abe . . . (*seriously*) . . . be-stir yourself, feller! Be-stir yourself! Th' fatal hour approacheth!

ABE.—(*Low*) Let it approacheth!

SPEED.—Mary's home gettin' her finery on includin' her weddin' clothes. Come on, get a-foot and let's get a-goin'!

ABE.—(*Blurting out*) I'm not . . . a-going anywhere, Speed.

SPEED.—(*Laughing*) Oh, yes, you are! You may not know it yet, but . . . you are! (*Laughter . . . then he stops short*) What you . . . s'pale for, Abe? What you . . . shiverin' in your stockin' feet for? (*Pause . . . then dead serious*) Abe . . . what did you mean you ain't goin' anywhere?

ABE.—I . . . I've decided . . . *not to get married*, Speed!

SPEED.—(*Half jokingly*) Whoa, now, Abe, and back up!

ABE.—(*Going on*) I've been sitting here thinking it all out, Speed!

SPEED.—I knowed I shouldn't of gone off and left you here alone to think!

ABE.—I've about decided it . . . it can't be! Speed . . . as I sit here amongst all my earthly possessions, I figure I'm about the poorest poor critter that ever breathed air two minutes to live to count 'em! Job's turkey was *nothing* in poor-ality to me!

SPEED.—Aw . . . you got a second shirt and a tophat, ain't you?

ABE.—(*Ruefully . . . bitterly*) And that's about all, and a clean pair of socks. *And* that carpet bag, this shirt, the chain and fob, and two pairs of underwear that all you people *gave* me to get married on and in!

SPEED.—(*Trying to minimize it*) Well, if Mary wants to chance it, why shouldn't *you?*

ABE.—Because she doesn't realize what chance she's really taking . . . *she's* never been poor, and I've never been anything else! What's been perfectly natural to me would be new and alarming and pretty disheartening to *her!* But . . . it's not all this so much, Speed. Not all this . . .

SPEED.—Abe . . . Lordy-massy, get your galluses on! We got to be goin'!

ABE.—(*Paying him no heed*) . . . Not being poor *now*, or next week. Maybe we *could* live with the Edwardses a while and dip into Mary's money a little now and then to keep things going. What counts more and . . . why I can't go through with this . . .

SPEED.—Don't (*scared*) say them words, Abe!

ABE.—There's no signs of my *ever* gittin *any richer!* There's no guaranty I'll ever get any more clients or be any more successful! There's no justification for me thinkin' I could ever support a woman of Mary's tastes and caliber and breeding as she's bound to demand!

SPEED.—Abe . . . you're just tryin' to argue yourself out of it because you're *scared* . . . just plumb *scared!* Lookit, now . . . Mary's got lots of swell connections and rich friends! *She'll* get out and get you clients, don't you worry! Abe, if it takes a woman to make a man out of a man, as they say, it takes a durned *good* woman t' make a lawyer out of him! And Mary's *durned good!* C'mon . . . (*pleading*) . . . let's go marry her!

ABE.—(*He is scared now*) I . . . I'd be bound to make a fool of myself! I'd look like a fidgety scarecrow standin' up there beside her in that church! I'd . . . (*crying out*) . . . Speed, we've not got the same interests nor ambitions nor backgrounds! We're not the same breed! We're . . .

SPEED.—(*Mad*) Well, this's a nice time to be thinking about *that!*

SOUND.—*Church bells far off, lively.*

SPEED.—There's the first church bells, for lord's sakes! Abe, listen now. You've got to get out of it now! You just don't mean all these things!

ABE.—(*Crying out*) Maybe not! Maybe it's *not* these things I mean! Maybe it's something . . . (*low, deep*) . . . *more important!* Keeping me from doing it!

SOUND.—*Bells ringing afar to fade in louder . . . fade up background noises of a small, quiet crowd passing by . . . brief thunder.*

VOICES OF MEN AND WOMEN.—Wel-l, I'm shore glad t' see *you* out t'day, Aunt Min! They gits tied up, and they gits on-tied up! La, these youngens! Ye-e-eh . . . looks like he *might* light in and rain. We need rain for th' crops! Has th' bride got here yet? Oh, she'll wait in the anteroom! Good afternoon . . . Oh, we never miss a wedding! How's the Edwardeses taking it? When's *Louisa* goin' to get her a man and be led down th' aisle, too? . . . Grmmp. Come on, Louisa! Yes, he's the groom! We all like him *so* much! They say Speed's th' best man . . . (*titter*) . . . but I don't b'lieve it! You stayin' for th' funeral, too? It 'minds me of Phelie's wedding . . . th' lilacs and all! How'd you happen to marry Hal, Sarah? If I ever knew, I sure don't remember now!

GIRL.—It's all so, so lovely, Mr. Whitfield . . . (*hinting*) . . . don't you think so? Has th' groom come yet, boys?

SOUND.—*Church bell up and fade down and out and into*

LIZZIE.—Oh, Mary . . . I'm so utterly nervous!

MARY.—Well, stop sticking me with those pins, dear! Here . . . how do I look in all my silk and flouncings?

WOMAN.—Lovely, Mary! Just so fresh and lovely! There never was a prettier bride, nor a wiser one! I declare, I wish almost I were getting married . . . *again!*

MARY.—You will, dear . . . you will! Just give Fancher *time!* And Lizzie, dear . . . see that all the little French cakes are placed on the opposite sides of the reception tables and the bonbons near by. And tell old Mrs. Julian *not* to *talk* as she pours or no one'll get served and Mr. Lincoln and I will miss the cars at 4:30!

WOMAN.—Oh, Mary, Mary, how do you do it? You look *so* radiant and happy!

MARY.—Perhaps it's only because *I am* so radiant and happy! (*Fade*)

SOUND.—*Bells fade up, fade down into*

SPEED.—(*Remonstrating loudly*) Love? Love? What's love, anyways, but "a smoke rais'd with the fume of sighs!" and "a rose petal dropped on th' quagmire of life!"

ABE.—You've got to remember, marriage is for a long time and that people's souls and hearts and gizzards and bootstraps are involved, and a good, noble young girl's person and life, and you don't go into a thing like this unless you . . . love her! (*Pause*) *Do you?*

SPEED.—(*Not answering, but not giving in*) Well, you loved her *once*, didn't you?

ABE.—I don't know! How does anyone know?

SPEED.—By golly, I've thunk of th' same item with regard to Fanny, and I wisht *I* knew! Howsomever, you *told* her you loved her, didn't you? Sure . . . !

ABE.—I don't recollect ever telling her that!

SPEED.—Then why'd you court her?

ABE.—(*Tragically*) I don't even recollect ever having done that!

SPEED.—Well, you must of given her good cause of *some kind* to think you'd marry her, Abe! You must of manifested it in some shape or form, or other! You must of thrown your heart at her feet, or something, Abe! I know she didn't just 'magine it, and *I've seen* you holdin' her hand and chitterchatterin' low so's I couldn't hear, nor th' moon!

ABE.—(*Lost*) I reckon so! I . . . (*A bit of a light*) . . . I reasoned myself into it, Speed! That's what I went and did!

SPEED.—Well, you can just *reason* yourself over to the church, now! Put on those galluses, by golly! Abe, they always say, "Love is blind and lovers cannot see the pretty follies that

187

themselves commit"! And they say, "Friendship often ends in love." And you can learn to love her later if you don't now, or love her better later, if you do! Here, let me button . . .

ABE.—(*Tragically*) But . . . what if I don't and can't, now nor later, Speed? It'd not be *fair* to her . . . now . . . nor then, nor ever! She'd soon discover it, because she's as wise as she is beautiful and I'm as open-faced as I am homely; and it'd only cause her misery and shame and utter contempt and hatred for me, me going through with it on those terms, treating her that way!

SPEED.—But you *have* been *happy* with her, Abe! I've seen you smile in the light of her presence and droop in the shade of her absence! You've quarreled, sure . . . but don't we all? And you know you've never been unhappier than when you was quarreling, and downright woe-besmitten! Look at that week you moped and drizzled when she was running about with Stevie Douglas, Abe! Aw . . . (*Trying to hearten Abe*) . . . you can be happy with her again, because you can't be happy without her! Come 'long, now, Abe . . .

ABE.—There's *always* been doubts and questionings, Speed . . . even when I was happy, because it seems *now* like I was only happy with her because there wasn't anyone else more congenial . . . or even anyone else at all . . . to be happy with, and I needed someone. Just . . . someone! Speed . . . (*deeply and sincerely*) . . . I can't go through with it, by golly!

SPEED.—(*Bitterly*) All right, all right. Maybe you're not thinking of that mighty fine and proud girl, probably over at th' church *right now* arrangin' her veil and flutterin' in her heart, gettin' all ready to give herself and her life, her weal and her woe unto you!

ABE.—It'll hurt her now, I know; but in the long run . . .

SPEED.—(*Contempt*) "In the long run," my leg! You've *got* to *go*, Abe! You've got to! It's a cruel and inhuman thing you're doin'! People'll despise and taunt you! They'll revile you and pity her . . . and that'll kill her! Maybe you're not thinkin' of the chagrin and mortification and pain and tears you'll cause *her*, Abe . . . leavin' her a-waitin' there . . . forsaken . . .

188

ABE.—Oh, Speed . . . Speed . . . ! I have thought of it . . . all of it! For God's sakes . . . what'll I . . . *do? What'll I . . . do?* (*Fade*)

SOUND.—*Sound of horses and carriage drawing up and stopping . . . Mary's laugh.*

MARY.—Come, get out of the carriage, Lizzie! Sakes, you look as peaked as a cambric kerchief!

LIZZIE.—I feel as limp as one, too! Oh, Mary . . .

MARY.—You can't be matron of honor sitting out here with old Daisy and Beauty!

LIZZIE.—Oh, I do *wish I could* . . . you know how Ninian and I feel about this marriage . . .

SOUND.—*People getting out of the carriage . . . carriage drives on.*

LIZZIE.— . . . *and* the groom, both!

MARY.—I know . . . you think they're *both* very unpropitious. Take my arm, Ninian.

LIZZIE.—Oh, oh . . . ! There's a little boy at the side entrance, motioning us to come in *that* way. I never heard . . .

MARY.—I'm sure it doesn't make any difference what way we go in if we can come out all together! I hope nobody's moved the lilacs nor touched that chancel rail! Ah . . .

SOUND.—*Door opens . . . Voices of young girls, giddy, excited.*

GIRLS.—O-o-oh, here's the br-ide! Oh, Mary . . . you're lovely! She's not as contrary as we used to think her, though, girls! Good luck, Mary! Aren't you ner-vous? You're going to have such a big, big wedding. The church's crowded, sakes!

MARY.—Well, darlings . . . I don't hear any weepings nor gnashings of teeth! I trust you do all have your teeth in and your brightest smiles on this afternoon!

GIRL.—(*Weeping*) But it's so sad, *losing* you this way, Mary!

MARY.—*Losing* me? Why, you ninny, I'm not going to be kidnaped nor murdered! Beulah, you look as fresh and pure as a newborn daisy, which you *are both*, I hope!

BEULAH.—La, Mary!

189

MARY.—It's just 4 minutes till time. Ninian . . . go see if Mr. Lincoln is all right. He's in the room off the baptistry.

GIRL.—The groom's not . . . (*giggling*) . . . here yet, Mary dolling!

MARY.—(*A bit disturbed*) Not here . . . yet? Well, I *supposed* it was the *bride's* prerogative to be late at the wedding . . . not the *groom's!*

GIRL.—He'll be here! He's got 4 minutes, and his legs are long, and . . . I suppose he'll consider the trouble worth the taking . . . though they do say that marriage's a feast at which the grace is sometimes better than the dinner! (*She giggles*)

MARY.—(*Suppressed, but furious*) I suppose it's not right that I should have mayhem in my soul at this happy hour; but, Lizzie, keep that silly, chattering vixen on the end of the procession and out of my eternal sight! (*Louder*) I don't like her, and I never have; and you asked her, not I!

LIZZIE.—(*Trying to hush and soothe Mary*) Now, now, Mary! Calm yourself now! You're overwrought!

MARY.—(*Going on, upset*) And where's this groom that's taking me for a bride in 3 minutes now?

SOUND.—*Low chatter of people . . . then the church bell off, fading down . . . church bell fades up but not near by . . . at distance.*

SPEED.—By golly, Abe . . . there's the last bell! Here . . . put on this vest. We'll be late, but not *much* . . . and they say it's better to be married late . . . if you can . . . than never to have been married . . . if you can! Now I've got everything packed. It'll take us about 2 minutes to walk over. Here . . .

ABE.—(*Low*) It's . . . getting dark outdoors.

SPEED.— . . . put your arm in this coat. Dag-gone, I thunk I was goin' to have a real time with you, you tryin' to rationalize yourself out of this happy, happy fracas. Don't you go worryin' about the weather, too . . . Why, th' sun'll be out before we get to th' church!

ABE.—It's started to sprinkle.

SPEED.—Yeh? Well, we'll *run* and make it in a minute! Here's your gloves . . . your hat. Dag-gone, you're about twice as hard t' dress as a newborn baby . . . bein' sommat over twice as big! Y'know, Abe . . . (*a bit piquant*) . . . I don't know how married people get along in them new-fangled sleeping cars, but when you git to Danville, you go put up at th' Delmonico. They say they load you up with good grub there, and they say (*lower*) their sleepin' facilities is fine . . . (*lower*) . . . if you want t' sleep. (*He bursts out laughing*)

ABE.—(*Bursting out*) Stop this, Speed! For God's sake, stop it!

SPEED.—(*Surprised*) Stop what, Abe? Your . . . coat . . . !

ABE.—Get that high-fallutin', hypocritical coat out of here . . .

SPEED.—But . . . Abe! And . . . watch out them gloves . . .

ABE.—Get 'em out! All of 'em! Stop tormenting me! I can't stand it any longer! I'm not goin'! I've told you a thousand times I'm not! You'd not believe me but . . . now maybe you'll know! I'm not! Decency won't let me, nor honesty! Get out of my way, Speed! Get . . . out!

SPEED.—Abe . . . look here! Let me help you! Let me . . . !

ABE.—Let go of me! Let me . . . go!

SPEED.—You can't! It's raining! You can't go, Abe! You can't do this to Mary!

ABE.—I can, because I must! And . . . *I am!* Hell nor high water can't stop me!

SPEED.—But where *you goin' to*, Abe?

ABE.—I don't know where! Except . . . anywhere . . . anywhere to get shut of this horrible doubt and shame and this splitting utter torment! Something's in me telling me I've . . . got to flee away . . . !

SPEED.—(*Determined*) I'll not let you do this to her! I'll not let you do it to . . . yourself, Abe!

ABE.—(*Warning*) You let go my arm, Speed!

SPEED.—(*Yelling*) Help! Someone help! Abe's . . . cr-azy! Hel-l-lp!

SOUND.—*A thud, as Abe strikes Speed.*

SPEED.—(*Going down, in pain and hurt*) A-abe . . . *no-o!*

ABE.—(*Vicious but kindly*) I had to! I . . . got to . . . go some-where else . . . away . . .

SPEED.—Go on, then . . . ! Go on . . . get out! She's well off rid of you . . . you . . . you yellow-livered coward! And that's all you are!

ABE.—(*Low, hurt*) Don't, Speed! Don't *you* say that . . . too! I've . . . (*fading*) . . . said it enough . . . to myself, God knows . . . ! (*Silence except*)

SOUND.—(*The bell, afar . . . a bit of rain*)

SPEED.—(*Low, as to himself*) . . . Tell 'em! I got to . . . go tell 'em!

SOUND.—*Speed . . . running . . . fade down bell and running . . . fade up bell and into distant organ music.*

MARY.—(*Muttering to herself, obviously walking up and down*) Where . . . oh, where . . . oh, where . . . oh, where . . . oh, where . . . *is he?*

GIRLS' VOICES.—(*Low*) Sakes, ain't it getting to be *something* now! Yes, and ain't *she?* Lord pity him when he does come!

MARY.—There's only *so much* waiting a woman can *stand!*

LIZZIE.—Wel-l, *we warned* you, Ninian and I!

MARY.—(*Gasping*) O-h, shut up, Lizzie! Just tell me *what's* keeping him, and maybe I can forgive him! If he's ill, or hurt, or . . . !

GIRLS.—Well . . . the music's pretty! You mean it *was.* This's only the fifth time the organist's repeated that piece that's supposed to lead right into the wedding march! He's only 10 minutes late . . . so far!

MARY.—And, of course, it'd have to rain, *too!* Surely *that's* not keeping him!

GIRL.—(*Loud, to another girl*) Oh . . . perhaps . . . (*giggling*) . . . perhaps he's like the frogs in Aesop's fable who were wise . . . for no matter how thirsty they were, they wouldn't leap into the cistern because they knew they . . . (*pointed*) . . . knew *they couldn't leap out again!* (*she giggles*)

MARY.—(*Furiously*) Lizzie, *I warn you* I'll . . . I'll do her body harm if you don't keep her out of my sight, sound, and . . . grasp! Where is he? Where's Speed? Where's the portmanteau? They're *all* three of a kind . . . lazy, shiftless luggage, all of 'em! Lizzie, Lizzie . . . why did it have to be spoiled . . . even this little way? It was going so beautifully . . . I planned it all to be so nice . . . so pretty . . . so *right* . . . so something to remember all one's life . . . like a flower that bloomed once, beautifully . . .

SOUND.—*Someone running in mud or slush far off . . . silence.*

MARY.—Oh, heavenly days, it's him! Heaven help keep me to be calm and sweet to him! He can't really help these things! He's a dear fellow, and . . .

SOUND.—*Footsteps close by.*

MARY.—Open the door for the groom, you huddled-up ninnies! Tell the organist . . .

SOUND.—*Door opening.*

MARY.—Tell . . . (*A second of silence*)

MARY.—Speed! What is it? Where's . . . Mr. Lincoln?

SPEED.—(*Breathing hard from running*) He's done . . . *gone!*

MARY.—(*Aghast*) *Gone?* (*Silence*)

LIZZIE.—O-oh, this is . . . awful! Ninian . . . !

MARY.—(*Trying hard to hold herself*) You mean he's not . . . *not coming,* Speed?

GIRLS.—(*Low, whispered*) Oh, oh, la! Listen! Gone! Oh, I'll *faint!*

SPEED.—(*Breathing loud*) He's not . . . coming, no. He fit the fight *with* hisself, and he lost *to* hisself, and he left . . . run out into the rain . . . wanderin' about . . . lost! He said he . . . he couldn't come.

LIZZIE.—This's preposterous!

GIRL.—(*Tenderly*) Sit here, Mary.

LIZZIE.—Ninian, go see what *you* can do! He's forsaken her!

MARY.—Stay here, Ninian! Let me . . . just let me be . . . a minute!

GIRL 1.—But, Mary! We must do something!

GIRL 2.—The audience . . . they're shuffling and buzzing and wondering!

MARY.—(*Bitter*) Go tell 'em the funeral will soon be moving in

GIRL.—Oh, ain't it awful!

LIZZIE.—(*Angry*) Oh . . . the horrible, indecent, cruel *boor!* The men of this town should horsewhip him out of town, and I'll see they do!

MARY.—Lizzie, be still. Shut up! *I* should be the angry, weeping-willow one . . . being the supposed offended one . . . not you!

LIZZIE.—But the shame; the insult; the waste! The cakes and bonbons and coffee! The presents!

MARY.—I'll just . . . go home and eat them myself, except the silver tea set, and be merry about it, and happy *I* have nothing to be wandering out in the rain about!

LIZZIE.—I'll never be able to raise my head again in society!

MARY.—Well, I'm sure *I've* got nothing to hang *my* head about nor be un-proud nor ashamed of! Go tell the crowd to look out the door and watch Miss Todd and her absent forsaken groom ride past in all her glory!

LIZZIE.—Mary! Where you going . . . in this rain . . . in your wedding dress . . . ?

MARY.—I'm going home . . . I'm going alone, also!

GIRL.—(*Fading*) Mary . . . come . . . back!

LIZZIE.—Oh, oh, oh . . . I can't . . . stand it! Don't let her! Go get her!

SOUND.—*Rain . . . a sort of sprinkle.*

MARY.—(*Calm, hurt*) Charles . . . drive me home.

MAN.—Yes . . . ma'am. You'll have the umbrella here, Missy Mary?

MARY.—No.

MAN.—But . . . the rain?

MARY.—The rain will . . . be kind to me today, Charles.

MAN.—Yes, ma'am. Giddap, Daisy. (*Cluck of tongue*) . . . Beauty!

SOUND.—*The carriage as it sloshes along . . . also horses' hoofs.*

VOICES.—(*Low but near by, as carriage passes at short distance*) Look at 'er sittin' there on th' back seat straight as an oak tree! Oh, it's perfectly scandalous, ain't it? Th' rain's on her dress and gleamin' in her hair! She looks like she's enjoyin' it, t' me! She's . . . she's . . . them's *tears*, ain't they? Na-aw, it's th' rain runnin' down her cheeks . . . (*pause*) . . . or ain't it? (*Carriage fades*) There . . . she goes! My sakes, Molly . . . *what happened?* Y' *read* of these things, but . . . t' *see* 'em! (*Low*) Look . . . now that she's past, she . . . she's sunken down on the seat, sure 'nough . . . a-cryin'!
(*Fade out*)

SOUND.—*The carriage going on . . . the light rain . . . a bit of thunder . . . the carriage fades out . . . the rain goes on and the thunder. Fade in the church bell, far, far off, as down in a valley, and now tolling as for a funeral. Fade in Abe's heavy footsteps . . . then they stop . . . the rain, lightly.*

ABE.—(*Deeply, in anguish*) Such a fool! Such a fool! (*With meaning, and not "reciting"*) "O that I were upon some desert coast! Where howling tempests and lashing tide would stun me into deep and senseless . . . Quiet! Come, madness! Come unto me, senseless death! I cannot suffer this! I . . . . "
(*Fade Abe's voice down . . . fade up*)

SOUND.—*Funeral procession . . . horses and carriages . . . tolling of bell far below.*

MAN'S VOICE.—"I am the resurrection and the death, and whosoever believeth on me shall not die, but have life . . . everlasting. There are many mansions . . . "

SOUND.—*The funeral procession fades out.*

ABE.—(*In anguish*) Lord God Almighty . . . as Thou dost help *the dead*, help now a *living* one! Give to a poor distraught, benighted, wandering soul a beacon light, a guiding hand, a glimmer of sanity to show him out of his dark way on earth! Help him to know what to do in *his* hour of distress as Thou didst know to do in *Thy* hour!

195

SOUND.—*The rain still.*

ANN'S VOICE.—(*Afar, mysterious*) Abe . . . dear Abe . . . !

ABE.—(*Puzzled, a bit afraid*) Yes . . . yes? Who . . . is it?

ANN.—Have you so soon forgot me? (*Silence*)

ABE.—(*Low, remembering*) Ann! Ann Rutledge! An . . . !

ANN.—Yes, Abe.

ABE.—(*Seeing the light*) It was *you* in my restless soul, Ann! It was the love of you that I can never put out from me that troubled me and I knew it not! Ann . . . Ann . . . why are you here in death? What shall I do? Ann . . . *tell me!* (*Silence*) Have I done wrong? Should what is earthly of me marry what is earthly of her? Tell me. Tell . . . me!

ANN.—(*Calm, patient, sure*) You must go on, Abe.

ABE.—Go . . . on? (*Silence*)

ANN.—You must face your . . . earthly destiny . . .

ABE.—(*Low*) Destiny! (*Pause*) Yes, Ann.

ANN.—Under the stones and grass *I* rest in peace . . . waiting for you till judgment day . . . (*Her voice fades out*)

ABE.—(*Breathless, calm*) Yes; yes. (*Pause*) Yes. (*Silence*)

SOUND.—*The rain stops.*

SPEED.—(*Distant, coming closer*) Abe . . . Abe, you hurt? You ain't gone and went cr-cr-azy, have you?

ABE.—(*Calm . . . a bit of a laugh*) I'm all right now, Speed. I'm ready to go back . . . to face things . . . to help make things right that I've done.

SPEED.—(*Cheerfully doubtful*) Well, Abe . . .

SOUND.—*The two walking.*

SPEED.— . . . Mebby *you can;* but it don't look *t' me* like there *was* any help for what you went and did! (*Fade*)

MUSIC.—*Full and down behind*

ABE.—I suppose every man is called upon, some time or other, to set his face toward a challenging and anguished future, and alone, before the anguish of the past has left burning his heart and soul. That is how I went back to Springfield . . . yea, an older and a sadder young man.

Music.—*Up and out.*

Announcer.—This is the thirty-fifth in a series of broadcasts dealing with the life of Abraham Lincoln. The stories are dramatized by E. P. Conkle and directed by Sidney Harmon. These sketches do not claim to be historically accurate in all their details but attempt rather to bring to listeners the true spirit of the man and the period in which we find him. We hope you will be with us again next week to enjoy the agreeable companionship of Abe Lincoln. This is the Columbia Broadcasting System.

Roadside

A free adaption for radio of the play by LYNN RIGGS
Presented by THE COLUMBIA WORKSHOP

MUSIC.—*Introduction.*

ANNOUNCER.—The year is 1905. It is near sundown of a day in
June, and the air is summery and sweet. By the side of a road,
through the woods in Indian Territory, there nestles a
covered wagon, Pap Rader's roadside home. Outside the
wagon are some battered camp chairs, a large three-legged
pot with a fire under it. Buzzey Hale, a little, bluish, dried-up
farmer is sitting disconsolately by the fire as Pap Rader, a
good-natured old man, comes from around the wagon . . .

PAP.—(*Fading in*) Set there a-pinin'. If you doan look like a ole
turkey buzzard! No wonder Hannie called you Buzzey.

BUZZEY.—Buzzey is short . . . fer beautiful.

PAP.—Beautiful! Huh! If you're beautiful, I'm a bob-tailed
witch! I doan see whut you make outa follerin' us around
anyway, Mr. Turkey Buzzard. There ain't nothin' dead
around here fer you to chaw on.

BUZZEY.—I'm gonna *be* around, though.

PAP.—Yeow! You'll be.

BUZZEY.—If it hadn't a-been fer you, Hannie wouldn't a-left me
in the first place. You done it with yer ole covered wagon.
Tellin' her about the roads again. You brung her up . . .
I'll say you brung her up, with her ways! Wonder why I
married her a-tall, an' her with an ole man like you couldn't
read a sign on a hitch post! Ridin' on the road, that's all
you think about!

PAP.—Whut you think about is plowin'. The road's better. I'm
tellin' you, Hannie'd orter divorced you like she did. She's
a strappin' girl that wants to roam, like me an' see life,
'stid of a milk churn!

Buzzey.—I'll git her back, you'll see.

Pap.—If you foller us too long, yer crops'll all be ruint!

Buzzey.—It's cut, pap. I got money to h'ar me h'ard hands An' when *I* h'ar men, I h'ar *men*. Red Ike an' Black Ike . . that's the kinda men I h'ar.

Hannie.—(*Off*) Pap!

Pap.—Whut is it?

Hannie.—Pap, come 'ere!

Pap.—Come 'ere, yerself, Hannie. I'm busy.

Hannie.—Gol darn it, pap! You heared me. Come a-runnin'. Cain't you hear nuthin'?

Pap.—Well, whut is it? Come out here and tell it.

Hannie.—(*On a little closer*) I ain't got so many clothes on. And I don't expect to come out and give that ole buzzard no free show. Case you'd like to know it, that hound of yourn is eatin' up yer hog shoulder.

Pap.—Well, why in blazes didden you say so!

Hannie.—I said so!

Sound.—*Dog wails . . . then short yelps.*

Pap.—(*Off*) I saved that dog from drownin', and this is the way he does me. A good hog shoulder plumb ruint! The yeller cur! (*In*) Looky here, Buzzey, you let Hannie alone. She ain't gonna have no truck with you's long's I'm around, you hear me?

Buzzey.—I hear you.

Pap.—You better heed me. (*Fading*) I'm goin' down along the crick bank and see whut I c'n see.

Sound.—*Footsteps fading in brush . . . then steps down wagon steps.*

Buzzey.—Hannie!

Hannie.—(*Fading in*) I don't know you from Adam.

Buzzey.—Hannie, cain't you come back to me?

199

HANNIE.—(*On*) Not to you ner to no one like you. I want me a man, not a broomstick. Besides, I had enough of bein' a farmer's wife.

BUZZEY.—You wouldn't a-got no divorce from me if someone hadn't fixed it up fer me to be found the way I was.

HANNIE.—Oh, woulden I? Who fixed it, then?

BUZZEY.—I ain't sayin'.

HANNIE.—Well, whoever fixed it, you fixed yerself with me!

BUZZEY.—Hannie, it won't never happen again.

HANNIE.—It can happen till you're blue in the face, fer all I keer. Whut I cain't figger out is how I ever come to marry you in the first place.

BUZZEY.—It was love, that's whut it was.

HANNIE.—Love? Lemme look at you.

BUZZEY.—Well, *look* at me, and you'll see.

HANNIE.—Is that a new suit you got on?

BUZZEY.—Brand spankin'!

HANNIE.—It don't seem to improve you none.

BUZZEY.—You coulda done worse. I had me plenty of land and a way to take keer of you, didn't I?

HANNIE.—Yeah. But I could take keer of myself the day I was borned. And if I ever marry again, it'll have to be to a world-slingin', star-traipsin' son of a gun that's more my match than you air. And when I run into sich a feller, I miss my guess if cracks of lightnin' don't burn up the country fer 14 miles around. So look out you don' get scorched.

RED AND BLACK.—(*Off* . . . *singing*)

BUZZEY.—Hannie, come on back to me. The calves an' the roan . . . they won't have nuthin' to do with me. They're missin' you, I reckon.

HANNIE.—(*Fading*) I never heard of no dumb animals dyin' of a broken heart. Quit a-botherin' me now.

BUZZEY.—Aw, Hannie . . .

200

RED AND BLACK.—(*Fading in*) They chew tobaccer thin in
        Kansas,
        They chew tobaccer thin in
        Kansas,
        They chew tobaccer thin, and
        they spit it on their chin,
        And they lick it in again in
        Kansas.

BUZZEY.—(*Mad*) Red Ike and Black Ike! Whut in blazes you
doin' here, anyhow? Whut'd you mean flyin' off leavin' my
farm to run itself?

RED.—Is this yore campin' outfit?

BUZZEY.—Campin'!

BLACK.—You a campin' man now, Mr. Hale?

RED.—You got some soup?

BUZZEY.—Soup?

BLACK.—We're powerful hongry. Ain't et in a day.

RED.—Been singin' to keep up our sperrits!

BUZZEY.—Singing!

BLACK.—Et some strawberries, though.

BUZZEY.—I don't keer if you starve! Whut'd you leave my farm
fur? Thought I could trust it to you.

RED.—We was a-lookin' fer someone else.

BUZZEY.—You git back quick's you c'n hotfoot it, both of you.
Git, I tell you!

RED.—We're gonna stay.

BLACK.—We're gonna set here and stay, ain't we, Red?

BUZZEY.—You're f'ard, both of you!

RED.—Suits me. Cain't make me mad.

BLACK.—(*Irrelevantly*) Chew Star Navy, an' spit ham gravy!

BUZZEY.—Look here, if I give you $10 apiece . . .

RED.—Woulden take it!

BUZZEY.—How much you tryin' to bleed outa me?

RED.—Not any.

BUZZEY.—Whut'd you come fer, anyway?

BLACK.—Oh, jist seen the purty road and started off a-follerin' it.

BUZZEY.—You got somethin' up yer sleeve.

SOUND.—*Footsteps in brush.*

HANNIE.—(*Fading in*) Howdy! Red Ike an' Black Ike! Thought I heard yer voices!

RED.—Thought we'd find you!

BLACK.—Knowed we'd find you!

RED.—If we looked long enough!

BLACK.—In the right place!

RED.—On the right road!

HANNIE.—If I ain't missed you! Tell me things!

BLACK.—Whut about?

HANNIE.—Oh, anything!

BLACK.—Wanta hear about Texas?

HANNIE.—Whut about Texas?

BLACK.—Well, we seen sich a sight, didden we, Red?

RED.—Down at the switch as we come through.

BLACK.—A man th'owed in the jail fer gettin' drunk!

RED.—He got drunk and crazy and wild. And he yelled. My, how he yelled!

BLACK.—How'd it go?

RED.—Wild and reckless,
Borned in Texas,
Suckled by a bear,
Steel backbone,
Tail screwed on,
Twelve feet long,
Dare any son of a gun to step on it!

202

HANNIE.—Purty good!

BUZZEY.—(*Disgusted*) Purty good!

RED.—Nen the marshal got a-holt of him, an' the jedge said; "Twelve days in jail, one fer every foot of yer long tail." So they went to t'ow him in jail, and he kicked the jedge offen the bench and made jist plumb hash outa the courtroom first, 'fore they got him in the calaboose.

HANNIE.—Good!

BUZZEY.—(*As before*) Good!

RED.—My, a big, hulky, curly-headed, han'some ring-tailed tooter, wuzn't he, Black?

HANNIE.—An' whur is he?

RED.—Down the road a piece.

HANNIE.—Outa jail?

BLACK.—Shore!

PAP.—(*Fading in*) Red Ike and Black Ike. I knowed it! I knowed it! Whut'd I tell you about h'ard hands, Buzzey! Hee, hee!

TEXAS.—(*Off . . . singing*) . . . Wild and reckless . . . (*etc.*)

HANNIE.—Hey, Pap, they's a man comin' along the road! Wild and reckless, borned in Texas! A tail 12 feet long! He fit his way into jail and outa jail, and he's coming along that road there, and heavens and earth, whut're you gonna do?

TEXAS.—(*On closer . . . singing*)

HANNIE.—Hear that! It's him! I'm gonna run in the wagon, quick!

PAP.—Whut you goin' in the wagon fer, Hannie?

HANNIE.—I'm gonna put flour on my face and purty myself up, that's whut fer.

SOUND.—*Footsteps up steps.*

BUZZEY.—Now, whut on earth's come over her?

PAP.—Danged if I know. Whut's this about a man?

TEXAS.—Howdy!

203

Pap.—Huh? Oh . . . howdy yerself, mister.

Texas.—Thought you might be the marshal. Shore don't want to see him again! It wouldn't be safe—fer *him!* Hello, if here ain't the two little twins I seen down the road a piece . . .

Red.—We ain't twins!

Black.—We're cousins!

Texas.—You look like twins to me. Is this here yer pap?

Red.—It's Pap Rader. He ain't *our* pap, though.

Black.—Not as we know of.

Texas.—Howd' do, Mr. Rader.

Pap.—We been hearin' about you, Mr. Texas. Hear you beat up the jedge an' broke outa jail and raised high water complete, down here in Verdigree.

Texas.—Oh, it wasn't so much.

Pap.—This here is Mr. Hale.

Texas.—Howd' do, Mr. Hale.

Buzzey.—(*Sullen*) Howdy.

Texas.—You look porely.

Red.—Guessed it right, that time, Mr. Texas! His wife jist divorced him!

Texas.—Oh!

Buzzey.—Shet up yer mouth, Red Ike, I'll knock yer down! (*Fading out*) Folks a-buttin' into business that don't concern 'em . . .

Texas.—He kinda takes it to heart, don't he?

Pap.—'Tain't no joke to lose a womern.

Texas.—She musta been blind if'n she married a man like that!

Red and Black.—Hee, hee, hee!

Pap.—Go an' git some wood, 'fore I smack you one. Both of you! Git a move on!

Red and Black.—(*Fading*) Hee, hee, hee!

204

PAP.—Have to excuse them little shavers. You never know whut they're gonna do next. Little off'n the head . . .

HANNIE.—(*Off*) Who's that with you, pap? Cain't make out nuthin' but a smudge an' a pair o' laigs.

TEXAS.—Reckon they're mine, lady.

HANNIE.—Well, I seen worse.

SOUND.—*Footsteps down wagon steps.*

PAP.—Make you acquainted to my daughter, Hannie, Mr. Texas.

TEXAS.—Howd' do.

HANNIE.—Mr. Texas? Thought that was a state?

TEXAS.—Oh, Texas is named after me! And I'm kina of a state myself, in a way o' talkin'.

HANNIE.—State of smart Alec, I'd call it.

TEXAS.—You got a kind of a jokin' daughter, ain't you, Mr. Rader?

PAP.—Blame if I know when she *is* or when she *ain't!*

HANNIE.—When you've saw as many funny-lookin' sights as *I* have, you'll turn to jokin', too, Mr. Texas . . .

TEXAS.—I think I'd sorta like you, 'f I could jist make out whut you was up to.

HANNIE.—Ain't that nice of you, though. Whur was you bound fer, Mr. Texas?

TEXAS.—Well, I had aimed to make it up to Claremore 'fore it got night.

HANNIE.—Is that so? Well, I guess the law down at Verdigree kinda helt you up a bit.

TEXAS.—Yeah, I guess it did.

HANNIE.—Is there anything a-hinderin' you now?

TEXAS.—If you was as smart 'th yer eyes as you air 'th yer tongue, you'd see it's comin' night on me.

HANNIE.—If you was smart, you'd ast 'f you could stay here all night an' sleep by the f'ar—so the varmints won't bother you.

TEXAS.—I might do that.

HANNIE.—How about tellin' me 'bout yerself?

PAP.—(*Fading*) Guess I'll jist mosey along and warter the horses while I'm able!

TEXAS.—You know, I don't think a ordinary man'd be safe around you! You're too smart! I was borned in Texas, an' I ain't got any present job, though I c'n do most anything I want to—if I want to—an' I'm on my way some'eres now, I don't know where.

HANNIE.—Look at them lightnin' bugs!

TEXAS.—I was tellin' you about myself!

HANNIE.—I c'n listen and look at the same time.

TEXAS.—Well, look at me 'stid of lightning bugs.

HANNIE.—I couldn't help myself, if you had a light on yore tail . . . like a lightnin' bug. (*Relenting*) I wanta hear about you, though, honest I do.

SOUND.—*Work in night sounds as background.*

TEXAS.—Onct I run a ranch in Texas as big as the state of Alabama. I ain't never been licked by mortal man.

HANNIE.—I take you serious, but I don't swaller that kinda fish bait. Not right at first. I got to git used to it.

TEXAS.—Oh, you're gonna git used to it! Whut I see I *see!* And I see a lot about me an' you that's been writ down some-eres for a long time. I wanta tell you sump'n I never told nobody . . . I wasn't borned!

HANNIE.—What!

TEXAS.—I wasn't borned in the ordinary way . . . Way out on the Texas prairie set a small cabin made outa oak. And in that cabin set a man and womern with a growed gal as purty as purty could be! Name was Liza, Mornin' come, she'd hop on her pony to ride the range, her old pap and mammy a-runnin' arter her to stop her. "Come on back, Liza," they'd say, "the plains is full of coyotes." And seein' she didn't answer, they'd say, "Don't go fur, then, and come back soon." And away she'd go! Greased lightning! Dynamite on wings! When she was 7½ mile away, she'd stop an' look around. Now a funny thing! She had rid into a valley whur a river used to flow in the year one. The tall grasses stood up like trees. A queer kind of a roarin' like lions came from somewheres among the tall grass. She'd git off her horse and go into that valley on foot. She'd stay all day. Who did she see there? Who did she meet there? Somebody! A secret man that roared when he talked and shuck the ground like an earthquake rumblin'. Finally, one night, Liza lay in her pappy's cabin, when all of a sudden there was a crash and a bang and a clatter. Thunder and hail, f'ar and brimstone! The cabin whur Liza lay cracked itself wide open from stern to stern, beam end to beam end, hind end to gullet! And when the smoke cleared away, out *I* stepped, full size, dressed to kill, in a 10-gallon hat, boots, and chaps, a gun in ary hand, and both guns a-poppin'! And that's how I got started!

HANNIE.—(*Carried away*) I believe to my soul you're tellin' the truth!

TEXAS.—Course I'm tellin' the truth!

HANNIE.—The truth and whut else?

TEXAS.—It's gospel . . . ever word I speak!

HANNIE.—Can you look over a tree?

TEXAS.—Whut's that got to do with it? I'm 6 foot tall!

HANNIE.—(*Relieved*) That's quite a size. Whur air you a-goin' after today, Mr. Texas?

TEXAS.—I ain't said—yit. It all depends.

HANNIE.—On whut?

TEXAS.—Oh, on which a-way the wind blows.

HANNIE.—Well, it pears to me the wind has died down complete.

TEXAS.—I been a-noticin' that. Trees ain't hardly a-movin'. I'd shore hate to exert myself more'n a tree.

HANNIE.—Well, you c'n sleep here by the f'ar 'th the rest of 'em, less'n you're afeard they'll bite! I'm goin' to bed. Good night, Mr. Texas.

TEXAS.—Good night.

HANNIE.—Tell Buzzey good night fer me, if you see him. And tell him I said he could sleep right bang up clost to the hot f'ar—and *imagine!*

SOUND.—*Footsteps up wagon steps . . . night sounds louder.*

TEXAS.—(*Laughs*) Funny, ain't it, the way you take to some people? And some people you cain't set down in eighty. I'm as easy in my mind as a newborn bronc! And sich a deep, dark hole of sleepin' as I'm goin' into will be wrote down in books! I bet I don't wake up till the sun goes down. And I bet I dream!

SOUND.—*Quiet except for the hoot of a night owl . . . a frog begins to croak. Cross-fade into*

MUSIC.—*Bridge.*

SOUND.—*Rooster crowing . . . slow footsteps in brush.*

PAP.—Whur you goin', Buzzey?

BUZZEY.—Sh!

PAP.—Whut're you up to?

BUZZEY.—Quit makin' a noise! You don't want a-lose Hannie, do you?

PAP.—I ain't a-losin' her.

BUZZEY.—Not yit! But it's a-comin'!

PAP.—Whut was you aimin' to do?

BUZZEY.—Go down here to Verdigree, rouse up the marshal, and tell him whur Texas is at. First thing you know this here Texas'll be runnin' off with Hannie, nen both of us'll be outa luck!

PAP.—Well, don't talk so much, you'll wake him up. Why didn't you go sooner?

BUZZEY.—I meant to, but I overslept.

PAP.—Overslept! Git on there, now, an' do whut you're a-gonna do.

BUZZEY.—I'm a gittin'!

TEXAS.—Oh, is that you, Mr. Hale?

BUZZEY.—Huh? Ye-yeah, it's me!

TEXAS.—Goin' some'eres?

BUZZEY.—Jist goin' down along the crick bank . . .

TEXAS.—Come 'ere, you sneakin' pike, don't you never try a trick like that on me again, or I'll make stew outa you!

BUZZEY.—W-whut kind of a trick, Mr. Texas?

TEXAS.—I heard you all right, both of you. And you, pap Rader, a-listenin' to a suck-egg mule like this here Buzzey. I'd a thought you had more sense!

PAP.—Well, blame me, I don't want you a-runnin' away with my Hannie! She's better off with me than she'd be with you.

TEXAS.—Oh, is that so? Well, I'm gonna learn you a lesson you won't fergit! Hadn't meant to take Hannie away with me a-tall. But I'll put her under one arm and claw my way to clear down in the Verdigree bottom some'eres outa sight. She'll jump at the chanct! She'd kick you both in the pants if I told her to and lay down and let me walk on her . . .

BUZZEY.—You quit . . .

TEXAS.—But after I git her well trained to ride proper, I'm gonna leave her some'eres to git along the best way she can! Learn you two a lesson!

SOUND.—*Steps down wagon steps.*

HANNIE.—How's that, Mr. Texas?

TEXAS.—(*Weak*) Eh . . . whut're you . . . whut?

HANNIE.—I'll tend to you! You don't look so big, and you don't look so handsome to me!

BUZZEY.—Give it to him, Hannie!

PAP.—Shet up, you!

TEXAS.—Now, Hannie . . .

HANNIE.—(*Blazing mad*) Don't you Hannie me! Gonna run off with me, and me under your arm, is that it? If I ever seen a lantern-jawed, cock-eyed idiot that couldn't say "Boo!" to a fly, you're it! Ever time I look at you, I git ringworm.

TEXAS.—Aw, Hannie . . .

HANNIE.—Whyn't you beat it up the road and find a place that'd suit you better?

TEXAS.—I wisht you'd listen to me . . .

HANNIE.—Gether your things and git!

BUZZEY.—And don't you never come around decent . . .

PAP.—Shet up, Buzzey! He ain't done nuthin' to you!

RED AND BLACK.—(*Fading in . . . shouting*)

RED.—Hey, Texas, man a-comin'!

BLACK.—The marshal from Verdigree!

RED.—Big man, 'th a hat and a pistol!

BLACK.—Comin' along the road like a bat outa thunder!

TEXAS.—How's that?

RED.—The marshal from Verdigree a-lookin' fer trouble!

TEXAS.—Oh, the marshal. Let him come.

RED AND BLACK.—Whut?

TEXAS.—Let him come, I said.

BLACK.—He'll git you!

RED.—Th'ow you in jail!

BLACK.—Shoot a hole th'ough you!

TEXAS.—We'll see about that.

PAP.—Tell you whut I'll do, pardner. 'F you git shot, I'll bury you nice—and put up a stone made outa aweepin' willer tree with a sign on it that says, "He fit and died."

TEXAS.—That'll be nice.

SOUND.—*Footsteps through brush.*

MARSHALL.—Hands up, the lot of you! You, too, lady. Now, then, Mr. Borned-in-Texas, I've got you again. And this time you ain't gonna git away. From the looks of that jail, you musta been full of elephant juice. You must be Mr. Samson before he got his hair cut! Is he a friend of yourn, pap?

PAP.—Yes, sir, he is.

BUZZEY.—He ain't!

PAP.—Yes, he is.

TEXAS.—We might jist as well hit the pike now as to stand here a-talkin'.

MARSHAL.—You got more sense than I give you credit fer. You hain't got a gun on you anywhurs, have you?

TEXAS.—You tuck my gun away from me before, didn't you?

MARSHAL.—Yeah, I did. The rest of you can put your hands down, 'f you want to.

HANNIE.—Looks like you could shet up talkin' so much and take this here crimernal outa here. I'd be right glad. (*With real disappointment*) I thought he was somethin' special . . . a 9-footer . . . stridin' along 'th his head so high. Now I know he's jist a thing on stilts . . . and the stilts is shaky and full of worm holes!

TEXAS.—Listen, Hannie, if I git outa this and come back, whut'll you do?

HANNIE.—Spit in yer face!

TEXAS.—You shore?

HANNIE.—Shore am!

TEXAS.—Well, I reckon I won't be back here, then. I reckon I won't be back *nowhur* now till I git my second wind. I been winded 'cause I run 17 mile thout stoppin' and by a cyclone smackin' me plumb in the face. But this is the first time I been knocked holler by a female. Kinda gits a feller down in the mouth!

MARSHAL.—Come on, Mr. Texas. And if you make one false move, I'll put a hole in you you c'n see daylight through!

TEXAS.—(*Fading out*) I reckon I'll jist try to keep from gettin' any more till the one I got is healed up a little bit.

SOUND.—*Footsteps out . . . pause.*

PAP.—Well, I'm a cow and a calf! Never lifted a finger! He mighta kicked the marshal on the shins onct, anyhow!

Buzzey.—I told you. I told you! A coward and a liar and a ring toom toom! (*with crazy exuberance*)

Hannie.—What a fool!

Buzzey.—Shore proud of you, Hannie. A womern after my own heart! Glad you come to your senses. Let's jump a train to Claremore, git spliced, hitched up together same as before! Nen after that, we'll hop another train and git home 'fore sundown!

Hannie.—Go home with you? (*Laughs*) Jawbone of a whale and hock of a terrapin! Go home with *you?* Why, you little dried-up blue-nosed old buzzard, smellin' of a dead cow in the summertime! Go home with a corpse!

Buzzey.—Hannie?

Hannie.—If you knowed whut I was gonna do, you'd have a conniption fit! Come on, you Ikes! We're a-goin' some'eres! (*Dashes off*)

Red and Black.—(*After her*) Hee, hee, hee! Wild and reckless, borned in Texas!

Buzzey.—(*Dazed*) My stars, *now* whut's come over her?

Music.—*Bridge.*

Sound.—*Banging of gavel.*

Judge.—Order in the courtroom! I ain't gonna pay no attention to the rightfulness or wrongfulness of procedure this mornin'. The court's been defied and spit on, and I'm gonna do some defyin' and spittin' myself! This here feller, Mr. Texas, has got drunk, which is agin the law. He's broke outa jail after beatin' up the guard, which is agin the law. He's smashed up the courtroom, which is agin the law. He's run plumb away, which is also agin the law. Fer gettin' drunk, I only sentenced him to 12 days in the calaboose. Now then, adding on to that, fer smashin' up the courtroom and fer breakin' outa jail . . .

Marshal.—And fer beating up the guard!

Judge.—Shet up! Nobody ast you to speak! Six months in jail and $200. Now, then, have you anything to say?

Texas.—Well, I ain't got $200 . . .

JUDGE.—(*Haughtily*) That ain't no excuse.

TEXAS.—And you ain't got no jail.

JUDGE.—Whut? Whut's the matter with the jail?

TEXAS.—(*Abashed*) Well, I . . . I reckon a cyclone struck it!

JUDGE.—D'you mean to tell me . . . ! Neb, come here. Whut'd you let him tear the roof offen your jail fer?

NEB.—(*Terrified*) He jist done it, jedge. He went an' tied me up first.

JUDGE.—(*Disgusted*) Tied you up? Neb Withers, I'm gonna turn this prisoner over to you, and you'll jist have to keep him '*thout* a jail.

NEB.—But, jedge, I cain't keep him with me 'f he doan wanta stay.

JUDGE.—You got handcuffs, ain't you?

NEB.—But, jedge . . . I cain't have *that!* I'm a married man!

JUDGE.—That don't make no difference!

NEB.—(*Righteously*) Jedge, I know that ain't gonna be right.

JUDGE.—Shet up! We gotta do sump'n with him.

NEB.—Well, now, the marshal here ain't married . . .

MARSHAL.—I'll break your neck!

SOUND.—*Gavel pounding.*

JUDGE.—Order in the courtroom!

SOUND.—*Door opens and closes.*

JUDGE.—Whutta you want in here, Miz Foster?

MRS. FOSTER.—(*Giggles*) Oh! It's a court, ain't it? Open to the public? Howd' do, prisoner? Glad to see you!

JUDGE.—Order!

SOUND.—*Gavel.*

MRS. FOSTER.—Don't you mind me, jedge. I ain't gonna be a mite of trouble. Jist go right on 'th yer jedgin'. My brother that used to steal hogs always said, "They ain't no use in

213

goin' up 'fore Jedge Snodgrass, fer yer sure to git 90 days in the calaboose, wh'er you're guilty or not."

JUDGE.—(*Outraged*) Order, I say!

MRS. FOSTER.—Course, Davy was always *guilty*, Jedge, I'll say *that* fer you! Davy jist couldn't keep his hands offen hogs. I'll never forgit, one time he . . .

JUDGE.—Miz Foster, ef you don't shet up a-talkin' about hogs and things, you'll have to leave the courtroom!

MRS. FOSTER.—(*Huffily*) I ain't interferin' 'th justice, am I?

JUDGE.—I jist said *shet yer mouth!* . . . As I was sayin' when Miz Foster come a-buttin' in . . .

MARSHAL.—You wasn't sayin' anything, jedge, it was *me!*

SOUND.—*Gavel.*

JUDGE.—Order, I said!

MARSHAL.—Neb, here, had been tryin' to put you up to handcuff this prisoner to me, and I jist said to Neb I'd break his neck . . . and I will too!

NEB.—You keep yore hands offen me!

JUDGE.—'F it ain't one thing, it's another. Order! Shet up, you two! Quit it!

MARSHAL.—Beg yore pardon, jedge. But if that little wart . . .

NEB.—Don't you call me no wart . . .

JUDGE.—Shet up!

SOUND.—*Door opens.*

HANNIE.—(*Fading in*) Well, Texas, if you hain't a purty one! No gumption! I'm ashamed of you! Jedge, you let this man alone, you hear, or they'll be trouble!

JUDGE.—(*With icy rage*) Here, lady! You run this court, you're so *smart!* Take this here gavel! I'm gonna get someone to repair the jail (*fades*), and if this prisoner's gone when I git back, I'll shore *crown* the lot of you!

SOUND.—*Door slams.*

214

HANNIE.—Well, of all the . . . what's the matter 'th *that* ole mustard plaster? What'd he give me this here thing fer? Run the court myself, he said. You heard what he said! That's a good un! I'd do it right, too! I'd turn all the prisoners loose, let 'em run hog wild. I'd show 'em the road. That's the kinda jedgin' I'd do!

MARSHAL.—You better stay down from the jedge's bench!

HANNIE.—I'd th'ow all the marshals in the crick!

MARSHAL.—Git down from there, I told you!

HANNIE.—I'd burn all the law books and start all over. I'd tell nobody whur to stand, and nobody'd tell me whur to set!

MARSHAL.—(*Outraged*) This hain't right, it hain't reg'lar! And if you don't shet up, I'll arrest you fer contempt!

HANNIE.—Come, on, you Ikes!

SOUND.—*Struggle . . . door opens.*

RED AND BLACK.—Wild and reckless, borned in Texas . . . (*Etc.*)

SOUND.—*Struggle . . . chair over . . . pistol falls.*

TEXAS.—Hold on to that marshal, you crazies! Gimme that gun! It's mine anyway! I thought I recognized it!

MARSHAL.—(*Mad*) I'll fix you, ever one of you! I'll have the law on you!

SOUND.—*Gavel pounding.*

HANNIE.—Here, here! Is it the law you're a-talkin' about, Mr. Marshal? Here's the law! This thing! A polished piece of post oak a-poundin' on a holler piece of pine! That's the law!

TEXAS.—(*Laughs*) Set down! All of you!

RED AND BLACK.—Hee, hee, hee!

TEXAS.—Shet up, you Ikes! Now, then! This is jist the kind of courtroom I like! The law . . . with its teeth pulled . . . and the prisoner with a shootin' arm! *This here is justice!* It don' come to a feller often. Now I'm myself again. I hadn't orter ever laid myself li'ble to the br'ars that scratch people like you-all. I'm savin' my blood—to make a worth while river outa it! I'm shore glad to've met you-all. And I don't wish you no more bad luck than the cholery morbus. See you all in . . .

HANNIE.—Jist a minute!

TEXAS.—Well?

HANNIE.—Don't be in no hurry!

TEXAS.—(*Grimly*) I've fooled around enough in these parts· It ain't healthy.

HANNIE.—Air you as blind's a bat?

TEXAS.—Well, no, I ain't.

HANNIE.—You air, too!

TEXAS.—I ain't!

HANNIE.—Here, take this piece o' oak!

SOUND.—*Gavel thrown over desk top.*

TEXAS.—Now I guess I got the law on *my* side!

HANNIE.—Now then, you c'n do things fer yourself. I'm th'ough with *you*. You're green as grass, you don't know two whoops about women, and whut you *don't* know about *anything* would make 30 million books full of close printing. When you first come along, I kind tuck to you . . . I thought you stepped right off a mountain some'eres. I thought you was full of shine like a scoured pot. I thought if you set, the sun'd set! *Course* you're blind as a bat! If you wasn't, you'd see I've hotfotted it clear here to Verdigree, waded th'ough weeds, and got chiggers on me all the way from my feet to whur I sit down! And whut fer? To try to git a fool of a man outa trouble that's had a landslide in his head and cain't even remember who he's supposed to be! Now git outa my way!

TEXAS.—(*Amazed*) Hannie!

HANNIE.—Don't you *Hannie me*

TEXAS.—I never seen a womern like you in all my life. You're crazy and reckless and wild. So'm I. You're walkin' the earth temporary like you know'd sump'n secret. So'm I. You got eyes and hair—*everything* a little better'n the next womern,

216

and you suit me down to the ground. I git awful lonesome bein' by myself, and it looks like you would.

HANNIE.—I ain't all by myself—say, air you invitin' me to travel with you?

TEXAS.—I was headed in that direction. We could swim in the cricks, we could watch it git sunup and sundown! See lightnin', hear thunder! Walk on th' wind! Burn yer tail feathers on th' sun! Feed natural, sing strong! Stop when you feel like stoppin'! Stay put when you feel like stayin' put!

HANNIE.—Well . . . that's sump'n . . . But I'd kick yer shins and pull out yer hair. I'd blister yer 'th my tongue ever couple o' days!

TEXAS.—(*Passionately*) I'd hate you 'f you didn't! Come on! *Go* with me! Wouldn't see another womern but you . . . wouldn't *think* of another womern but you.

HANNIE.—Look out now . . .

TEXAS.—*You—you*—all the time, day in, day out! Me and you! Like it ort to be! Like it was wrote down! Makes me dizzy!

HANNIE.—(*Breathless*) Don't talk that a-way . . .

TEXAS.—*You*—in my arms! I'd make love to you! Kiss you the way you never was kissed before . . .

HANNIE.—(*Responding, passionately*) Kiss me then . . .

TEXAS.—Hannie! (*Kiss*) . . . I'm blind! (*Rapturously*) Lightnin's struck! The world's ended! Kiss me!

HANNIE.—Whur air you? (*Kiss*)

TEXAS.—The trees is smokin'! My feet's burnin!

RED AND BLACK.—Hannie's got a feller! Yanh! Yanh! Hannie's got a feller!

MARSHAL.—I hain't gonna stand any more of this! I never seen sich goin's-on in a court of law! Making a fool outa me, and the courtroom, too! Blamed if I don't . . .

TEXAS.—Set down, and don't you move a eyelash, or I'll shoot it off!

217

HANNIE.—Texas! Quick, we got to be movin' from here! Ef the jedge gits back, they'll git you agin!

TEXAS.—I'd fergot all about it!

HANNIE.—I hadn't!

TEXAS.—Well, am I goin' with you, er air you goin' with me?

HANNIE.—I cain't run off an' leave pap.

TEXAS.—No, I reckon not! That means I'm goin' 'th you and pap, then. Less'n you're goin' home 'th Buzzey.

HANNIE.—I don't know him from Adam!

TEXAS.—Do you know me from Adam?

HANNIE.—No.

TEXAS.—No?

HANNIE.—As fur as I'm concerned—you *air* Adam!

TEXAS.—Yip-eee! We'll git pap, hitch up the wagon, and stamp out the f'ar! We're leavin' this place! I was borned on th' side of th' road! I like to walk fur and to cut up jake and let out my lungs considerable! Like to walk on th' hills that no one can locate!

MARSHAL.—Jist fergit I'm here, why don't you!

TEXAS.—You're too good a man to marshal. You ort to go back to farmin'. Hannie, you know whut'll happen to him someday?

HANNIE.—Whut?

TEXAS.—(*With tense exaggeration, visualizing it*) Someday he'll start to arrest a feller . . . a mean 'un! Start to put the handcuffs on . . . and that feller'll reach out like a cat and grab him! Claw him to ribbons! Tie his arms in a hard knot!

HANNIE.—(*Catching his excitement*) Jump on him 'th hobnails!

TEXAS.—Break his laigs!

HANNIE.—Cut off his years!

TEXAS.—Crack his ribs! And nen that feller'll shoot the marshal six times! (*To marshal*) Kill you daid, that's whut he'll do!

MARSHAL.—(*In alarm*) You keep yore hands offen me!

TEXAS.—You don't want *me*, Mr. Marshal. You don't want me!

MARSHAL.—(*Baffled*) No?

TEXAS.—There! (*Ecstatically*) I knowed you'd come to yer senses! Good ole marshal! Come on, you Ikes, let's . . .

MARSHAL.—Here, here, I never said you could go . . . Here you!

NEB.—Don't you let that crimernal go! I'll tell the jedge . . .

MARSHAL.—Shet up, Neb Withers! Don't you tell me whut to do! I guess I know whut I *can* and *cain't* do!

RED AND BLACK.—Wild and reckless, borned in Texas . . . (*Etc.*)

TEXAS.—Come on, Hannie! Good luck, Mr. Marshal! Keep outa trouble!

MARSHAL.—You better beat it, 'fore I change my mind . . .

TEXAS.—Jist a minute! Here . . .

MARSHAL.—Whut's that?

TEXAS.—This here hunk of wood's the law. We hain't got a mite of use fer it. Take it!

MARSHAL.—(*Evasively*) I . . . I got my hands full!

TEXAS.—Leave it fer the jedge, then . . .

SOUND.—*Gavel thrown on desk.*

HANNIE.—Good-by, Mr. Marshal!

TEXAS.—Here we go! Rarin' to step! Come on, Hannie! Come on (*fade*), you Ikes! Good-by, you-all! I bet you wish you was us!

RED AND BLACK.—Wild and reckless, borned in Texas . . . (*Etc.*) (*Fade out*)

MUSIC.—*Top with bridge.*

And Six Came Back

by RANALD R. MACDOUGALL*
Presented by THE LISTENER'S PLAYHOUSE

MUSIC.—*Playhouse theme.*

ANNOUNCER.—The Listener's Playhouse.

MUSIC.—*One tone.*

ANNOUNCER.—"And Six Came Back."

MUSIC.—*Another tone.*

ANNOUNCER.—By Ranald R. MacDougall . . .

MUSIC.—*Resolves and sweeps into ice theme.*

ANNOUNCER.—Far north of here . . . north of Hudson Bay, of Baffin Bay, of Kane Sea . . . lies Lady Franklin Bay. For 300 years, only the English had gone farther north than this. Near by is Cape Sabine . . . and the withered bones of 18 men . . . Americans who broke that English record . . . Almost forgotten now, those bodies . . . but they had names and were heroes in their time. A few . . . a very few geographies mark the farthest north achieved by the Greely arctic expedition in 1881, but what has become of those names? Men, who would answer when called . . . Schneider.

SCHNEIDER.—Present.

ANNOUNCER.—Jewell.

JEWELL.—Present.
(*Roll call up as it fades into heavy background*)

ANNOUNCER.—Ellison.

ELLISON.—Present!

ANNOUNCER.—Whistler.

* From the published diary of General David L. Brainard, edited by Bessie Rowland James, "Six Came Back."

WHISTLER.—Present!

ANNOUNCER.—Connell.

CONNELL.—Present!

MUSIC.—*Out cleanly.*

ANNOUNCER.—(*Calmly*) No subject lends itself so well to dramatization, as man against the brutal force of nature. Such a conflict is the subject of this evening's production by the Listener's Playhouse of the National Broadcasting Company. Our story concerns the Greely expedition in 1881 and is based upon the diary of General David L. Brainard, only living survivor of that heroic group of men, who on this day, in 1883, started south from the Arctic zone. This diary, up to the present only available in part, will in a few days be published complete in book form. Thanks are due to Bessie Rowland James, editor of the Brainard diary, for permission to use the material contained and for her invaluable assistance in preparing this program . . . "And Six Came Back," by Ranald R. MacDougall, with especially written music by Tom Bennett.

We are on our way south . . . south to meet a rescue ship already at the bottom of Kane Sea . . . south to pick up winter supplies which are not there . . . south to Cape Sabine, where 19 men will die and from where only—6 came back.

MUSIC.—*Ice theme, which fades for*

READER.—August 10, 1883. We are on our way south. I was the last to leave the station and nailed the door securely. The ice was closing in as we started and we fought for our advance foot by foot. An unexpected bump spilled Rice overboard. After many narrow escapes, winding through the rapidly drifting ice, we reached a large floe a half mile from shore, onto which we hauled our boats to prevent their being crushed in the ice field . . .
(*Fade gradually under following*)

ANNOUNCER.—As the Greely expedition traveled southward, after waiting 2 years for a rescue ship which did not come, they were forced into a tremendous ice field of Kane Sea, and for 34 days they drifted helplessly in the frozen pack. As the long nights fell down, a young sergeant laboriously scribbled into a tattered notebook all that had happened during the day. That was Sergeant David L. Brainard—and this is his diary . . .

SOUND.—*Behind the following, the music melts into the sound of wind and the endless grumble of the ice pack . . . sudden crackling noises and low rumbles distinguishable.*

READER.—September 29, 1883. Shore at last! We are on land once more, after being lost in the sea ice over a month. Early this morning a sudden long gash in our icy prison allowed us to push 4 miles to the shore. The boats are ruined and must be abandoned, but the entire party is happy to be on land. Lieutenant Greely has taken our bearings and fixes our position as directly south of Leffert Glacier . . . *(fading) . . . Many miles south of Cape Sabine, our actual destination . . .*

GREELY.—*(Cross-fade) . . . directly south of Leffert Glacier . . . many miles south of Cape Sabine, our actual destination.* However, it can't be helped, Brainard. Have the Eskimos returned yet?

BRAINARD.—Jens came back an hour ago, Lieutenant Greely. He says the game is taking to the ice pack . . . frightened of our appearance probably.

GREELY.—*(Dryly)* We're not what might be termed an inspiring sight, are we?

BRAINARD.—It takes enough energy to live, sir, without bothering about cleanliness.

GREELY.—Even so. Did Jens have any luck?

BRAINARD.—No, sir . . . didn't kill a thing. He's pretty tired, sir.

GREELY.—Ayah . . . so are we all. But give him an extra gill of rum—he deserves it. All right, Brainard, you can attend to that, if you will.

BRAINARD.—*(Going off)* Yes, sir.

GREELY.—*(Calling)* Lieutenant Lockwood, will you come here, please. I'd like to have a talk with you.

LOCKWOOD.—Yes, sir. Shall I get Lieutenant Kislingbury?

GREELY.—No—not yet. This is the nature of a private conversation. First of all, I want you to know that I place the greatest of confidence in you.

LOCKWOOD.—Thank you.

GREELY.—But your behaviour during that trip on the ice indicates that you do not reciprocate my confidence. In other words, Lockwood, you seem to have developed a strong feeling that Dr. Pavy knows more about my business than I do.

LOCKWOOD.—Sir. I . . .

GREELY.—Let's understand one another, Lockwood. I have reason to suspect that Dr. Pavy desires to have me replaced as leader of this expedition, by himself. Your friendship with him, indirectly at least, aids his purpose.

LOCKWOOD.—I don't know what you mean . . .

GREELY.—I think you do. While in the boats, and with no thought of the effect on general discipline, you openly discussed our situation with Dr. Pavy and supported his various foolhardy suggestions. You told Dr. Pavy that you and Brainard could have gone even farther north—might even have reached the Pole, if I had given you permission to take a chance. Is that not correct, sir?

LOCKWOOD.—Well, those were my words, but I didn't mean . . .

GREELY.—Those were your words, sir, regardless of what you may or may not have meant. Well, understand me, Lockwood—it is not my custom nor my orders to take chances with this expedition. If an element of gamble is involved in measures having to do with the men's safety, I must refuse to countenance the suggestion. And further, I will not tolerate your public discussion of my procedures with a mutinous subordinate.

LOCKWOOD.—(*Stiffly*) I understand, sir.

GREELY.—(*Relaxing*) And for heaven's sake, my boy, when you disagree with me on matters that concern us all, come to me privately. Have respect for my dignity, at least, if you cannot bring yourself to respect my judgment.

LOCKWOOD.—(*Instantly relaxed*) I owe you an apology, Lieutenant Greely. (*Embarrassed but determined to do the right thing*)

223

I was disappointed that Brainard and I couldn't reach the Pole on our dash—but I certainly had no right or reason to criticize anyone but myself . . . and it was foolish of me to listen to Dr. Pavy . . . I am sorry . . . I can only plead stupidity.

GREELY.—Come—come—there's no need to take it so seriously. You have my full confidence and are second in command. I assure you, neither honor, doubtful as they are, would be yours if I thought you stupid. Now—do your best to forget the entire incident, as I will forget it.

LOCKWOOD.—Yes, sir—and thank you, sir.

GREELY.—Right. And now, if you'll be so good as to summon Lieutenant Kislingbury, we'll discuss our situation.

LOCKWOOD.—Very well, sir, I'll get him. (*Fades*)

GREELY.—(*Calling*) Sergeant Brainard?

BRAINARD.—(*Off*) Sir?

GREELY.—Will you step this way, please?

BRAINARD.—(*Coming in*) Yes, sir. I've given Eskimo Jens an extra dollop of rum, sir. Eskimo Fred came back also, and I took the liberty of issuing a ration to him.

GREELY.—Good man. It wouldn't do to make the Eskimos jealous of each other. Treat them both equally, Brainard, but when one brings in more game than the other—treat him a trifle better. Rivalry is good for the soul—especially an Eskimo soul.

BRAINARD.—(*Grinning*) Neither one of those Eskimos will admit the other *has* a soul, sir.

GREELY.—(*Coughing away his amusement*) Yes—quite so. I called you over because I want you to be in on our plans for the winter camp. I think that—oh, here's Lockwood.

LOCKWOOD.—(*Coming in*) Lieutenant Kislingbury will be here directly, sir.

GREELY.—(*Dryly*) That's good of him. By the way, Brainard, sometime this afternoon fit out Corporal Salor and Eskimo Fred for a trip south to Wade Point. Have the corporal test the ice for traveling by sledge and determine whether or not stores were cached at Ross Bay.

BRAINARD.—Yes, sir. If I . . .

KISLINGBURY.—(*Coming in . . . drawling*) You wanted me, Greely?

GREELY.—(*Precisely*) Yes, *Lieutenant* Kislingbury. You have my gratitude for responding.

KISLINGBURY.—Quite all right . . . I had nothing better to do.

GREELY.—Lieutenant—it so happens that you are with us by accident.

KISLINGBURY.—Quite. And if that somewhat obvious observation was a prelude to a demand that I do my duty, I hope you'll allow me to point out that you have already relieved me of duty and that I'm here against my own wishes.

GREELY.—Your attitude in the past few weeks has made that very plain, lieutenant, and I assure you that I find no particular delight in your company. However, I feel it necessary to remind you that if you had not overslept on the day you were to leave the expedition, you wouldn't have missed the return ship.

KISLINGBURY.—(*Laconic*) For the past 2 years, commander, I've had numerous opportunities for reminding myself of that regrettable tardiness . . . there's little need for you to point it out.

GREELY.—I merely wish it clearly understood that I do not accept any responsibility for your presence here. (*Annoyance*) However, all that is an old story, and I didn't ask you here for the purpose of quarreling with you.

KISLINGBURY.—Really? You astonish me.

GREELY.—(*A flash of temper*) Hold your tongue, sir. (*Pause*) Forgive me . . . I should not have said that. (*A low voice*) Lieutenant—our situation makes it impossible for any indulgence in personal grudges. For the common good of our party, I ask you to restrain your animosity, as I shall restrain mine. I beg you—I beg you, Kislingbury, to give me the benefit of your judgment and training.

KISLINGBURY.—(*Briskly*) Of course . . . of course . . . I am at your disposal, commander.

225

GREELY.—Thank you. Now—all of you—here is our position
. . . a precarious one as you all know. There is no rescue
ship here . . . and it is doubtful that there will be one for
some time to come. We are on a barren land with little food.
Brainard . . . how *are* the stores?

BRAINARD.—Enough for 30 days, sir.

GREELY.—And it's more than likely we'll be here all winter.

KISLINGBURY.—We might cross to Littleton Island—there may
be a cache of food there.

GREELY.—And if there isn't?

LOCKWOOD.—We'll be marooned.

GREELY.—Quite. My thought is that we wait for Rice to return
from Cape Sabine. If no food is found on this side within
20 days, we cross to Littleton Island.

KISLINGBURY.—Agreed.

GREELY.—Brainard? Lockwood? (*They agree*) Now—in the event
that food supplies are found—what then? Any suggestions?

KISLINGBURY.—We can only go south, if we go anywhere.

BRAINARD.—And if we go south, we run a risk of being locked in
the drift ice again. Next time it's probable that we'll end
up in Baffin Bay, 1,000 miles from land.

GREELY.—I agree. Well, Lockwood?

LOCKWOOD.—Surely they're doing something about us back
home? If we wait here a relief ship is sure to come for us.

GREELY.—You're suggesting that we hole up for the winter. Do
you think the men can stand it?

LOCKWOOD.—Yes, sir. Their morale is excellent, commander—
with the exception of Cross.

GREELY.—Has that man been drinking again? Why haven't you
taken precautions . . .

LOCKWOOD.—I've done everything but put a cork in his throat,
commander. The medicinal rum is locked up . . . I don't
know where he gets it.

KISLINGBURY.—I do. Did you ever notice how much alcohol the cook stove uses?

LOCKWOOD.—Yes, but I thought it was getting old and leaky; do you mean . . .

KISLINGBURY.—(*Dryly*) Cross will drink anything that has a headache attached to it.

BRAINARD.—His crushed foot pains him constantly . . .

GREELY.—Drinking lamp alcohol won't cure it, Brainard. However, I don't think the man deserves official reprimand . . . just watch him carefully, Brainard.

BRAINARD.—Yes, sir.

LOCKWOOD.—I wish Rice would come back. I'm not particularly worried about our situation, but knowing that there are supplies at Cape Sabine would do the men a world of good.

KISLINGBURY.—If I may suggest such a thing, Lieutenant Greely, I'd advise that the men be kept busy—let them build a camp for instance.

GREELY.—Here? But it's unlikely that we'll remain here very long.

LOCKWOOD.—I agree with Lieutenant Kislingbury, sir. Whether or not we stay, I think the men should have something to keep them occupied.

GREELY.—Hmm—I think you're both right. Brainard—will you start the men building a camp?

BRAINARD.—Yes, sir.

MUSIC.—*Meanwhile, far in the background someone is singing "Three for Jack."*

GREELY.—That sounds like Cross . . .

SOUND.—*Fighting and yelling in background.*

GREELY.—Come along, everybody!

SOUND.—*Running footsteps . . . fighting closer.*

BRAINARD.—Sergeant Cross!

CROSS.—Aw, lemme alone.

227

GREELY.—What's the trouble, Dr. Pavy?

PAVY.—(*Excitable creole . . . slight French richness to voice*) This pig has drunk lamp alcohol. I try to save his foot, and he do stupid things like this. I cut off his foot with pleasure —I also . . .

GREELY.—All right, Dr. Pavy.

PAVY.—(*Subsides with a few final grumbles in French*)

GREELY.—Cross, can you understand me?

CROSS.—Sure, commander, sure . . . certainly . . . feel like singing . . . feel like singing all the time. (*He does so*)

GREELY.—Brainard, take two or three men and douse him with sea water. Cool him off, and lock him up in the boat.

BRAINARD.—Yes, sir. Come along, Cross . . . we'll give you something to drink . . . something that will do you good . . .

CROSS.—My friend—you're my friend, Brainard. Don't know what I'd do thout you. Got no friends—got nothing but my beau-ful voice . . . (*fades singing . . . then screams offstage and kicks up a general fuss*)

HENRY.—(*Running in*) Commander—they've just seen Rice . . . (*A spontaneous reaction . . . high excitement*)

CROSS.—(*Off*) Lemme alone—I'm all right now . . . I wanna see Rice come in . . .

GREELY.—(*An undertone*) Well . . . we'll soon know now. There he is—just coming over the ridge . . . (*A cry of excitement . . . "There he is . . . Good old Rice . . . knew he'd make it," etc. . . . . Silence*)

LOCKWOOD.—Why doesn't he say something? Why doesn't he . . .

GREELY.—Hang on, Lockwood. Hang on. (*A pause . . . silence except for pack ice*)

RICE.—(*Far off*) Food! Food at Cape Sabine! Foooood!

SOUND.—*Wild excitement . . . music sweeps over . . . fades into sound of wind behind following.*

228

READER.—October 20. Temperature minus 13. Our winter camp at Cape Sabine is finished. The hut is 25 feet long and 18 feet wide. The walls about 4 feet high—pretty cramped quarters for 25 men, but easy to keep warm. Rice, Linn, Elison, and Fredericks started for Cape Isabella at 8 A.M. to bring back an English cache of 140 pounds of meat, left there in 1878, according to the records found at Cape Sabine. (*Fading*) Someone broke into the storehouse last night . . .

GREELY.—(*Talking loudly*) Someone broke into the storehouse last night, and a small quantity of hard bread was taken. I can sympathize with the hunger which drives a member of our party to commit such a despicable act, but the culprit must be found and punished.

SOUND.—*Grumbles and agreement.*

GREELY.—I'll say no more on the matter at present, but I sincerely hope there is no repetition of this unfortunate occurrence. Now Sergeant Brainard has something to say.

SERGEANT.—Men—in view of the fact that we only found enough provisions here at Cape Sabine to last us for a little over a month, our daily food allowance has to be cut to 14 ounces from the stores. That's all from me.

GREELY.—The party is dismissed. If you like, I suggest an entertainment is in order. Will you play your violin for us, Schneider?

SOUND.—*Groans.*

SCHNEIDER.—(*Very embarrassed*) Aw, heck, commander, I ain't good enough to play in public . . . (*Laughter and "You said it"*) I just play for my own amazement. But if you insist, I'll be glad to. (*More groans*) I got one piece here I think you fellows will all like . . .

MUSIC.—(*Chorus*). *"Over the Garden Wall"* . . . *Pause.*

SCHNEIDER.—(*Surprised*) Yeah—that's right. I guess maybe you're sick of hearing it . . . maybe I better not . . .

SOUND.—*Ad-libbing* . . . *"Go ahead . . . go on . . . we're dying to hear it,"* etc.

SCHNEIDER.—Thanks, fellers . . . just a second . . . I tune up . . .

SOUND.—*Tuning of fiddle . . . a trifle flat.*

SCHNEIDER.—Well, here I go—"Over the Garden Wall."

MUSIC.—*Solitary fiddle scrapes through tune.*

HENRY.—Boy, don't I wish I was back home now . . . How about you, Dr. Pavy?

PAVY.—Oh, me—what does it matter? I am too cold here and too hot home. In a few months you ask me again, Henry.

LOCKWOOD.—Is it hot down in Louisiana, Dr. Pavy?

PAVY.—Yes, in summer it is hot.

HENRY.—Just imagine being hot. I forgot what its like.

PAVY.—I think I like the trees best. You know, they whisper all the time in the bayou . . . and the Spanish moss . . . how it rustles and talks in the evening . . . and the air . . . warm and heavy with perfume . . . and woman's shoulders glistening in the moonlight . . . ahhhhh.

HENRY.—Boy . . . I wish I was home. What you gonna do when you get back, Ralston?

RALSTON.—Well, we got 3 years' pay coming, and I figure I'll start a settlement at Independence, Kansas.

HENRY.—I'm gonna open a saloon in Minneapolis. I got it all figured out. The beer is right there, and those guys that work in the breweries can drink more than anybody else in the country.

JEWELL.—I think I'd like to run a grocery. Maybe I could have one in Ralston's settlement, if he don't mind.

RALSTON.—Sure not . . . glad to have you, Jewell. Anybody else wanna come they're welcome. How about you, Long?

LONG.—Well, I'll think about it, but I had a idea I'd open a restaurant in Ann Arbor. You know, my girl works there now. She knows the business, and we could buy that place cheap.

HENRY.—A girl—gosh. Three years (*bitter*) . . . it's like being in prison.

LOCKWOOD.—That's enough of that, Henry

230

HENRY.—(*As violin stops*) Aw, whadda I care? I'm fed up, see? Orders—orders—orders—well, I'll talk about anything I like, see?

GREELY.—Henry! You're out of line.

HENRY.—I don't care. I'm fed up on this army stuff—this ain't the army here. Orders—orders—and the relief ship puts in a copy of the army regulations with the food so the boys will have something to read. Ain't that sweet of them? (*Low voice*) I may not ever get home again . . . I may not never touch a girl's skin again . . .

GREELY.—All right, Henry—that's enough of that. Come on, Schneider, start up the music again.

SCHNEIDER.—Yes, sir!

MUSIC.—*Fiddle again . . . sinks into rising wind . . . which sinks into music . . .*

READER.—Sunday, November 4. Although this is the Sabbath, we began work on a new commissary storehouse. Someone has again been purloining provisions. It is well we are preparing to lock up what food remains . . . (*fade*)

MUSIC.—*Up and down . . . fade into wind noise gradually.*

READER.—November 8. The walls of the storehouse are not progressing as rapidly as they should, but we are all so weak that one cannot in reason expect severe labor to be done rapidly. Dr. Pavy refuses to give medical sanction to such a scanty diet. He says we cannot live long on it in this cold climate . . .

PAVY.—(*Cross-fade*) . . . we cannot live long on it in this cold climate.

LONG.—And if we don't conserve our food, we'll live an even shorter time.

PAVY.—Do not talk back at me, Long!

LONG.—(*Gently*) You're kind of upset, doctor. I'm not talking back—I'm just telling you what's what.

PAVY.—My apology, sergeant. You are right. I should not talk to you of this. I will speak to Commander Greely . . .

GREELY.—(*Coming in*) Go right ahead, doctor. What's the trouble?

PAVY.—I will not allow the rations to be cut again. No man can live on less than a pound of food a day. I will not allow it. I myself am willing to take less, but how can I bring these sick men back to health if they do not eat?

GREELY.—The sick have extra rations . . .

PAVY.—It is not enough!

GREELY.—(*Gentle*) It can't be helped, doctor, I wish it might—but it can't.

PAVY.—(*Stiffly*) Then I resign from the expedition. I withdraw myself from this endeavour.

GREELY.—Going to walk home, doctor?

PAVY.—Never mind—I resign all the same. Brainard, you come and help me fix up Kislingbury. Then I will resign permanently.

BRAINARD.—All right, doctor. What do I do?

PAVY.—Help me lift his body.

KISLINGBURY.—(*Groans*)

PAVY.—It is all right, old man . . . just take it easy . . . That's it . . . over a little, Brainard. Fine . . . hmm.

KISLINGBURY.—(*Weakly*) Well, you old horse doctor? What do you guess is wrong with me?

PAVY.—(*Sternly*) You should not make jokes with me, Kislingbury. (*Gentle*) You have been a bad boy . . . a very bad boy . . . you should not work so hard . . .

KISLINGBURY.—Rupture?

PAVY.—It will heal. (*Sharply*) But you must stay in bed and rest. You will ruin my reputation with this work of yours—Brainard, bring my mattress here. (*Sure*)

KISLINGBURY.—I will not be pampered, doctor!

PAVY.—Pamper! You men have frostbite, gangrene, ruptures, and you starve, but when I doctor you it is pampering! Nom du nom! When you all get well, I resign this expedition!

232

KISLINGBURY.—(*Chuckling*) You're a faker, Pavy, an arrant old faker.

PAVY.—(*Hurt*) That's right—insult the hand that heals you, pig.

BRAINARD.—Here's the mattress. Shall I put it here?

PAVY.—Yes.

KISLINGBURY.—No—I refuse to take Dr. Pavy's mattress!

PAVY.—If you don't take it, I amputate your leg. I cut it off like that and teach you a lesson. Here—help me with him, Brainard. Easy now . . . that's right . . .

KISLINGBURY.—Doctor, I . . .

PAVY.—You talk too much. Go to sleep and get well. I have said you will get well. Do not make a monkey of me.

SOUND.—*Violin and "Over the Garden Wall" . . . far away.*

GREELY.—(*Off stage*) Brainard! Come here—some of you other men, too!

CAST.—*Some talk . . . questions.*

GREELY.—(*Coming in . . . grim*) I think we have found our thief. Look there—in the storehouse . . .

BRAINARD.—Schneider!

HENRY.—He oughta be shot. (*Agreement*)

GREELY.—Sergeant Brainard, will you go out there and get him, please? Don't harm him.

BRAINARD.—Henry—Jewell—and Cross—come with me please. (*They fade . . . the violin stops*)

SCHNEIDER.—(*Off . . . coming in*) Say, whatsa big idea? Lemme go . . . I ain't done nothing . . . lemme alone . . . (*In*) Whatsa matter with everybody? Who you staring at?

GREELY.—Close the door, Brainard.

SOUND.—*Door closes.*

GREELY.—Schneider. What were you doing in the storehouse?

SCHNEIDER.—(*Somewhat sober*) Why, I was playing my violin . . .

JEWELL.—Is that all—sure you weren't messing about with the food?

233

MEN.—(*Growls*)

SCHNEIDER.—Oh, hey—you fellers don't think—honest to goodness, I was onny playing the violin. I know how you guys are sick of hearing that tune. I went out there so I wouldn't bother you. Honest, I was just playing the violin.

GREELY.—You've been drinking, haven't you? Where did you get it?

SCHNEIDER.—It . . . I . . . somebody give it to me.

GREELY.—Who gave it to you?

SCHNEIDER.—I . . . I ain't saying.

GREELY.—Was it one of the men here . . . in front of you?

SCHNEIDER.—I ain't say . . . I can't. Lemme alone. I was onny playing the violin.

MAN.—(*Ad lib threats*)

GREELY.—Just a minute. After all, a man doesn't steal and then advertise his presence by playing a violin—not unless he's much more clever than I think Schneider is . . .

SOUND.—*Door opens . . . wind up and down . . . door closes.*

LOCKWOOD.—I found this out in the storehouse, commander.

GREELY.—What is it?

LOCKWOOD.—A can of milk. Someone's been trying to open it with a knife. You can see the marks where the knife dug into the metal.

GREELY.—Ayah—and there were evidently nicks in the knife that made these marks. Schneider—let me see your knife.

SCHNEIDER.—I . . . I ain't got it.

HENRY.—I have it, commander. Schneider lent it to me just a while ago.

GREELY.—Now I don't know what to think. But I do know this. One of you men is a thief.

HENRY.—(*Very firmly*) It's not me, commander.

SCHNEIDER.—(*Mumbling*) I was just playing the violin—that's all.

SOUND.—*A scratching on door . . . feeble rapping.*

GREELY.—Maybe that's Rice and his party—open . . .

SOUND.—*Door opens.*

GREELY.—Rice! Help him in . . . he's nearly frozen . .
(*Reaction*)

SOUND.—*Door closes.*

LOCKWOOD.—Rice, where are the others?

RICE.—(*Wheezing heavily*) Can't—can't talk . . .

LOCKWOOD.—Tell us what happened.

GREELY.—Let him recover himself, Lockwood.

RICE.—(*Almost unintelligible*) Fredericks . . . Linn . . . frozen
into . . . ice. (*Rests momentarily*) Still . . . alive . . . Elison . . . dying.

MUSIC.—*Bursts heavily and fades behind for wind.*

READER.—November 10. Eskimo Fred and myself were immediately ordered out by the commanding officer to carry food
and relief to Elison. As I left, Rice told me that Elison would
probably be dead before help reached him. He had gotten
his feet wet, and they had frozen as the party came back
with the stores found at Cape Isabella.

Gradually, Elison lost the use of his limbs, and Fredericks
and Linn crawled into the sleeping bag with him to thaw
him out, one on either side. Rice had walked 17 miles for
rescue, after dragging a heavy sledge all day long. It was a
noble, courageous act. Rice says that as he left . . . he
could hear Elison screaming in pain . . .

ELISON.—(*Cries of pain and delirius murmurs*)

FREDERICKS.—You all right, Linn?

LINN.—(*A trifle hysterical*) Yeah—yeah . . . I'm all right . . .
It's cold.

FREDERICKS.—Yeah. (*Pause*) I wish he'd stop screaming.

LINN.—How long we been here?

FRED.—It's a night and a day since Rice left.

235

LINN.—Think he'll get through, Fredericks? Sure . . . he'll get through, won't he?

FRED.—Yeah . . . he will . . . nothing can stop Rice.

ELISON.—(*Subsides to a dull murmur*)

LINN.—Hey, Elison—don't do that! Elison! Do you know what he's doing?

FRED.—Yeah, I know.

LINN.—(*An expression of disgust*)

FRED.—He can't help it, Linn . . . He doesn't even know . . .

LINN.—I've got to get out of here. I'm going home. I won't stay here. After all, there's a moon at home and the newspaper every morning . . . and girls . . . you know . . .

FRED.—(*Sharply*) Snap out of it, Linn!

LINN.—(*Dreamily*) I love singing . . . There's a cherry tree in our backyard . . . and baked potatoes . . . I'll never eat ice cream again . . .

FRED.—Linn! Linn!

ELISON.—(*Dull*) What's the matter with him?

FRED.—Hysterical. How do you feel, Elison?

ELISON.—I don't know . . . can't feel anything hardly. Why don't you guys go away . . .

BRAINARD.—(*Far off*) Se-coh! Se-coh!

ELISON.—Please kill me, Fredericks. Please kill me, Fredericks. Please kill me, Fredericks.

FRED.—Shut up—both of you! (*A silence*) Naw . . . nothing. Go ahead and howl for all I—(*Se-coh*) They've found us! Se-coh! They've found us. Elison—Linn—Se-coh!

SOUND.—*Linn, Fredericks, Brainard, off, yell back and forth into*

MUSIC.—*Rises and falls into wind.*

READER.—December 25. A merry Christmas! This has been a wonderful day for us all, except possibly Elison and Linn. Dr. Pavy says that Elison will probably recover, but he will lose both his feet and most of his fingers. Linn is slowly going crazy. He has never fully recovered his mind from that horrible night, frozen into the sleeping bag with Fredericks and Elison. Today is Lieutenant Kislingbury's birthday and thus became a double cause for celebration. Accordingly, an extra ounce of bread was issued to each man. The best of good feelings prevailed, and three cheers were given for Lieutenant Greely, Elison, Rice, and the cooks . . . (*gradual fade*)

MEN.—(*Feeble cheers*)

GREELY.—Thank you, men. This hasn't been what might be called the ideal Christmas dinner, but it was good, wasn't it? (*Reaction*) I suggest that we all make out menus for next year's Christmas dinner. We'll be back home by then, and we'll meet again for a celebration . . . the best menu . . . the most complete menu . . . will form our dinner . . .

LINN.—I want baked potatoes, commander. Promise me we'll have baked potatoes.
(*An awkward pause*)

GREELY.—(*Cheerfully*) You shall have them, Linn. Now—how about some entertainment?
(*Response from men*)

SCHNEIDER.—Well, commander, I'd be pleased to play the violin . . .

MEN.—"Over the Garden Wall"
(*General objection and laughter*)

GREELY.—(*Amused*) No, Schneider, thanks all the same, but I think you'd better save the violin for next Christmas.
(*A feeble cheer*)

BRAINARD.—Why so soon?
(*Laughter*)

GREELY.—Now—anybody else want to entertain? How about you, Fredericks? I understand you were a cowboy once . . . Tell us about it.
(*Agreement*)

FREDERICKS.—Aw . . . there ain't much to it. It was all right . . . punchin' cattle . . . There was lots to eat, and on Saturday nights everybody would get dressed up and go to town. Then you'd have spitting contests . . .

237

BRAINARD.—*Spitting* contests?

FRED.—Oh, sure . . . you take a wad of chawin' tobacco, and you let fly at a target. It costs a nickel a chance, and if you hit without splashing, you get a box of candy or something . . . it depends. Sometimes they have candy . . . sometimes they have cigars. Anyhow, there wasn't much excitement, except when the Indians got drunk and went off the reservation. Or else maybe some bad man would shoot all the winders out of the Silver Dollar saloon—say, you had ought to see that place . . . had real cartwheels set in the bar. That's what I'm goin' tuh do when I get back . . . gonna buy me a pretty house and a saloon. I guess that's about all . . . Thanks for the kind attention.

SOUND.—*Applause.*

WHISTLER.—Now it's my turn . . .

HENRY.—Who wants to hear about you?

WHISTLER.—Oh, yeah? You're such a wise guy . . . Maybe you'd like to get your face pushed in . . . Come on outside and I'll do it. Come on out, wise guy.

BRAINARD.—Go ahead with your story, Whistler—I'd like to hear it.

WHISTLER.—(*Belligerent . . . just waiting for someone to say something*) Well, I was a fireman, see? A good fireman, too, and if any of you wise guys don't think so . . .

BRAINARD.—That was in New York, wasn't it?

WHISTLER.—(*Relaxed slightly*) Yeah . . . they had three fire companies in my district. The one that got to a fire first got paid for putting it out, see? Well, it got so each company used to have men race to the fires and sit on the hydrants until their company came up. Boy, did we used to have fights. I remember one day, me and my kid brother was down in Flatbush when a fire broke out . . . him and me sat on the fire plug for half an hour, keeping the other companies away with baseball bats, until our company came up.

JEWELL.—Did you put the fire out?

WHISTLER.—Naw . . . it burned out itself before our company got there.

SOUND.—*Laughter.*

HENRY.—Yeah . . . that's the way they do things in New York. You take Chicago now—they got the best fire fighters in the country.

WHISTLER.—Yeah, sure they have. The Chicago fire proves that.

HENRY.—Never mind that. Didn't our firemen have to go to New York to show them the business?

WHISTLER.—Listen, you—don't you say nothing against the New York fire department. I'll bust you in the teeth. Come on outside, wise guy.

BRAINARD.—None of us have enough energy for fighting, Whistler. Calm down.

WHISTLER.—Whaddya mean, no energy. Well, *you* come outside, Brainard, and I'll show you whether I got energy or not. Come on outside, wise guy . . . come on.

BRAINARD.—(*Laughing*) No, thanks . . . it's too cold out there.

MEN.—(*Ad-libbing*) Aw, lie down, Whistler . . . you're making a draft . . . Shut up, Whistler . . . you're spoiling the party . . . (*Etc.*)

WHISTLER.—(*To the world at large*) Bunch of wise guys, aren't you? Well, I'll take any one of you outside, any one. I'll show you . . . Come on outside somebody. Well, any two of you then . . . and if Henry comes, I'll take on any three of you . . . well, whaddya say . . . how about it? Who wants his block knocked off?

MEN.—(*Assorted laughter and "Twenty-three for you, kiddo . . . In your hat, kewpie"*)

WHISTLER.—(*Grumbling*) Buncha wise guys—just because a guy's got a little frostbite, they think he can't fight. Guess I showed them . . . wise guys . . .

KISLINGBURY.—(*Weakly*) Gentlemen . . .

BRAINARD.—Can I help you up, Lieutenant Kislingbury?

KISLINGBURY.—It's all right, thanks—I'd rather stay lying down. Gentlemen . . . this being my birthday . . . and an occasion for peace on earth and good will toward men . . in spite of Whistler not thinking so—(*Laughter*)

WHISTLER.—(*Mumbles*) Buncha wise guys.

KISLINGBURY.—It being Christmas and my birthday, I'd like to give each of you a gift. To each man I give my best wishes and a cigarette. Or if you don't smoke, I've saved up some raisins for you.

SOUND.—*Reaction from men . . . fades into*

MUSIC.—*Fades behind following into wind.*

READER.—January 1, 1884. Temperature, minus 35. We enter the new year under particularly favorable conditions. Most of us were awake at midnight to greet the New Year. How are our friends spending the day, we wondered. Do they think us alive? The storehouse has been broken into again. About 5 pounds of English bread and 2 pounds of bacon . . .

GREELY.—(*Cross-fade*) About 5 pounds of English bread and 2 pounds of bacon are gone.

MEN.—(*Mutter*)

WHISTLER.—(*Off slightly . . . enraged*) Somebody will hang for this!

JEWELL.—Shoot him like a dog!

WHISTLER.—It's that monkey Schneider . . . We oughta throw him into the lake and let him freeze . . .

MEN.—(*Agree*)

SCHNEIDER.—Now look, fellers—I was onny playing my violin that time . . .

GREELY.—(*Quietly*) Never mind, Schneider, it's all right. (*Up*) That's enough, men. Quiet down. (*Muttering subsides*) We'll catch whoever it is sooner or later, and we'll know how to punish him. Right now, there's nothing to do but wait.

LOCKWOOD.—And while we wait, somebody is getting more to eat than us . . . Somebody is getting strong on stolen food . . . getting strong while we get weak . . . getting so strong, maybe, that we won't be able to punish him when the time comes. (*Men respond*) Listen here, you men . . . somebody here is a thief . . . One of you is shaking inside right now for fear we'll find out . . . Why don't you come forward like a man? We won't punish you now . . . whoever you are . . . I'll even share my rations with you so you won't be tempted any more . . . but come forward now. (*A silence*)

GREELY.—That won't do any good, Lieutenant Lockwood. Sergeant Brainard has a better idea . . . tell them, sergeant.

BRAINARD.—I've hidden a gun in the storeroom. It's set on a spring and attached to every barrel of food except one. I'm the only man who knows which barrel is safe. Anybody else who breaks into the storehouse will find a bullet through him.

WHISTLER.—(*Off*) Attaboy, serge—now you're telling him!

MEN.—(*Agree*)

GREELY.—That's all, men. Party is dismissed.

SCHNEIDER.—(*Fading to background*) I tell you I was onny playing the violin in there . . . that's all, so help me.

WHISTLER.—(*Fade*) You better not play the violin in there any more . . .

JEWELL.—(*Fade*) Say, Fredericks, how about a game of checkers?

FRED.—Yeah . . . okay.

HENRY.—Wait a minute, Shorty. I remembered a good joke I heard in San Francisco just before we left . . .

FRED.—I heard all your dirty jokes a thousand times. (*Fading*) I don't wanna hear them anymore . . . Why should I torment myself listening to dirty jokes . . .

LONG.—(*On . . . nervous*) Say, Sergeant Brainard, can I speak to you, private, please?

BRAINARD.—Sure. Come over here. Now, what is it, Long?

LONG.—You know, sergeant, I'm a pretty good cook—I don't get much to cook, but I do the best I can, don't I?

BRAINARD.—You sure do. I'm not complaining. What's on your mind?

LONG.—Well . . . this has been bothering me an awful long time . . . and I gotta get it off my chest . . .

BRAINARD.—(*Harsh but low*) Are you the man who's been stealing the . . .

LONG.—No! No—not me! This is something else . . . I wouldn't . . .

BRAINARD.—(*Relaxed*) I know you wouldn't, I'm sorry. Go ahead.

LONG.—Well, it happened on Christmas . . . You know how the tea rations have been cut way down lately . . .

BRAINARD.—Yes.

LONG.—(*Nervous and reluctant*) Well—I don't know how to say it —how did you like your tea on Christmas?

BRAINARD.—It was all right, I guess. I drank it—why?

LONG.—That's just the point . . . It wasn't tea . . . it was just hot water. I forgot to put any tea in it.

BRAINARD.—(*Laughing*) What?

LONG.—Yeah . . . I been so worried about it . . . but nobody seemed to notice it . . . I just wondered.

BRAINARD.—(*Chuckling*) It's all right, I guess—as long as no one noticed it. Forget it, Long.

LONG.—Thanks—aw, thanks, sergeant. (*Fading*) Boy that's a load off my mind . . .

BRAINARD.—(*To himself*) Tea—without any tea. (*He chuckles*)

GREELY.—You seem rather happy, Brainard.

BRAINARD.—Yes, sir. Private Long was just telling me a funny story, sir.

GREELY.—I see. Brainard . . . about that gun trap you said you set in the storeroom.

BRAINARD.—Yes, sir?

GREELY.—Did you set such a trap as you described?

BRAINARD.—(*Reluctant*) Well, sir . . . I don't know that I . . .

GREELY.—(*Low voice*) Brainard . . . while I am commander of this expedition, all matters concerning the expedition are my business. Do you understand?

BRAINARD.—Yes, sir. But . . .

GREELY.—I perceive that you suspect *me* of having broken into . . .

BRAINARD.—No, sir!

GREELY.—Then—is there a gun trap in there?

BRAINARD.—No.

GREELY.—Very well. Don't tell anyone else.

ELISON.—(*Off . . . very weak*) Hey, fellers—hey, one of you guys . . .

GREELY.—(*Up*) What is it, Elison? Anything I can do?

ELISON.—(*Shy*) Naw, commander . . . I just wanted a favor done . . . but you shouldn't . . .

GREELY.—We're all the same here, Elison. What is it you want . . . Do your feet pain you?

ELISON.—A little, but that ain't what I wanted. I can't ask you to . . .

GREELY.—What is it, Elison?

ELISON.—Well . . . would you scratch the bottom of my feet . . . they itch something fierce . . .

GREELY.—Scratch your feet . . .

ELISON.—I hadn't oughta asked . . .

GREELY.—No . . . no, that's all right. I'll scratch them, of course . . . How's that? Any better?

ELISON.—Much better . . . They was itching something fierce . . . (*fading*) Thanks a lot, commander.

GREELY.—(*Low voice*) Oh, dear Lord in heaven . . . did you hear that, Brainard?

BRAINARD.—Yes, sir. It's funny about him thinking his feet itch—he doesn't know they dropped off from gangrene last week.

MUSIC.—*Hits full and subsides into wind behind*

READER.—January 17 . . . temperature minus 39. That is what the thermometer registered, but the mercury was frozen, so we have no means of knowing how much colder it really is Lately, at times, the mercury disappears in the bulb entirely and cannot be seen at all. For the first time this winter, we had our hair cut. The cut was comfortable, if not artistic. Those wishing to be cropped crawled on their hands and knees to the foot of their sleeping bags and held their heads in the alleyway. The tonsorial artist passed along the line, armed with a huge pair of shears, and devoted about 10 seconds to each head. My hair was over 6 inches long. Some of the others were too weak to rise from their sleeping bags. Ellis, Linn, Ralston, Cross, Jewell, and Lockwood are all broken down in strength. They seldom move except when absolutely necessary . . . *(Fade)*

SOUND.—*Wind . . . up and down.*

READER.—January 19. Clear and calm. Mercury frozen again. Cross is dead. The first member of our party to go. He died of dropsical effusion of the heart and a slight scurvy.

GREELY.—*(Cross-fade)* . . . died of dropsical effusion of the heart and a slight scurvy.

HENRY.—*(Off)* That's what you call it—I call it starvation.

GREELY.—*(Dryly)* I'm sure your opinions are of great value, Henry, but I for one can do without them. We all know what Cross died of, but it sounds better not to say so. Brainard . . . has the grave been . . .

BRAINARD.—Yes, sir. The ground was frozen, but we managed to dig down about 6 inches.

GREELY.—All right. Men—we are about to bury a comrade—the first, and, I am certain, the last of our party to die. Cross was a valuable member of our party, and until the hardships of our journey overcame him, was a popular and conscientious worker. Let us all remember him as he was then and forget the weakness of character—the drinking—that contributed so heavily to his death. He was a noble fellow, and we do him honor. Schneider, will you play?

MUSIC.—*Fiddle . . . scraping "Over the Garden Wall."*

GREELY.—*(A very long fade)* We have no organ, Lord, and Schneider can only play one tune, but we ask you to consider this a church . . . where the 24 comrades of this noble·

member of our expedition ask you to accept him and enter him unto your Grace. Like all your children, this man has strayed from the paths of righteousness, but we remaining kneel in prayer and ask your blessings on him and on those who live after him . . .

MUSIC.—*Up and over violin . . . fade into wind.*

READER.—March 25. A clear beautiful day. I issued the last of the corn, soup, tomatoes, lard, and potatoes. Rice made three trips to the shrimping grounds today, adding to our supplies about 7 pounds of shrimp . . . (*fade slowly as counting comes in*) A terrible scene occurred this morning in the hut. While cooking breakfast . . .

JEWELL.—(*Counting monotonously*) Six hundred fifty-nine . . . six hundred sixty . . . (*Etc.*)

BRAINARD.—What's that you're doing, Jewell?

JEWELL.—(*Monotonous*) Counting them shrimp . . . See how many there is to an ounce . . . over six hundred so far . . . never saw shrimp like them. An ordinary housefly looks like their big brother. Lost forty of them in a crack of the table . . . Six hundred . . . (*Etc.*)

BRAINARD.—What are we having for breakfast, Long?

LONG.—Tea.

BRAINARD.—You didn't forget to . . .

LONG.—Naw . . . I put the tea in this time, sergeant. Not that it makes much difference . . . Say, it's kinda stuffy in here this morning, ain't it? (*Sniff*) Smells like . . . (*Sudden exclamation*) Jewell forgot to take the ventilator off the roof when he turned on the stove . . .

BRAINARD.—(*Shouting*) Wake up, everybody! You'll smother to death! Commander!

SOUND.—*Coughing in background.*

GREELY.—(*Off*) Open the door, Brainard! Get these sick men out —everybody outside!

SOUND.—*Confusion . . . shouts and cries.*

DR. PAVY.—(*Shouting*) Do not anybody more go outside! The fresh air will make you faint—stay inside by the door!

Beiderback . . . bring Lieutenant Greely and those other men back in here . . . They'll freeze out there . . . Mille tonneres . . . they faint like women in that fresh air. Gardiner, help me with Israel. Kislingbury, you take the ventilator off the roof, and let some air in here.

BRAINARD.—*(Fainting)* Anything I can do, Dr. Pavy?

PAVY.—Yes . . . go sit down, Brainard, and stay there. You get up and fall down like a pugilist. Make the commander sit too. Gardiner . . . put some water on Connell . . . Nom du nom! what a terrible thing. Take it easy, commander. *(The excitement has subsided)*

GREELY.—I'm all right now . . . are the men . . .

PAVY.—They will be all right . . . but that was a close squeak, commander. Jewell.

JEWELL.—Yeah?

PAVY.—You forgot the ventilator. Do you want us to smother?

JEWELL.—I forgot . . . I'm sorry.

GREELY.—That's all right, Jewell . . . no harm done, fortunately . . . Be more careful in the future.

JEWELL.—*(Fading)* Yes, sir. Wouldn't that slay you . . . I lost count of them shrimp. It's a good thing I divided up the piles. *(He goes back to counting from "six hundred thirty")*

JENS.—*(Eskimo)* Greely boss . . .

GREELY.—What is it, Jens?

JENS.—Bacon gone from table . . . Man steal him.

GREELY.—What? It's true—someone has stolen the bacon. I won't stand for anymore of this. Brainard, call the men together.

BRAINARD.—Everybody in, please. Jewell—stop that counting for a while . . .

JEWELL.—Six hundred seventy-three . . . six hundred seventy-three—okay, I'll remember. What's the matter?

GREELY.—Men—in the past few months, as you all know, some thief has been deliberately robbing our storehouse. Today, during the excitement, a half pound of bacon was taken from the table.

MEN.—(*React*)

GREELY.—Just a moment. I think you all agree with me that a man who will steal food from his starving companions, deserves whatever—what do you want, Henry?

HENRY.—(*Off slightly . . . ill*) Please, commander, may I go out? I feel sick.

PAVY.—(*Whisper on*) Do not let him go, Lieutenant. I think it will be very interesting if he stays.

GREELY.—The open air will only make you feel worse, Henry. Stay in here. Now, men . . .

HENRY.—(*Desperate*) But I've got to get out into the open—I . . . I . . .

BRAINARD.—Look out—he's going to faint.

PAVY.—(*With great satisfaction*) No—he will not faint . . . he's going to be ill—very ill.

HENRY.—I . . . I . . .

PAVY.—(*Sharply*) Don't let him out, you men! Keep him here . . . ahh! (*This last is caused by Henry's retching*)

SOUND.—*Since Henry is ill, there is first a murmuring by the men . . . then a dull silence . . . Henry subsides into a sobbing cough.*

BRAINARD.—(*Quietly*) You ate too fast, Henry. Bacon is bad on the stomach.

WHISTLER.—String him up!

GREELY.—(*Sharply*) Shut up, Whistler! (*Calmly*) So it was you, Henry.

HENRY.—No . . . no . . . honest . . . That's the first thing I've ever stolen . . . honest!

GREELY.—Three weeks ago, Henry, Dr. Pavy and I went through your belongings, because we noticed a strong smell . . . We found some English meat, 2 pounds of bread, and a quarter pound of butter . . .

HENRY.—I saved them up from my meals . . . (*Silence*) You believe me, don't you—you believe me, don't you fellers? (*Silence*) You've got to believe me . . . I've been perfectly honest!

247

GREELY.—We have evidence of your honesty in front of us, Henry.

WHISTLER.—Why we waiting—string him up!

GREELY.—(*Angrily*) Another outburst of that nature, Whistler, and you'll be confined to your sleeping bag! (*More quietly*) Well, men, how do you vote on Henry?

MEN.—(*Chorus*) "*Guilty.*"

HENRY.—Now wait a minute, fellows—you've got to . . .

GREELY.—(*No particular emotion*) Henry . . . you are under arrest. Under no conditions are you to leave your sleeping bag without permission, nor will you go outdoors unaccompanied. Under the circumstances, I must warn you that violent measures will be in order if the confinement is broken. Do you understand?

HENRY.—(*Brokenly*) All right . . . all right. Can I play checkers?

GREELY.—Yes. That's all, men.

WHISTLER.—(*Fading with men*) Play checkers . . . he'll have some job finding somebody to play with him, the dirty son of . . .

LONG.—I thought he was staying pretty fat on that stuff I been cooking.

GREELY.—(*Low voice*) Watch him closely, Brainard.

BRAINARD.—Yes, sir.

GREELY.—And be careful . . . He's had a good deal more to eat than any of us and consequently is the strongest man in the party.

BRAINARD.—Yes, sir.

SOUND.—*In the background Jewell is counting shrimp.*

MUSIC.—*Comes in over and fades as before.*

READER.—April 5. Temperature, minus 39, the lowest recording on the thermometer. Eskimo Fred died this morning at 9 A.M. (*Fade with*) Although not unexpected, his death was very sudden . . .

248

Music.—*Up and down.*

Reader.—April 6. Linn, our comrade and trusted friend, passed away quietly at 7 p.m. (*Fade with*) During the winter, Linn had been out of his mind on numerous occasions . . .

Music.—*Up and down.*

Reader.—April 9. Lieutenant Lockwood became unconscious early this morning and at 4:20, breathed his last. Death in our midst has ceased to arouse emotion. After his death, Rice and Ralston slept soundly in the same bag with the corpse. Noble Lockwood, with whom I went farthest north, is no more . . .

Music.—*Up and down.*

Reader.—April 12. Jewell died at 10 a.m. Burying these poor fellows is becoming an almost daily task . . .

Music.—*Up and down.*

Reader.—April 13. We have become accustomed to death, but gloom settled down over the party today, as Fredericks returned from an expedition for food with the news that our beloved friend Rice is dead. Many times, when the party seemed doomed to death of starvation, Rice saved us all with his brilliant hunting. Now he is dead—and some of our hope dies with him . . .

Music.—*Up and down.*

Reader.—May 24. Eskimo Jens is dead. Also Ellis, Ralston, and Whistler. We are all too near death ourselves to be conscious of any great difference between us and them. Schneider succeeded in counting the shrimp . . . there are over 700 to an ounce. Sealskin thongs cut into small pieces were made into a stew this evening. This life is horrible . . .

Music.—*Up and down . . . fade into wind behind.*

Reader.—June 5. Israel is dead. He was twenty-three years old. Lieutenant Kislingbury and Salor are also dead. I passed by Cemetery Ridge this morning and saw that the wind has blown the dirt away from the graves. Lieutenant Lockwood's uniform buttons seem to have been polished by the escaping gravel, and Linn's feet stick out. During the last few days I have eaten a great deal of rock moss. Lieutenant Greely says that they contain some nutriment . . .

249

GREELY.—(*Not cross . . . very weak*) Do you good, Brainard
. . . won't hurt you a bit.

PAVY.—(*Also weak*) Nonsense, they will harm your stomach,
sergeant.

GREELY.—(*Laughing like an old man*) Physician—cure thyself.
You are sicker than any of us.

PAVY.—(*Indifferent*) We are all the same. I may die first, Greely,
but you will not be far behind.

GREELY.—Shut up!

PAVY.—Aha—our gallant commander hates to die as much as
any man, eh?

GREELY.—If you don't shut up . . .

PAVY.—Pooh! A dying man doesn't have to salute, Greely. Why
don't you admit that you're no more than a plain ordinary
bundle of bones like all of us? Look at Brainard there . . .
he wouldn't even make a good hat rack . . . and I saw him
crying this morning—Brainard . . . the strong man.

BRAINARD.—(*Low voice*) It is true that I cried, doctor. I saw
myself in the mirror . . . I am not as I used to be.

PAVY.—No—you are not. You will soon join us, Brainard. Me
and Greely. (*He laughs*)

GREELY.—Sir . . . if you were not the surgeon of this expedition,
I would shoot you!

BENDER.—He doesn't mean any harm, commander. Why don't
you leave him alone?

GREELY.—(*Furious*) Now my men are giving me orders. By
heavens, Bender, I'll shoot you too! Long—give me your
rifle—that's an order, Long!

BRAINARD.—No . . . let me have it, Long. Bender, you go back
to your sleeping bag. Now . . . let's talk about food. You
know, it's funny but I don't seem to remember anything I
didn't like in the way of food.

PAVY.—Me neither. I once disliked cabbage, I recall, but no
longer.

GREELY.—And what I wouldn't do to a plate of greens. Say,
doctor, did you ever eat chicken à la creole?

Pavy.—Did I not? Oh, my dear Greely, let me assure you that my tissues are almost 90 per cent chicken à la creole (*Stops then in a low voice*) Le cochon! Le diable!

Greely.—What is it?

Pavy.—Henry . . . he just gobbled down Elison's chocolate . . . that pig is stealing again.

Greely.—Brainard . . . write this down for me. To sergeants Brainard, Fredericks, and Long. Private Henry having been repeatedly guilty of stealing the provisions of this party, it is imperatively ordered that if this man be detected in any further crime, you will at once shoot him and report the matter to me. Any other course would be a fatal leniency, the man being able to overpower any two of our present force. Signed. A. W. Greely. (*Fading*) Lieutenant, fifth cavalry, A.S.O. and

Music.—*Up and over . . . down into wind behind*

Reader.—June 6. I fished over 7 hours for the tantalizing little shrimps and caught only 2½ pounds. My baits are almost worthless. What are we to do? I have tried everything at hand but with no favorable results. Henry was caught this morning, stealing shrimps from the stew pot. He was also detected eating sealskin lashing and sealskin boots stolen from the public stock . . . (*Fade*)

Henry.—So what? You'd think I took something worth while.

Greely.—Henry . . . those sealskin boots may seem insignificant as food when compared to steak, but let me point out that we have no steak . . . only sealskin boots. To use such articles means life.

Henry.—I'm sorry, commander. I won't do it again . . . I promise you.

Greely.—You've promised me that several times, Henry.

Henry.—I know I have, but this time I mean it.

Greely.—All right. But I want you to take back all the things you've stolen . . . take them back to the storehouse. And when you're through doing that, pick some seaweed for tonight's stew.

Henry.—Yes, sir (*fading*) I'll never do it again, commander.

251

GREELY.—(*Softly*) No, Henry, you won't. Brainard!

BRAINARD.—Sir?

GREELY.—Give me some paper and a pen, and stay by me until I write an order for you.

BRAINARD.—Here you are, commander . . . Let me put this pillow under . . . That's better.

SOUND.—*Pen scratching*

BENDER.—(*Weakly*) Brainard?

BRAINARD.—Yes, Bender?

BENDER.—There's a caterpillar crawling on my sleeping bag . . . The summer must be coming, eh?

BRAINARD.—Yes, I think it is . . . I saw some birds this morning.

BENDER.—Wish I had one . . . I'd eat everything . . . even the feathers. Look, Brainard . . . that caterpillar . . . there's too much meat on him to waste . . . He's mine, isn't he? He's on my sleeping bag . . . You won't eat him, will you?

BRAINARD.—No . . . I won't.

BENDER.—Well, I will. Put him in my mouth, Brainard.

BRAINARD.—You don't want to eat a—caterpillar?

SOUND.—*Scratching stops.*

BENDER.—Oh, they're good, Brainard. Please, Brainard . . . I want him. (*Deep gratitude*) Oh—thank you.

GREELY.—Brainard . . . read this, and then carry it out. Get Fredericks and Long to help you.

BRAINARD.—(*Reading in a mumble*) Yes, sir. Where is he, commander?

GREELY.—Out by the storehouse, picking seaweed. Be careful, Brainard.

BRAINARD.—Yes, sir. I'll leave the order with you, sir. (*Fading*) Long . . . Fredericks . . . come with me.

GREELY.—(*Up weakly*) You other men . . . I have an order to read you. Near Cape Sabine. June 6, 1884. Sergeants Brainard, Long, and Fredericks. Notwithstanding promises given by Private Charles B. Henry yesterday and this morning, he has since acknowledged to me having tampered with seal thongs, if not other food at the old camp.

SOUND.—*Off stage there is an indistinguishable yelling.*

GREELY.—This pertinacity and audacity is the destruction of this party, if not at once ended. Private Henry will be shot today, all care being taken to prevent his injuring anyone, as his physical strength is greater than that of any two men. This order is imperative and absolutely necessary for any chance of life. Signed. A. W. Greely, First Lieutenant, Fifth Cavalry. Commanding Lady Franklin Bay expedition.

SOUND.—*The yelling off stage quiets down . . . there is a 5-second silence . . . only the wind is heard . . . then a shot.*

MUSIC.—*Up and over . . . fade into wind behind*

READER.—June 21. Tent has blown down. We have no strength to raise it. No one can walk now . . . and we seldom crawl. Bender, Dr. Pavy, Schneider, and Gardiner—all are dead. (*Cross-fade*) There are only seven of us left, and the living are as dead. We could not remove Schneider's body from the tent, except for his head, which we pushed out as best we could . . .

BRAINARD.—(*Weakly . . . cross-fade*) . . . there are only seven of us left, and the living are as dead. We could not remove Schneider's body from the tent, except for his head, which we pushed out as best we could . . .

GREELY.—What are you mumbling about, Brainard?

BRAINARD.—Reading what I wrote in my diary last night . . . can't write any more . . . My fingers won't hold the pencil.

GREELY.—Brainard . . . how are the others?

BRAINARD.—Bad.

GREELY.—And Elison?

BRAINARD.—(*A ghastly chuckle*) No hands . . . no feet . . . but he's the strongest.

GREELY.—Tie a spoon to his wrist, Brainard. If we die, he'll be able to manage for himself.

SOUND.—*Very faintly . . . steam whistle . . . three times.*

BRAINARD.—Yes, sir.

GREELY.—(*Idly*) What was that sound? Like a whistle?

BRAINARD.—I didn't hear anything.

GREELY.—I thought I heard something . . . you and Long had better go to the top of the ridge and see . . . (*minor excitement*) it may be a ship at last.

BRAINARD.—(*Excited*) Long! Come with me to the top of the ridge!

LONG.—What's the matter?

SOUND.—*Stumbling, crawling, sliding footsteps on gravel.*

BRAINARD.—The commander hears something like a whistle—it may be a ship . . .

LONG.—Just a little way now, and we'll know . . . Here we are . . .
(*A silence*)

BRAINARD.—(*Dull*) Nothing. Nothing anywhere. Let's go back.

LONG.—No . . . I'll stay here for a while. You go back, Brainard.

BRAINARD.—All right . . . I'll probably break my neck going down this slope . . .

SOUND.—*Rolling and tumbling of gravel . . . it stops.*

BRAINARD.—(*Starts to cry like a child*)

GREELY.—(*Far off . . . barely heard*) Brainard! Brainard! What is it?

BRAINARD.—(*Crying bitterly*) Whistles . . . ships . . . . there aren't any ships, and there aren't any whistles . . .

SOUND.—*Low moaning of wind in tin can.*

BRAINARD.—Whistles . . . there's the whistle . . .

SOUND.—*Tin cans being knocked aside . . . whistling stops.*

GREELY.—(*Closer*) Brainard . . . is that you?

254

BRAINARD.—Yes . . . I'm coming.

GREELY.—Did you see anything?

BRAINARD.—Nothing.

GREELY.—But the whistle . . .

BRAINARD.—It was the wind blowing over the water tins—that's all.

GREELY.—(*Dull*) Oh. I thought it was a ship. Well . . . go to sleep, Brainard. We won't . . .

SOUND.—*Running footsteps off.*

GREELY.—Someone running—that's strange . . .

NORMAN.—(*Off*) Greely. Are you in there, Greely?

BRAINARD.—That sounds like—it's Norman—Norman?

SOUND.—*Weak shouts of "It's Norman."*

NORMAN.—(*In*) Greely . . . is that you?

GREELY.—Here—yes—yes—seven of us left—here we are . . . Did what we came to do—beat the best record . . .

NORMAN.—You're all right now—there are two ships waiting to take you home.

MEN.—Food! Food!

NORMAN.—Corporal—give them some dried meat . . . not too much.

CORPORAL.—Yes, sir.

GREELY.—Aren't you Englishmen?

NORMAN.—Don't you know me, commander? I'm Norman. I was on the ship that brought you here—remember? We've had the devil's own time finding you—been looking for 6 weeks.

GREELY.—I'm glad you came. Those lemons your wife so kindly put up for us. (*Mumbles*)

NORMAN.—His mind is wandering. (*Calling*) Get the boat's crew, corporal, and bring up those stretchers. We need them. (*In*) Sergeant Brainard, give me the names of the survivors . . . I can't recognize anyone here by appearance.

BRAINARD.—Call the roll.

NORMAN.—Lieutenant Frederick F. Kislingbury.

BRAINARD.—Dead.

NORMAN.—Lieutenant James B. Lockwood.

BRAINARD.—Dead.

NORMAN.—Dr. Octave Pavy.

BRAINARD.—Dead.

NORMAN.—Sergeant Edward Israel.

BRAINARD.—Dead.

NORMAN.—Sergeant Winfield S. Jewell.

BRAINARD.—Dead.

MUSIC.—*Throughout this reading the music builds slowly and forcefully as the two men speak . . . they fade gradually until only the music remains.*

NORMAN.—Sergeant David L. Brainard.

BRAINARD.—Living and present.

NORMAN.—Sergeant David Linn.

BRAINARD.—Dead.

NORMAN.—Corporal Nicholas Salor.

BRAINARD.—Dead.

NORMAN.—Private Roderick Schneider.

BRAINARD.—Dead.

MUSIC.—*Sweeps up and out.*

ANNOUNCER.—Biederbeck, Fredericks, Long, Connell, Greely, and Brainard came back from the north. Elison died on board the rescue ship. Twenty-five went—and six came back. Of these six, only David L. Brainard is still alive, a retired Brigadier General of the United States Army, the only man, either active or retired, holding a commission received for distinguished service to his country. This week the diary of General Brainard, upon which this program was based will be published under the title "Six Came Back." May we

256

again extend our thanks to Bessie Rowland James, editor of the Brainard diary, for permission to use the material contained in this dramatization . . . "And Six Came Back," by Ranald R. MacDougall.

The musical interludes on the program were especially composed by Tom Bennett.

Next week the Listener's Playhouse will be heard at its customary time, 8:30 E.D.S.T. This was a presentation of the National Broadcasting Company.

The Little Wife

by William March

eeeeeeeeeeeeeeeeeeeeeeeeeeeeeeeeeeeeeeeeeeeeeeeeeeeee

MUSIC.—*Theme . . . up . . . then to background.*

ANN.—Nelson Olmsted brings you The World's Greatest Short Stories.

MUSIC.—*Up . . . then to background.*

ANN.—In the past century and a half, authors of the world have provided us with an invaluable heritage of good entertainment through the precise and exacting medium of the short story.

Occasionally these authors imbued in their work a spark which is instantly evident but difficult to describe. Such stories Nelson Olmsted presents. Such is the story tonight by William March—a simple narrative, simply told, entitled "The Little Wife."

MUSIC.—*Out.*

OLMSTED.—Joe Hinckley selected a seat on the shady side of the train and carefully stowed away his traveling bag and his heavy black catalogue case. He looked at his watch: 2:28—the train was five minutes late in getting out. If he had known the 2:23 was going to be late he might have had time to pack his sample trunk and get to the station, but he couldn't have anticipated that, of course.

Joe noticed that one end of his catalogue case protruded slightly. With his foot he shoved it farther under the seat. It was a battered, black case, made strongly to withstand constant traveling and reenforced at its corners with heavy copper cleats. One of the handles had been broken and mended with newer leather.

On the front of the case there had once been stamped in gilt the firm name of Boykin & Rosen, Wholesale Hardware, Chattanooga, Tenn., but time had long since worn away the gold lettering.

258

That telegram had upset Joe; it had come so suddenly, so unexpectedly. He felt vaguely that somebody was playing a joke on him. He felt confused and helpless. It was difficult to believe that Bessie was so desperately sick. He sat for a time staring at his fingernails.

It was very hot in the coach. The small electric fan at the end of the car droned and wheezed sleepily but succeeded only in stirring up the hot air.

Joe took from his pocket the telegram that he had received from his mother-in-law and read it again. It said: "J. G. Hinckley, American Hotel, Montgomery, Ala. Come home at once. Doctor says Bessie not expected to live through day. Will wire again if necessary. It was a boy. Mother."

Joe's hands clenched suddenly and then relaxed. It had all happened so suddenly; he couldn't quite get it through his head, even yet. He had taken a buyer to lunch that day and they had laughed and talked and told each other stories. Then at two o'clock he had gone back to the hotel to freshen up and the clerk had reached in his box and taken out the key to his room and the telegram. The telegram had been waiting for him for two hours, the clerk said. Joe read it through twice and then looked at the address to make sure the message was really for him.

He hadn't understood. Bessie was getting along so nicely—she had no trouble at all—and the baby wasn't expected for a month. He had arranged his itinerary so that he would be with her when the baby was born. They had gone over all that and had arranged everything.

Joe leaned his head against the red plush of the seat. He felt numb and tired.

When he had married Bessie her mother had come to live with them as a matter of course. He was rather glad of the arrangement; he was really fond of the old lady in an impersonal sort of way. Then, too, it was pleasant for Bessie to have someone with her while he was on the road. His work made it impossible for him to get home oftener than every other week end, and many times it was difficult for him to get home that often, but he had always managed to make it. He couldn't disappoint Bessie, no matter what happened. Their year of married life had been the happiest that he had ever known. And Bessie had been happy too. Suddenly he had a clear picture of her lying on their bed, her face white with suffering, and a quick pain gripped his heart. To re-assure himself he whispered: "Those doctors don't know everything. She'll be all right. Mrs. Tompkins was just excited and frightened. Everything's going to be all right!"

Just then, the Negro porter brought him a telegram. Joe's throat felt tight and he noticed that his hands were shaking. He placed the unopened telegram on the seat beside him and stared at it for a long time.

At last he reread the first telegram very slowly. "It must be from Mrs. Tompkins, all right. She said she'd wire if . . . It might not be from Mrs. Tompkins at all; it may be from somebody else; it may be from Boykin and Rosen, about that cancellation in Meridian. That's who it's from; it's from the House; it's not from Mrs. Tompkins at all!"

He arose from his seat feeling weak and slightly nauseated, the opened telegram in his hand. He passed through several coaches until he reached the end of the train and went out on the rear vestibule.

The rails clicked rhythmically and the wilted countryside flew past. "There's no need of going so fast . . . we've got all the time in the world." He felt sick.

He kept turning the telegram over in his hand, thinking: "I've got to open it now; I've got to open it and read it." Finally he said aloud: "It's not true! I don't believe it! It's from the House about that cancellation in Meridian—it isn't from Mrs. Tompkins at all." He tore the unopened telegram into tiny bits and threw the pieces from the end of the train. A wind fluttered and shimmered the yellow fragments before they settled down lightly on the hard, hot roadbed. Immediately he felt better. He drew back his shoulders and sucked in lungfuls of the country air. "Everything's all right," he said. "I'm going home to see the little wife and everything's all right." He laughed happily. He felt like a man who had just escaped some terrible calamity.

When he could no longer see the scraps of paper on the track he went back to his seat, humming a tune. He felt very gay and immensely relieved.

Joe reached his seat just as the conductor came through the train. He nodded pleasantly as he gave up his ticket. "Don't let anybody talk you out of a free ride."

"Not a chance of that, Cap'!" said the conductor.

Joe laughed with ringing heartiness and the conductor looked at him in surprise. Then he laughed a little himself. "You sure are in a good humor, considering how hot it is."

"And why shouldn't I be in a good humor? I'm going home to see the little wife. It's a boy!"

"That's fine, that's simply fine!" And the conductor put his papers and tickets on the seat and shook Joe's hand. Joe blushed and laughed again. As the conductor moved off he nudged Joe's ribs and said: "Give my regards to the madam."

"I sure will," said Joe happily.

Joe was sorry that the conductor couldn't stay longer. He felt an imperative need of talking to someone. He felt that he must talk about Bessie to someone. He saw an old lady and her husband in their seat up the aisle, eating a lunch which they had brought, and he decided to go over and talk with them.

"Can I come over and talk to you folks?" asked Joe.

"Certainly, sir," said the old gentleman.

"I've just got a telegram saying that I was a parent for the first time."

The old people congratulated him heartily. Then Joe started talking rapidly. He told in detail of the first time he met Bessie. Joe talked of his wedding. It had been very quiet. Bessie was the sort of a girl who didn't go in for a lot of show. There had been present only a few members of the family and one or two close friends. George Orcutt, who traveled a line of rugs out of New York, had been his best man. Bessie was afraid that someone would try to play a joke on them; something like tying tin cans to the automobile that was to take them to the station or marking their baggage with chalk. But everything had gone off smoothly. The Barneses had been at the wedding, of course; he had met Bessie in their home and they were such close neighbors that they couldn't overlook them, but almost nobody else outside the family was there.

Then he told of the honeymoon they had spent in New Orleans; all the places they had visited there and just what Bessie had thought and said about each one. He talked on and on and on. He told of the first weeks of their married life and how happy they were. He told what a splendid cook Bessie was and what an excellent housekeeper, how much she had loved the home he had bought for her and her delight when she knew that she was going to have a baby.

The old gentleman was staring at Joe in a puzzled manner. He was wondering if he hadn't better call the conductor, as it was his private opinion that Joe had a shot of cocaine in him.

Joe had lost all idea of time. He talked on and on, rapidly, excitedly.

He had got as far as Bessie's plans for the child's education when the porter touched him on the arm and told him that they were pulling into the station at Mobile. He came to himself with a start and looked at his watch: 7:35! He didn't believe it possible that the time had passed so quickly.

"It's sure been a pleasure talking to you folks," said Joe.

"Oh, that's all right," said the old man.

Joe gave the porter a tip and stepped off the train jauntily. As he turned to pick up his bag he saw that a woman with a huge goiter was staring at him. He walked over to the window that framed her guant face. "Good-by, lady; I hope you have a nice trip." The woman answered, "The doctors said it wasn't no use operating on me. I waited too long." "Well, that's fine . . . that sure is fine," said Joe. He laughed gaily and waved his hand. He picked up his bag and his catalogue case and followed the people through the gate. The woman with the goiter stared at him until he was out of sight.

On the other side of the iron fence Joe saw Mrs. Tompkins. She was dressed in black and she wore a veil. Joe went over to her briskly and Mrs. Tompkins put her arms around him and kissed him twice. "Poor Joe!" she said. Then she looked at his smiling, excited face with amazement. Joe noticed that her eyes were red and swollen.

"Didn't you get my telegram?" she asked. Joe wrinkled his brow in an effort to remember. Finally he said: "Oh, sure. I got it at the hotel."

"Did you get my second telegram?" insisted Mrs. Tompkins.

She looked steadily into Joe's eyes. A feeling of terror swept over him. He knew that he could no longer lie to himself. He could no longer keep Bessie alive by talking about her. His face was suddenly twisted with pain and his jaw trembled like a child's. He leaned against the iron fence for support and Mrs. Tompkins held his hand and said: "You can't give in. You got to be a man. You can't give in like that, Joe!"

Finally he said: "I didn't read your telegram. I didn't want to know that she was dead. I wanted to keep her alive for a little longer." He sat down on an empty baggage truck and hid his face in his hands. He sat there for a long time while Mrs. Tompkins took guard over him, her black veil trailing across his shoulder.

"Joe!" she said patiently . . . "Joe . . . "

A man in a dirty uniform came up. "I'm sorry, mister, but you'll have to move. We got to use that truck." Joe picked up his catalogue case and his bag and followed Mrs. Tompkins out of the station.

MUSIC.—*Interlude . . . slow . . . sad.*

ANN.—This has been the story of "The Little Wife," as presented by Nelson Olmsted.

NBC presents Nelson Olmsted three times each week, on Monday, Tuesday, and Wednesday nights at this same time, over most of these stations. Tomorrow night try to be with us for another of Edgar Allan Poe's startling narratives, entitled "The Case of M. Valdemar."

Moll Flanders

by DANIEL DEFOE

INVITATION TO LEARNING

~~~~~~

Daniel Defoe is the most prodigious literary journeyman on record. Besides writing with his own hand the whole of an important newspaper for many years and besides creating the profession of journalist as it still is known after two hundred years, he was the author of approximately a thousand books and pamphlets, many of them influential in their day and several of them still living classics. "Robinson Crusoe," one of the most popular books ever written, is the best known instance of his power to imagine and convey the details of a life, not his own, lived under special conditions. He was seldom recognized in his own time as a writer of fiction, so convincing were the "biographies" he turned out in such great profusion. Any narrative so plain and circumstantial must be true, the feeling was; and only with time have his superb merits, his invention, and his verisimilitude been given the credit due them. "Moll Flanders" has nothing of Defoe in it except his genius; it is in Moll and her career that we are absorbed; it is she that we believe without ever asking whether it is possible not to do so. Her disreputable days become a portion of general human experience, while Defoe's art is taken for granted. His art is of the highest, and it will always be studied by those who want their stories to carry conviction. He is also a reminder that prose fiction, of which he is one of the creators, had better remain prose. The poetry of Defoe is unseen, though it is always clearly felt, beneath a deceptively commonplace exterior.

(*Miss Katherine Anne Porter, guest*)

CAIRNS.—I could not help associating Moll Flanders with Robinson Crusoe when I reread Defoe's novel. He is so realistic that I felt I was reading a true story. Perhaps I ought not to admire Moll Flanders, but I feel that on the whole she is an excellent person, and it occurred to me—although I am not altogether certain—that Moll would have made a fine wife for Robinson Crusoe. I wonder, Miss Porter, if you would agree with that.

PORTER.—Oh, yes, I do, but I think that she made an excellent wife for all her husbands.

VAN DOREN.—And would for any man, perhaps?

PORTER.—Oh, I think so. I think she had the qualities that men like.

VAN DOREN.—I'm sorry I came 200 years too late.

TATE.—Every man is apt to feel that way. Miss Porter, what do you think that Moll had in her character that made her such a good wife, although she was a wife so many times?

PORTER.—Well, she was a woman extremely friendly to men, and she was very resourceful. She was self-supporting. I don't think that's a small matter.

CAIRNS.—She was self-supporting in a strange fashion.

PORTER.—Well, yes, in odd ways. But I think if she had been on a desert island, for example, she would have shown the same kind of ready wit and resourcefulness and a cool head in a crisis, and a very practical mind.

VAN DOREN.—Would she have complained about the difficulties?

PORTER.—She never did.

VAN DOREN.—She never seems to be that kind of woman.

CAIRNS.—I had only one reservation about Moll Flanders being the wife of Robinson Crusoe. I thought she would make an excellent wife for any man except, perhaps, Robinson Crusoe. Do you think that she would have been content to live on a desert island? Wasn't the mainspring of her action excitement?

PORTER.—Well, yes. But I think she would have found excitement on a desert island, too, without much trouble. You remember how happily and comfortably she lived quietly when she was young. Then she got a great deal of excitement, even so, out of life.

VAN DOREN.—She was no Emma Bovary, was she? Nothing neurotic about her.

PORTER.—Oh, no.

TATE.—She was not a frustrated woman at all, but if that is true, why, do you think, had she so many husbands? Why didn't she stick to one of them?

VAN DOREN.—It was not her fault perhaps.

CAIRNS.—It may have been her craving for excitement. I gather it is more exciting to have many husbands than merely one. Defoe seemed to think so. His advertisement of the book stressed the plurality of husbands as an exciting aspect of the novel.

TATE.—She was constantly being "done in" by her men, wasn't she?

PORTER.—Well, in a way, but it was mostly a question of the marriage portion, you remember. The money always got in the way, and one thing and another. They couldn't last because they had no money, and they separated.

VAN DOREN.—Her husbands were always dying, too.

PORTER.—Some of them were dying, and some of them were going away to seek their fortunes. Their troubles were largely what we now call economic.

TATE.—But isn't it true that the only husband who was well-to-do turned out, by one of those malignant chances of fate, to be her half brother? And she had to separate from him.

CAIRNS.—Moll had a characteristic that Robinson Crusoe possessed. She was a solitary person. She was solitary in society because she was an outlaw, and of course Robinson Crusoe was solitary in nature. He was alone—until his man Friday appeared—on an island. And I am still not satisfied that you have answered my question.

PORTER.—Well, I can only remember one thing that she said about herself: that she could never work with a partner. Do you remember? Twice, I think it was, she went with a partner, and each time she came to disaster.

CAIRNS.—Yes, but she had perhaps a semipartner at the end— her governess. I forget the name, if any, that she applied to her.

VAN DOREN.—She calls her her governess.

TATE.—By the way, Miss Porter, don't you think the governess is a rather mysterious character? She's a person of great worth. At the same time, she is Moll's confederate in crime. I can't place her. She is the only character, I think, in the entire story who may perhaps be not quite convincing.

VAN DOREN.—My notion is otherwise. It seems to me that she was one of the most convincing. I wonder why that is. I should say that here this woman is, by chance, perhaps, and by circumstance, doing certain things, following certain trades of which we might disapprove, and yet carrying into those trades, into those occupations the character that she was born with, that she always had. She is a very clear-headed and very faithful woman, very faithful to her friends.

TATE.—That's true, but let me see if I can make the point a little more clearly. Moll, of course, does not lead an ordinary social life. But the governess is obscure because Defoe doesn't spend as much time upon her as he does upon Moll. He doesn't give you enough detail about her. She moves forward and backward, moves up a little into the foreground, then disappears again.

VAN DOREN.—That is what I like about the way he handles her. For instance, suddenly you find her very active for no special reason. Do you remember the occasion when she goes to the man whom Moll has robbed? Her main intent is to blackmail him. Suddenly she has the passion to do that. It isn't explained, just as it isn't explained that she wants to help Moll on this occasion or some other occasion. The coming and going of this woman, to me, attests her vitality.

TATE.—I don't feel that Defoe ought to explain her. I think one of the great virtues of this book is that no action is really motivated. It's like life, because you don't see where the action comes from. You can't predict the consequences. Yet it's all beautifully clear.

CAIRNS.—I thought you might suggest that that was a defect of the book, that he doesn't really put us inside his characters. We only know them through their actions.

PORTER.—No, I think the great virtue of that book is that his characters explain themselves with their actions and their speeches, and you know as much about them as you could possibly know. You know a great deal more about them than someone you know in life, really, and you understand also their motives; I don't think he has to explain.

VAN DOREN.—I quite agree with you, Miss Porter. We find out about the inside of a person, so-called, by his outside. I think it is the outside that tells us. There is nothing else.

CAIRNS.—How would you differentiate the characters in this book? It seems to me they are all alike because they are all leading the same kind of life.

VAN DOREN.—Well, are her husbands alike? I should say not.

TATE.—I think they are very different.

PORTER.—They're all as different men as you could possibly imagine.

VAN DOREN.—Two of them are, respectively, a banker and a highwayman. I find nothing in common between those two men.

CAIRNS.—You may be letting a mere label mislead you.

PORTER.—Their characters are very different.

VAN DOREN.—One is a good banker and one is a good highwayman.

TATE.—They tend to be types.

CAIRNS.—That is exactly my point.

TATE.—That's all right. I have no objection to types.

CAIRNS.—I have no objection to types either—in their place. Aeschylus created types and they are magnificent. Do we want the novelist to give us nothing but types? Don't we want the novelist also to be able to give us individuals?

PORTER.—They tend to be types in everything except the most important thing in a novel, and that is the difference in their human emotions. They all have a different set of feelings about things, which they express very clearly. In their relations, for example, with Moll, each one is quite different and quite separate. They all have a kind of amiability and a kind of benevolence almost, you know, which Moll's personality inspired in them all alike; but they are quite different really, and the characters of the men come out in their speeches and in their actions. They don't seem in the least alike to me, and I thought I knew them very well.

268

VAN DOREN.—Wouldn't you say, Miss Porter, speaking as a novelist, that any character in a novel must be a type first of all?

PORTER.—Oh, naturally.

CAIRNS.—I would not deny that a completely unique individual might not appeal to us. We ought to be able to recognize some common characteristics in him.

VAN DOREN.—Perhaps he must be 75 per cent type.

TATE.—If he's not a type first, we don't understand him; we can't possibly get hold of him; we can't recognize him; he is a monster.

CAIRNS.—But the modern novelist would attempt to give individuality to his characters, would he not?

TATE.—I think, Mr. Cairns, that Virginia Woolf's characters tend not to be types, and for that reason it is very difficult to remember the action of a novel by Mrs. Woolf, although while you are reading the novel it is immensely impressive.

VAN DOREN.—Yes, but it's all Mrs. Woolf.

TATE.—And it's very hard to remember it a year later.

VAN DOREN.—The inside of Mrs. Woolf's characters is the inside of Mrs. Woolf.

CAIRNS.—That may be a reflection upon Mrs. Woolf as a novelist.

VAN DOREN.—It's a reflection upon the theory of novel writing which says that you should get at the inside of your people. A great artist gets the outside. It's the most difficult thing in the world.

CAIRNS.—It is difficult also to get the inside. Difficulty does not seem to me to be a sound test.

PORTER.—By getting the outside very clearly and perfectly, there is a sort of radiation. The radiation of personality through the being as presented from the outside.

TATE.—When we talk about this objective quality of Defoe's, it's not quite the same thing that we get in the ordinary realistic novel of today. It's a very different thing, isn't it?

269

CAIRNS.—The element that is lacking, I think, is introspection, in large part. That is an element that the modern novelist has added which I don't find here to any appreciable extent.

VAN DOREN.—But, Mr. Cairns, my objection is that this element of introspection which you speak of has not given us the insides of the characters. It has given us the inside of the author's mind.

CAIRNS.—Because second-rate novelists have used this method. But in the hands of a first-rate novelist, it seems to me a valuable element that we should not arbitrarily exclude.

TATE.—I think I agree, Mr. Cairns.

PORTER.—I think that Joyce is a first-rate novelist, and I think that he has come as near to getting completely into the blood stream of his characters as anyone in the world, and for the most part, I find his characters very monotonous and not half so interesting as an objectively presented character like Moll Flanders. Now I'm not going to interrupt anyone again.

CAIRNS.—Miss Porter, we want you to.

TATE.—Well, Miss Porter, what do you think about this? You've mentioned Joyce. What about Henry James? He seems to combine very subtly these two things, the external observation of the character and the interior monologue. I'm not sure that we remember the interior monologues of James's characters. I remember his novels as a succession of scenes. That's what you take away, and of course the scene is preeminently what Defoe gives us.

VAN DOREN.—But the interior monologue in James is again, I would say, James himself. The interior monologues in his novels are almost indistinguishable from his prefaces to those novels.

TATE.—They all have the same style, the same tone—yes.

CAIRNS.—To repeat—that may be a reflection on James. However, I enjoy his prefaces as much as his novels.

VAN DOREN.—Take a person who is done completely from the outside, as Hamlet, for instance, about whom I think we know nothing except the way he looks, the way he talks, what he says, and so forth. Even the soliloquies, I should say, are not indications of what he is inside. And yet we know everything about him.

TATE.—It seems to me, Miss Porter, that this novel is a "dramatic" novel. That is, it is presented in one scene after another, and the author never appears in it at all. That is a great thing to achieve in fiction.

PORTER.—I like the introspective novel very much. I think it has its place, and I think we'd be much poorer without it, but I do think that the weakness of it is that when a novelist gets inside of a character, he finds only himself, and the great art really is to be able to look at the world and individuals and present characters that readers will recognize and will know or feel they know. That is a tremendous feat.

VAN DOREN.—Once you're inside a person, you cannot see him, literally speaking. You see organs or motives or what not that are just like yours. It seems to me very clear that this is the case.

CAIRNS.—Would you not like some soliloquies from Moll Flanders?

TATE.—The whole book is a soliloquy.

CAIRNS.—Not in the sense in which we are talking.

VAN DOREN.—Mr. Cairns, why do you believe in soliloquies? Why do you think they tell more about a person than his conversation with other persons? I don't see why they should.

PORTER.—Moll is always saying, "I thought this. I said that to myself. I was grieved," and she describes her grief. "I repented," and she describes her repentance in a passage which gives me more the feeling of real grief for sin and a real sense of the soul approaching death than anything else I know in the English language, and she does it all by saying, "I thought this and that. I said that."

CAIRNS.—Yes. They are all descriptions about something, but you are never taken inside that something.

TATE.—Mr. Cairns, doesn't Moll go into a soliloquy occasionally?

CAIRNS.—She does occasionally.

TATE.—She moralizes, and she says that she is going to repent, but they are the least interesting passages.

CAIRNS.—I can't tell, Mr. Tate, whether you are for me or against me. Where do you stand on this question of introspection?

TATE.—I think it all depends on who does it and how successful it is. But the safest, and at the same time the most brilliant, thing in fiction is this objective method.

VAN DOREN.—Mr. Cairns, I'd like to know more about this inside that you speak of. Character originally means an outline drawn of someone. To be able to draw an outline of someone you have to be outside him, obviously. When we're inside him, there is nothing to see. There is no point of view. But also, what is there inside of a person? If you take a person's skin away from him, what is there?

CAIRNS.—I think Miss Porter has given us an example in Joyce's novel. The whole novel is about what's inside Mr. Bloom and Miriam Bloom.

VAN DOREN.—I'm interested in your word "about."

CAIRNS.—What do you mean?

VAN DOREN.—I think you're confessing right there that it isn't the inside. It's about the inside, and so I think the inside of Mr. Bloom is still at a distance from Joyce.

CAIRNS.—You must admit that there is certainly a distinction. A distinction can be drawn in this manner: The novelist says, "*A* does something"; that is one approach. The other approach is: *A*, a character in a novel, says, "I am going to do so and so for the following reasons," and thinks about it. His thoughts are recorded in the novel. That latter element is what I find lacking in "Moll Flanders."

VAN DOREN.—But why do you believe people when they tell you what their reasons are for what they do? I don't know what my motives are.

CAIRNS.—That depends on the art of the novelist.

TATE.—Yes, I think so, too, Mr. Van Doren. For example, a character in a novel states explicitly his motive. The author shows that it is not his real motive. The false motive becomes dramatically interesting.

272

VAN DOREN.—Of course. But in both cases you're on the outside of that person. You hear him say, "This is my motive," don't you? It's something that happens between you and him.

TATE.—But don't you think the upshot of the matter is something like this—that the introspection, the soliloquy, is likely to be no good unless it is firmly grounded in a realistic setting? That is to say, unless the character is very distinct from the outside, you don't believe his soliloquy.

CAIRNS.—Let us attack that problem from the point of view that you have just suggested, from the point of view of Defoe's realism. Do you think his realism is the result of his shop-keeping experience, or is it a conscious art such as Flaubert employed?

PORTER.—I think Defoe was a first-rate artist.

CAIRNS.—I think he was, too, but how about his realism? Was it because he was a shopkeeper that in the book he gives you the cost of the stockings, how much the linen was worth, or was his realism a deliberate art?

PORTER.—That may have something to do with his background, his training, because, after all, he was using a very good method. He was writing about what he knew. Of course, though, that may have something to do with his choice of a character, too, because, after all, Moll was intensely interested in the price of things and getting a little money and knowing what things were worth.

CAIRNS.—So was Defoe himself.

VAN DOREN.—And so was his new audience.

CAIRNS.—You would not say that his realism was the realism of Flaubert, would you?

PORTER.—No, I don't think so. It's on quite a different level.

VAN DOREN.—I should say that there was very little difference in degree; that is to say, Flaubert looks at a certain class of French people of the nineteenth century with a theory about that class. He doesn't describe that class without the aid of feeling and a theory about the middle class, the bourgeoisie. So, however, does Defoe have a feeling and a theory about the class of person whom Moll represents. I think he was

273

conscious that he was introducing into fiction a new type of person.

TATE.—But at the same time, don't you think that, unlike Flaubert, Defoe is not interested in giving you an analysis of society? You don't see the English social system of the early eighteenth century at all. The realism is close up. It is realism about Moll's immediate surroundings.

CAIRNS.—His realism was the realism of the journalist. It is photographic and is designed to picture the society Defoe knew at first hand.

PORTER.—With respect to some of the laws, I always thought that he made rather a good criticism of a certain phase of society when Moll makes her speech to the judges just before the death sentence is passed upon her. He puts into her speech a real criticism of the criminal code; and he does quite often criticize society—rather obliquely, that is true—but he does say that the poverty and the bad upbringing of people is the cause of crime. He does say so, plainly.

VAN DOREN.—And weren't you impressed, too, by the fact that he seems to have a certain knowledge—which I should say was social—of the habits of people in a certain quarter of London with reference to marriage?

TATE.—Yes, but he doesn't draw it up systematically, for example, the way Zola did.

VAN DOREN.—Oh, no. I think Flaubert did not do it systematically either.

TATE.—Zola did, however. He documented his books in great detail.

CAIRNS.—Flaubert, of course, was selective for his effect, and Defoe is cumulative in his effect.

PORTER.—But both are very good methods which the artist can use.

CAIRNS.—I am not condemning either. I am making a distinction.

VAN DOREN.—Can you say any more about the method of Defoe as a novelist, Miss Porter?

PORTER.—I love especially that cumulative method, one episode following another until you find at the very end you have a complete picture, exactly what he wanted you to see, and you realize that you've had it in a procession of small pictures that build up to the whole.

CAIRNS.—What do you think about the fact that he gives no descriptive detail, no scenery, no houses, no descriptions of people?

PORTER.—He was a city man, for one thing.

TATE.—Don't you think that there is another reason for that, Miss Porter, and that it proves Defoe's superiority? One vice of the modern novel is the long descriptive passages.

VAN DOREN.—Description is always the resource of someone who does not know how to tell a story.

TATE.—I'm afraid that's true. Fielding has no description.

VAN DOREN.—A first-rate novelist never needs description.

CAIRNS.—I hope we bring up this point when we discuss Proust.

PORTER.—I don't pretend to know how Defoe does it. It is really beyond me. I've tried to put my finger on it, but when Moll goes on her ship you see that ship.

CAIRNS.—But he does not describe it.

PORTER.—No; he doesn't have to.

VAN DOREN.—He creates the ship.

PORTER.—He gives you the ship. You see the coach she travels in. You see the house she lives in. She goes into a street, and in the strangest way you know the street.

CAIRNS.—Flaubert creates the same effect on me, but his method is entirely different.

TATE.—Paradoxically, don't you think you see the streets and the ship and the coach because he refuses to describe them? He selects one object. Moll puts her hand on one object and holds it. The whole scene comes to life.

VAN DOREN.—Or that famous place in the novel where she suddenly sees her Lancashire husband from her window in the inn. She simply walks to the window because she needs air, she says. It is a curious thing. That little statement creates the room, the inn, the street, and the husband.

275

PORTER.—And when she goes along the country road and meets the honest man, you know, who is going to sell her a horse. There is the country road, and there is the man. And not only that, she is trying to deceive him; she is trying to escape; and she has her little thoughts about the way she is deceiving this man and her motives for it, and the whole scene is clear.

CAIRNS.—Do you think he is a very great artist?

PORTER.—One of the greatest.

VAN DOREN.—I would say that what we have just been saying suggests that he is a great artist. God does not describe the world. He creates it. He doesn't need to describe it.

CAIRNS.—No, because He hands it to us, and we have to take it. If Defoe does not appeal to us we can put him aside.

TATE.—Doesn't Defoe give you the scenes almost as if they weren't communicated through words? You tend to forget the language. The object shines through the words.

VAN DOREN.—The words are a perfectly transparent medium.

CAIRNS.—If he is such a great artist, how do you reconcile his art and his morality? Is he reducing art to a tool of morality?

PORTER.—I think he made quite a few little bows in the direction of the moral fashions of his time.

CAIRNS.—You think he is not serious in his morality?

PORTER.—Well, he was a man who wrote political pamphlets for hire, that's true, and he went with the side that seemed to promise him the best advantage, and all that. But I think his morality was strong and sincere; certainly a little commonplace, but real.

CAIRNS.—How do you reconcile the happy ending of "Moll Flanders" after such a life of sin and wickedness? How do you reconcile that happy ending with the morality he is preaching in the book?

PORTER.—She repented, don't you see? And it is true that there is a religious idea that repentance is sufficient. Of course, it shouldn't lead to a happy ending as a usual thing, but you remember that in those days—I notice it in studying the Puritans—they really did believe or seemed to believe that God rewarded earthly virtue with earthly good.

276

CAIRNS.—But Moll did not repent until she had a sum of money in the bank and an attractive husband.

TATE.—Didn't she repent before that?

PORTER.—She repented when she was facing death and thought she was going to be hanged next week. There is almost no religion that will refuse a sinner on his deathbed. Oh, no, she repents at exactly the right moment.

CAIRNS.—You mean the right moment at the end of the book when she had all this money or the moment when she was facing death? She repented, of course, both times.

PORTER.—No, her real scene of repentance, which I think is one of the most exciting things in the book—Defoe promised he would make it interesting, and he did—the great passage in that book is from the time the minister comes to talk with her about her soul and persuade her to repent until the time he returns to bring her news of her reprieve. Then again she becomes immediately the busy woman of the world—counting her possessions, encouraging her husband, making plans for the future.

CAIRNS.—So her repentance wasn't sincere, was it?

PORTER.—Yes, she behaved much better after that. She had a few habits left over that she tried to curb.

TATE.—She had several habits. Don't you think, Miss Porter, that Defoe may have something else in mind? Is he showing us that a virtuous woman can also on occasion be a thief, that a certain kind of virtue doesn't consist solely in conventional behavior?

VAN DOREN.—Yes, and, of course, it is also fair to remember that his morality was a morality of success. These new people whom he introduces into the world, these middle-class people for a new middle-class audience, are people who have to make their way in the world—a thing that we still have respect for, I should say.

PORTER.—Yes, indeed. It's certainly part of our national faith.

CAIRNS.—She was goaded, of course, by poverty, and there is a very fine sentence that I recall from the book. She said, "The terror of approaching poverty lay hard upon my spirits." Perhaps she can be excused on that ground.

TATE.—Perhaps it's more than a conventional excuse that Moll was deceived in her girlhood by the young country gentleman. From then on it was almost impossible for her to recover and be a respectable woman. She had to live in the underworld from that time on.

CAIRNS.—But she did become a respectable woman at the end.

TATE.—In a way, yes, but I don't think her respectability is really convincing, Mr. Cairns, I must say.

CAIRNS.—That is the question I raised, whether or not he is sincere in his morality. I take it we agree that he is not.

VAN DOREN.—The use of the word "gentleman" reminds me that when she was a little girl in the workhouse, she said she wanted to be a gentlewoman, and it turned out that she meant she wanted to be a woman who could make her own way.

PORTER.—To make her own living.

VAN DOREN.—Speaking of the style of this man, I should like to read a paragraph in which he has created a scene, created all over again the governess whom we were talking about a minute ago, made her talk so that we seem to listen to her talking. The occasion is that on which Moll has been disguised as a man. She runs from those who are chasing her into the governess's house and is not identified there because she has changed her clothes. "When they had thus searched the house from bottom to top and then from top to bottom and could find nothing, they appeased the mob pretty well, but they carried my governess before the justice. Two men swore that they saw the man whom they pursued go into the house. My governess made a great noise that her house should be insulted and that she should be used thus for nothing, that if a man did come in he might go out again presently for aught she knew, but she was ready to make oath that no man had been within her doors all that day, as she knew of (and that was very true indeed). But it might be indeed that if she was above stairs any fellow in a fright might find the door open and run in for shelter when he was pursued but that she knew nothing of it, and if it had been so certainly went out again, perhaps through the other door, for she had another door into an alley, and so had made his escape."

278

Edward R. Murrow*

MURROW.—Mr. Ernest Brown, the Minister of Health, appealed today for more women to open their homes to workers in need of billet. In the course of a discussion about the problems of evacuation, the minister read a letter from a ten-year-old East London boy, now living in the country. You will recognize the subject of the essay. Here it is:

"The cow is a mammal. It has six sides—right, left, and upper and below. At the back it has a tail on which hangs a brush. With this it sends the flies away, so that they do not fall into the milk. The head is for the purpose of growing horns and so that the mouth can be somewhere. The horns are to butt with, and the mouth is to "moo" with. Under the cow hangs the milk. It is arranged for milking. When people milk, the milk comes and there is never an end to the supply. How the cow does it, I have not yet realized, but it makes more and more. The cow has a fine sense of smell. One can smell it far away. This is the reason for the fresh air in the country. The man cow is called an ox. It is not a mammal. The cow does not eat much, but what it eats it eats twice so that it gets enough. When it is hungry it moos, and when it says nothing it is because all its inside is full-up with grass."

Now that essay was, tonight, included in the principal news bulletin broadcast in this country.

* Excerpt from The World Today, broadcast October 29, 1941.

Elementals

by STEPHEN VINCENT BENÉT

MUSIC.—*Up and under.*

ANNOUNCER.—The Authors' Playhouse!

MUSIC.—*Theme up and under.*

ANNOUNCER.—Presenting Stephen Vincent Benét's brilliant short story "Elementals"!

MUSIC.—*Theme.*

ANNOUNCER.—Tonight the National Broadcasting Company presents its new dramatic series, The Authors' Playhouse . . . radio adaptations of great modern short stories . . . tales written by acknowledged masters of their craft . . . stories by writers famous for their ability to excite, to amuse, to alarm, and, above all, to entertain!

We are privileged to open our series with a tale from one of America's foremost writers, Stephen Vincent Benét, poet, critic, novelist, short story writer. His novel-length narrative poem "John Brown's Body" is perhaps the most popular poem of our time . . . and his short stories of America's past are without equal in their power to bring to life the shadowy and often legendary figures of our history. In "Elementals"—our story tonight—he departs from his widely known historical fiction and offers a picture of modern times . . . a vivid and dramatic study of conflicting personal philosophies. (*Pause*) The Authors' Playhouse presents "Elementals," by Stephen Vincent Benét!

MUSIC.—*Full, dramatic . . . brought to abrupt conclusion.*

SLAKE.—Would *you*, Mr. Latimer?

SHERRY.—I don't believe I understand what . . .

SLAKE.—(*Interrupting*) You have been contending that the two lovers described by Guiccardini . . . Antonio and Lucetta

. . . that their love was of a lesser intensity. You say that some people in love *could* withstand Alessandro's test of elemental hunger.

SHERRY.—I'm certain of it.

SLAKE.—(*Purring*) I wonder . . . I very much wonder, Mr. Latimer, just what people you mean?

SHERRY.—(*Vaguely*) Ohhhhh . . . dozens . . . there are many who could . . . most people. Or half of them at any rate.

SLAKE.—More coffee, Mr. Latimer? It's still warm.

SHERRY.—Yes . . . thank you.

SOUND.—*Pouring coffee.*

SLAKE.—Ummmmm . . . you chose to avoid a question I put to you a moment ago . . . but I'll try again . . . Would you?

SHERRY.—Why—why, I don't know, Mr. Slake. The . . . the premise is preposterous, Of course . . . such a thing couldn't happen now—

SLAKE.—(*Purring*) But suppose it could, Mr. Latimer, suppose it could? Would you be willing to wager—oh, your future professorship, say . . . that seems important to you . . . would you be willing to wager that against—uhhhh . . . $10,000 on the ability of you and one woman to endure Alessandro's test?

SHERRY.—Y-yes.

SLAKE.—You are wholly certain of that?

SHERRY.—(*Defiantly*) Yes! (*Pause*)

SLAKE.—(*Quietly*) Very well, then . . . suppose we try it.

SHERRY.—What!

SLAKE.—No, really, I'm not suggesting anything so impossible as it seems.

SHERRY.—Your suggestion would be fantastic . . . if it weren't so insolent, Mr. Slake.

SLAKE.—A man of my means often may venture what others would consider . . . I believe you used the word "fantastic."

281

SHERRY.—(*With amusement*) I'll be frank, Mr. Slake. If you'd made your insane offer to myself alone I'd have jumped at it. Ten thousand dollars . . . I should say! But to ask . . .

SLAKE.—(*Slyly*) Of course. Miss . . . Miss . . .

SHERRY.—(*Mechanically*) Vane.

SLAKE.—Miss Vane is to be considered. She could not bear it of course.

SHERRY.—Catherine would view your proposal as I do. It's absurd.

SLAKE.—Yes . . . Catherine . . . Then I may take it that you are turning down my offer.

SHERRY.—You may.

SLAKE.—(*Elaborate thought*) Catherine Vane. Not one of the Newport Vanes, I presume. There were Vanes in Philadelphia, but I really don't seem to . . .

SHERRY.—Oh, you wouldn't know. She's working in the secretary's office at Columbia.

SLAKE.—(*As he writes*) Catherine Vane—secretary's office, Columbia University.

SHERRY.—(*Angrily*) Say! What are you doing!?

SLAKE.—Just a notation, Mr. Latimer. I should like very much to find out what Miss Vane would say to this trifling experiment of mine . . . Brandy, Mr. Latimer?

MUSIC.—*In . . . fade briefly to*

SOUND.—*Telephone bell . . . receiver lifted.*

SHERRY.—English department.

CATHERINE.—(*Through filter*) You, Sherry?

SHERRY.—Oh, hello, Cathy. I was just going to call you about . . .

CATHERINE.—(*Interrupting*) I know about it, Sherry. John Slake was just here—and, oh, Sherry, isn't it *wonderful*?!

SHERRY.—Wonderful? Cathy . . . you didn't say you'd be *willing* to . . . (*break*) Stay in your office . . . I'll be right over.

MUSIC.—*Up briefly . . . out behind.*

CATHERINE.—Just *think*, Sherry. It's everything we want—everything now . . . and it's ours if we only have the little courage to take it.

SHERRY.—(*A snort*) A little courage!

CATHERINE.—Ten thousand dollars. It means we could marry at once. We could have a home and children safely, without fear, without having to spend every summer tutoring.

SHERRY.—But Cathy . . .

CATHERINE.—You may like the *idea* of "honorable" poverty—but you wouldn't like it as an actuality. (*Pause*)

SHERRY.—Just how did Slake describe the test to you?

CATHERINE.—(*Recalling the details*) Well . . . he said we would be in adjoining rooms on the third floor of his house. There would be a glass window between us, so that we could see each other but not talk together . . .

SHERRY.—I should imagine that touch would appeal to him.

CATHERINE.—(*Going on*) We would have three books . . . the Bible, the Koran, the Zend-Avesta . . . all the water we need . . . but no food.

SHERRY.—If I had only myself to consider I'd accept in a minute.

CATHERINE.—Just 7 days, Sherry.

SHERRY.—You don't know what 7 days of ceaseless hunger is. I don't. We can't even surmise.

CATHERINE.—A 7 days' fast . . . There are health cranks who undergo a fast of that length . . . voluntarily . . . seven times a year.

SHERRY.—We're not capable of self-hypnosis! I won't listen to you. Ten years in virtual bondage to Slake if either of us fails. Consider that.

CATHERINE.—My love for you is so great that the possibility of failure doesn't enter into my thinking. (*Pause*)

SHERRY.—Did . . . did Slake tell you of the climax of the 7-day fast?

CATHERINE.—(*Tight-lipped*) Yes . . . he did.

SHERRY.—After 7 days of starvation, 7 days of ceaseless hunger, we would be brought to the same room—and a piece of bread would be placed between us . . . Cathy! it's ridiculous . . . You didn't read the translation of the sixteenth century pamphlet by Guiccardini that I made for Slake . . .

CATHERINE.—Only part of it.

SHERRY.—You should read the chapter on the (*irony*) Merry Diversions of His Highness Prince Alessandro.

CATHERINE.—I don't see . . .

SHERRY.—Let me finish. In his court there were two lovers—Antonio and Lucetta—and their love for each other was court legend, it was so intense. Prince Alessandro challenged them to make precisely the same test Slake is asking us to try.

CATHERINE.—Were you discussing it with him . . . is that how he happened to make the proposal?

SHERRY.—Ummhmmm . . . but let me finish. (*On slow fade*) On the tenth day . . . theirs was a 10-day fast . . . Alessandro and two attendants went to one of the adjoining compartments . . . (*Out*)
(*Fade in. Echo chamber*)

MAN.—(*Off slightly*) The girl is not sleeping, Your Highness. Her eyes opened when I touched her . . . but there was no recognition in them . . . and I knew her well.

ALESSANDRO.—They are not so weak that they cannot move, I trust.

MAN.—Of that I cannot say, Your Highness.

ALESSANDRO.—The sight of this bread is quite likely to result in strange behavior, Antonio . . . Antonio . . .

ANTONIO.—Food. Please . . . for the love of God . . . food.

ALESSANDRO.—(*Unpleasantly*) Are you not eager to hold your beloved Lucetta in your arms, Antonio?

ANTONIO.—Food . . . Please, please give me food.

ALESSANDRO.—(*Smiling*) Renaldo, could it be that this unsightly piece of bread can have more attraction than the beautiful Lucetta to this most faithful of all the suitors in my court?

MAN.—It would seem so, Your Highness.

ALESSANDRO.—Raise the partition . . . and we shall see.

MAN.—(*Off*) Yes, Your Highness.

ALESSANDRO.—See, Antonio—see what I have in my hand? . . . Bread. You would like to have it, would you not?

ANTONIO.—Bread . . . bread . . . give it . . . I'm so hungry . . .

SOUND.—*Gears and clanking of chains . . . partition raised . . .*

ALESSANDRO.—Lucetta . . . there is bread on the floor for you.

LUCETTA.—(*Off*) Bread . . . bread for me . . . my bread . . .

ANTONIO.—(*Exertion*) My bread . . . it is mine . . . food . . . I am hungry.

LUCETTA.—(*Screams*) Mine! Mine!

SOUND.—*Grunts and screams of struggle.*

ANTONIO.—It's mine! I'm hungry! My bread . . . my food!

LUCETTA.—(*Screams*) Mine—mine! (*Her scream is cut off as Antonio closes his grip on her throat*)

MAN.—Your Highness! Each will strangle the other if we do not separate them!

ALESSANDRO.—(*Sardonically*) Most faithful in love! Yes . . . tear them apart. (*On fade*) What an unbeautiful picture. Hmmp . . . most faithful in love.
(*Out . . . fade in*)

SHERRY.—It took the combined strength of the three to tear Antonio and Lucetta from their death grips.

CATHERINE.—Sherwood Latimer! Do you think *we* would be like *that?* Sherry . . . I'm disappointed in you.

MUSIC.—*Appropriate transition . . . out.*

SHERRY.—What the deuce! Three days of this boredom, and I'm biting my wrist . . . just to watch the little white dints appear and fade away. Boredom . . . there's another "elemental" for John Slake to add to his list. Boredom and nervousness. (*Amused*) Slake would think that my 3 days without food has caused me to consider the flesh on my wrist as a possible future source of nourishment . . . No more of that, brother Latimer . . . you had better count the bluebirds on the wallpaper again . . . Wonder how Cathy is? She wouldn't count bluebirds on the wallpaper to pass away the time. Not Cathy. She would lose herself in reading . . . the sensible thing . . . Why don't *you* read, Fra Latimer? Better than counting bluebirds . . . those idiotic bluebirds . . . no occupation for a sane man. (*Suddenly quite serious . . . then, speaking aloud*) Sane man? (*His voice, reverberating in the bare room, startles him . . . causes him to sustain the sound of the last syllable in fascination . . . his thoughts continue*)

Ohhhhh! Even if I should doubt my own sanity, there's Catherine. Catherine is sane . . . that's a verity . . . even if my sanity is slightly suspect for allowing her to undergo this ridiculous test. Yes, Catherine Vane is sane, sane . . . Catherine Vane is sane, is sane. (*He speaks the foolish rhyme aloud . . . and again is startled by his voice*) Catherine Vane is sane, is sa—(*He stops short . . . snorts ruefully*) Three days and I'm doing that. I'd better count my wallpaper birds again . . . maybe there'll be 85 if I count again . . . 83 . . . Three days without food, and my head's rattling with silly jingles . . . and it isn't 3 days yet. It has been 2½ days. Daylight fading. In a few minutes the lights will be turned on—and Slake will come in. Then it will be *exactly* 2½ days . . . There! The lights. Two and a-half days. Cathy will be expecting to see me at the window . . . (*exertion*) so I'll just . . . (*he sinks back momentarily*) I . . . I'm getting a little weak. (*Exertion*) There.

SOUND.—*Footfalls . . . slowly across bare wooden floor.*

SHERRY.—Did too much pacing about these first days. From now on I'll conserve my strength.

SOUND.—*Walking stops.*

SHERRY.—Just as I thought . . . she's lost herself in reading. Maybe I shouldn't break her concentration . . . She closed her eyes!

SOUND.—*Tapping . . . fingernail on glass pane.*

SHERRY.—(*He forms words with his mouth . . . half utters them*) Good . . . evening . . . darling. (*To self*) That smile. She's just the same . . . or is she just a little paler? Yes . . .

she is . . . just a *little* paler . . . (*Forms words, half speaks*) I? I'm . . . fine . . . f-i-n-e. (*Aloud*) Don't get up! (*Forming words*) Don't get up. Save . . . your . . . strength. (*To self*) This is absurd . . . pantomiming with Catherine through a pane of glass. She would get up . . . just to show me she's all right. (*Forming words*) Yes . . . dear . . . I can . . . see . . . (*To self*) Pointing out words in the Bible! What a maddening way we have to converse, when we have so much to say to each other . . . Yes, yes, I see. Good . . . evening . . . dear . . . Her smile is weak. I'll bet mine is weaker. I mustn't let it be . . . (*Half aloud*) Wait.

SOUND.—*Footfalls on floor.*

SHERRY.—(*Continues to self, over sound*) I marked the pages in my Bible . . . some things I want to show Cathy . . . Here . . .

SOUND.—*Riffling book pages.*

SHERRY.—I marked the places . . . I'm sure I did . . . Yes . . . yes . . . here. (*Half aloud*) Look, dearest . . . this . . . (*He stops*) Eyes closed . . . her eyes are closed again.

SOUND.—*Tapping pane with finger.*

SHERRY.—That smile. How like her. Oh, Lord, if only I could *get* to her . . . just for a kiss . . . a few words . . . (*Forming words*) Look, dearest . . . She's reading . . . (*On fade*) The . . . lions . . . do . . . lack . . . and . . . suffer . . . hunger . . .
(*Out . . . fade in*)

CATHERINE.—The lions do lack and suffer hunger. (*Forming words*) Yes, Sherry . . . we do . . . we lions. (*To self, with vocal moue*) We . . . lions. (*Passionately, to self*) Oh, Sherry, Sherry . . . it's not my hunger, it's *your* hunger that tortures me. If only I could tell you how much stronger my love is . . . than this gnawing hunger . . .

SOUND.—*Riffling pages of book.*

CATHERINE.—Where is that sentence I was going to point out to him? . . . He's waiting . . . he's relying on me to transmit just a hint of what's in my heart . . . through this glass barrier . . . Here. (*Half aloud*) This, Sherry . . . read this . . . (*fading*) Happy shalt thou be, and it shall be well with thee . . .
(*Out . . . fade in*)

SHERRY.—(*Reading slowly*) Happy shalt thou be, and it shall be well with thee . . . Yes . . . I see . . . What's that she's underscoring with her thumbnail?

MUSIC.—*Start Slake theme softly.*

SHERRY.—She means that as a signature. (*Reading*) Thy wife.

SOUND.—*Kissing finger tips lightly . . . blowing gently . . .*

SOUND.—*Dialogue and sound in following scene resounds as in bare room . . . key in lock . . . away . . .*

SHERRY.—(*Forming words*) Slake's coming, dearest . . . Slake . . . Yes . . . yes . . . after he's gone.

SOUND.—*Door opened . . . away . . .*

SLAKE.—(*Off*) Good evening, Mr. Latimer.

SHERRY.—(*Stiffly*) Good evening, Mr. Slake.

SLAKE.—Everything perfectly all right, I suppose, Mr. Latimer?

SHERRY.—Everything entirely satisfactory, Mr. Slake.

SLAKE.—How charming! You are admirable guests indeed, Mr. Latimer . . . you and Miss Vane. You make so little demand on one's hospitality.

SHERRY.—I . . . I'm glad you find us so.

SLAKE.—Errrrr . . . aren't you concealing something behind your back, Mr. Latimer?

SHERRY.—Eh? Oh, yes . . . the Bible . . . (*lamely*) . . . I've been reading.

SLAKE.—Yes . . . reading. It must pass the time. You *do* find time heavy on your hands, do you not, Mr. Latimer?

SHERRY.—I have been . . .

SLAKE.—(*Interrupting*) May I have the book?

SHERRY.—As a matter of fact, Miss Vane and I have contrived a way to communicate . . . using the book to . . .

SLAKE.—(*Abruptly*) The book, Mr. Latimer . . . may I have it? . . . Thank you . . . I didn't overlook the possibility that you might converse by pointing to words and phrases in the books I have given you. It's quite all right. I'm not Alessandro.

SHERRY.—No . . . you're not.

SLAKE.—I imagine you find that means of communication quite lacking in spontaneity and . . . uhhh . . . in warmth. (*Pause*) Ummmmm . . . Well! what is this, Mr. Latimer?

SHERRY.—It was just nervousness. It was done unconsciously . . . You do mean the . . .

SLAKE.—(*Picking it up*) Yes . . . I do mean the teeth marks on the leather binding. That *is* something I hadn't reckoned with.

SHERRY.—(*Stiffly*) I certainly hadn't considered . . . eating a leather bookbinding.

SLAKE.—(*Purrs*) Of course. I'm sure you didn't . . . but you wouldn't mind if I tear the leather cover from this volume. (*Slight exertion*)

SOUND.—*Leather cover torn from book.*

SLAKE.—A shame—but then you wouldn't want to eat dyed leather . . . no matter *how* hungry you get. It would be terribly unpalatable.

SHERRY.—As I said . . . I hadn't considered doing it.

SLAKE.—Then I have helped you—by removing the temptation.

SHERRY.—(*Murmuring*) Thoughtful of you.

SLAKE.—I'll bid you goodnight now, Mr. Latimer. Is there any message I may carry to Miss Vane for you?

SHERRY.—No . . . no message.

SLAKE.—It would be simpler than seeking out words and phrases in your books to point out to her. But just as you say. (*Going away*) I'll drop in on you tomorrow morning at the usual time, Mr. Latimer.

SOUND.—*Door opens.*

SLAKE.—(*Off*) Good night.

SHERRY.—Good night.

SOUND.—*Door closes . . . echo out.*

MUSIC.—*Slow, weary, pulsating softly behind.*

289

SHERRY.—Slake . . . John Slake—Oh! why did I listen to him . . . let him persuade me . . . to do this. Elementals . . . how sure he is of his elementals . . . Fear . . . hate . . . hunger. Yes, he has all three on his side now . . . but we have something that can laugh at the three, Cathy. We'll beat him. We'll erase that smug smile of his. We'll win, Cathy. We'll win . . . (*Then, a trifle desperately*) We have to!

MUSIC.—*Up . . . hold for transition . . . slow clock motif . . . sustain behind.*

SOUND.—*Door opens . . . away.*

SLAKE.—Good morning. Everything perfectly all right, I suppose, Mr. Latimer?

SHERRY.—Everything entirely satisfactory, Mr. Slake.

MUSIC.—*Up briefly . . . fade briefly for*

SLAKE.—Good evening, Miss Vane. Everything perfectly all right, I suppose?

CATHERINE.—Perfectly, Mr. Slake.

MUSIC.—*Up briefly . . . sustain behind.*

SLAKE.—Good morning, Mr. Latimer. Everything perfectly all right, I suppose?

SHERRY.—(*Noticeably weakened*) Everything . . . entirely . . . satisfactory.

MUSIC.—*Up and out.*

SOUND.—*Tapping on glass pane . . . repeated.*

SHERRY.—Cathy . . . (*Alarm*) Cathy! (*Aloud*) Cathy! (*Then, rapidly to self*) She's asleep! It can't be anything else! She *is* asleep . . . I shouldn't waken her—but if she isn't asleep . . . ? She must be . . . she must be . . . What else could . . . (*In sudden great fear he shouts as he pounds*) Cathy! Cathy, darling!

SOUND.—*Frantic pounding fists on glass . . . stops suddenly.*

SHERRY.—(*With great relief*) Ohhhh . . . she was just asleep . . . and I've wakened her . . . That smile . . . brave . . . brave. (*Forming words*) Don't . . . get . . . up. I . . .

just . . . wanted to . . . say . . . I . . . love . . . you.
(*To self*) And I do . . . I do . . . so much. How could I
let her go through this! (*Forming words*) I'm all right . . .
fine. Don't worry about me. Don't *worry* . . . Yes—yes,
good evening, dearest. (*To self*) I must get away from the
panel, or she'll try to get up and come over to me. (*Intensely,
tearfully, to self*) Oh, Cathy, Cathy . . . why did I let you
go through this? Why! I never knew that hunger could be
like this.

And I love her—I *love* her—and I let her do this crazy thing.
I'm mud! I'm a thing made of mud who happens to be wearing clothes! No man with—with the will of a vertebrate
animal would let the one he loves go through torture like
this. Why did I? What happened to me? How did this come
about?! I must have been mad! I—I can't even remember
what led me to enter this wild, fantastic agreement. I can't
remember. Five days without food. Five days with . . .
(*break*) *Is* it 5 days? Oh, God—it could be 4! I don't remember! I can't remember. It could be 4 days. (*Trying to get a
grip on himself*) No . . . I'm sure . . . it's 5 . . . 5 days.
Yes, 5 days . . . (*pitifully*) . . . but I could be wrong. If
it's 4 . . . I shall ask Slake when he comes in . . . and if it
had been only 4 days . . . (*rehearsing it*) then I will tell
him that, because I fear the effect this starvation will have
on Cathy, that I am giving up the contest, that I am completely resigned to serving him for the 10 years . . . (*Hol-
lowly*) Ten years. He couldn't compel me to keep that
promise. It would have to be taken to court and he wouldn't
dare do that—he would have to tell of this . . . this test.
He wouldn't . . . (*break*) Those contracts . . . all the
terrible meanings hidden away under the drift of ordinary
legal phrases. Subtle, too . . . very binding. In considera-
tion of a task to be performed, Sherwood Latimer and
Catherine Vane are to receive a sum of $10,000. If the task
is not performed . . . (*Distraught*) He would lie ! And no
one would believe us . . . it would seem fantastic! (*Suddenly . . . frantically*) But there's nothing else to do! I
can't stand it . . . knowing how Cathy is suffering! I'll
serve my 10 years! To the devil with my career! I'll have
Cathy! (*Pitifully*) Oh, Cathy . . . Cathy!

MUSIC.—*Short transition . . . out behind . . . echo.*

SOUND.—*Key in lock . . . door opened . . . off.*

SLAKE.—(*Off*) Good evening, Mr. Latimer.

SHERRY.—(*Struggling to feet*) Good evening.

SLAKE—(*Coming in*) You needn't stand if you are weak, Mr. Latimer. (*Pause*) Everything perfectly all right, I suppose? (*Pause*) I wished for you at dinner this evening . . . I really wished for you. The bisque had a trifle too much whipped cream for my personal taste, but the fish was perfection . . . baked bluefish, you know. And the roast . . .

SHERRY.—Stop!

SLAKE.—(*He's smiling*) Dear, dear, I forgot. My apologies . . . So it has really begun to touch you—my elemental.

SHERRY.—(*Trying to disguise his question*) Not more than I had expected on the fifth day. (*Pause*) This is the fifth day isn't it?

SLAKE.—Don't you *know*, Mr. Latimer?

SHERRY.—Yes—I do. This *is* the fifth day. (*Pause*) I am right.

SLAKE.—Perhaps—though it may be only the fourth.

SHERRY.—(*Losing control*) Tell me, you devil! Tell me just that! (*Pause . . . then, under control*) I . . . I'm afraid we shall have to withdraw from the contest, Mr. Slake.

SLAKE.—Really? When only a few more hours would have brought us to the most interesting part?

SHERRY.—Yes.

SLAKE.—May I ask why?

SHERRY.—Catherine.

SLAKE.—I presume you have discussed this matter through the partition in your painfully slow way.

SHERRY.—Miss Vane doesn't know of my decision. She's brave . . . she'd never give up . . . but I can't allow her to be tortured this way.

SLAKE.—According to our contract, Mr. Latimer, both must agree to the withdrawal. One can't speak for the other.

SHERRY.—(*In a rage*) Damn our agreement! And you—and you—and you—you devil from hell!

292

SOUND.—*Scuffling of feet . . . a slap . . . man falling to floor . . . footfalls going away . . .*

SLAKE.—(*Going away*) I will ask Miss Vane how she feels about your decision.

SOUND.—*Door opens . . . away.*

SLAKE.—(*Off*) What an exhibition of temper you gave, Mr. Latimer. (*Fading*) What a pitiful exhibition . . . (*Out . . . fading in*)

SLAKE.—Miss Vane. Miss Vane!

CATHERINE.—(*Weakly*) Yes? . . . I was not asleep. Everything is perfectly satisfactory . . . perfectly.

SLAKE.—A little matter, Miss Vane. Mr. Latimer is concerned over your condition and has asked me to inform you that he will agree to withdraw . . . if you insist.

CATHERINE.—(*Slowly*) Everything . . . is perfectly satisfactory.

MUSIC.—*In with impact . . . fade slowly on weary, clock motif.*

SHERRY.—(*Weakly*) One more day . . . or two at the very most . . . . I wish I could be sure . . . if it's two . . . (*He stops*) Oh, Cathy . . . if you could be spared this . . . it's like the pressure of a dull knife against the pit of my stomach. It must be worse for Cathy . . . it must be. She's thinking of me . . . she thinks of what the 10 years might do to me. Oh, Cathy . . . don't think of that. It's all right. I'll have you. And she'd die before she would let me know that she suffered. I let her do this! I did! I'll spend the rest of my life making it up to her . . . But we'll win . . . we'll win . . . and our future together will be assured. This is the sixth day . . . just one more . . . If I'm right . . . if this *is* the sixth day . . . I'm so weak . . . (*Wryly*) He who sleeps dines, the French say. I'll see. I'll see . . . and tomorrow when I wake . . . If I sleep . . . If I sleep . . .

MUSIC.—*Soft, melodic, becoming gradually strange, unreal . . . The music reverberates in echo chamber . . . softly behind.*

SHERRY.—I'm not asleep . . . but I feel . . . different . . . and it isn't a dream . . . because I'd not even think it might be a dream . . . if it were a dream. It isn't really a dream . . . because I know it's a dream . . .

293

CATHERINE.—Then it is a dream.

SHERRY.—(*Not too surprised*) Cathy . . . You see, Cathy, it isn't a dream . . . because I can stop it whenever I want to . . . whenever I want to.

CATHERINE.—I'm so hungry, Sherry . . . sooooo hungry.

SHERRY.—You needn't be. This is my dream. And I can do in it whatever I choose. Only it isn't really a dream, because I can *control* everything . . . We will go to a restaurant.

CATHERINE.—Yes—let's.

SHERRY.—This *is* a restaurant. Here's the waiter. Tell him what you would like.

SLAKE.—(*Coming in*) Everything perfectly all right, I suppose, Mr. Latimer.

SHERRY.—Everything entirely satisfactory, waiter.

CATHERINE.—(*Whisper*) That isn't the waiter, Sherr—that's Mr. Slake.

SHERRY.—(*Giggles fatuously*) In my dream he is the waiter. I am not really asleep, so things are as I want them to be. (*Chuckles*) One of the wealthiest men in the world, Cathy— our waiter.

SLAKE.—Don't you know me, Mr. Latimer?

SHERRY.—You were John Slake—but now you are our waiter.

ALESSANDRO.—Non sai' dove sei, Antonio?

SHERRY.—Certainly. We're in your restaurant . . . and my name is not Antonio. Tell His Highness my name, Catherine. (*Alarm*) Catherine!

SOUND.—*Pounding on pane of glass.*

SHERRY.—(*Frantically*) Catherine! Catherine!

ALESSANDRO.—Lei nonti sente, Antonio.

SHERRY.—She *can* hear me!

ALESSANDRO.—Non e possible!

SHERRY.—It's not impossible. She's right here. This is a dream. I know it's a dream . . . and I can do in it whatever I choose . . . and so can Lucetta.

ALESSANDRO.—A spetta un momento . . .

SHERRY.—(*Translating quickly*) In just a moment . . .

ALESSANDRO.—Cerchero muevere la finestra . . .

SHERRY.—(*Translating*) I will have the glass partition removed.

ALESSANDRO.—Allora vendremo quanto e grande questo tuo amore!

SHERRY.—(*Translating*) Then we shall see how great is this love of yours.

ALESSANDRO.—Vendremo come si paragona un competizione con mie forze elementari!

SHERRY.—(*Translating*) *We shall see how it fares in competition with my elementals.* (*Chuckles*) Yes, we shall—we shall. Lucetta and I will prove you wrong, Your Highness.

SLAKE.—You translated the pamphlet for me . . . you know the ending of this tale.

SHERRY.—You are confused. *Guiccardini* wrote of your Merry Diversions. *I* am Antonio . . . No—I am confused also. *I* am Sherwood Latimer. You are . . .

SLAKE.—(*Picking it up*) Prince Alessandro.

SHERRY.—No—no . . . You're not going to muddle me again. You are John Slake.

ALESSANDRO.—Abasta . . .

SHERRY.—(*Translating rapidly*) Enough of this . . .

ALESSANDRO.—(*Going away*) C'ai fame!

SHERRY.— . . . You are hungry.

ALESSANDRO.—Guarde per la finestra.

SHERRY.—How *can* I look through the partition?

SLAKE.—(*Interrupting*) See Lucetta's hungry eyes.

SHERRY.—That is not Lucetta—that is Cathy. My Cathy . . . and *her* eyes are not hungry.

SLAKE.—She won't recognize you when I put the bread between you.

SHERRY.—Again you're wrong. This is my dream. Nothing happens unless I want it to happen.

SLAKE.—(*Away*) Raise the partition!

MUSIC.—*Accelerates in tempo, heightened dramatically, with sound.*

SOUND.—*Gears and clanking of chains.*

SHERRY.—Cathy! you do know me, don't you? Say you do.

CATHERINE.—Of course I do, my silly Sherry. Here comes the waiter again with our order. I'm so hungry, Sherry darling . . . so hungry . . .

SLAKE.—(*Coming in*) You ordered . . . uhhh . . . the bread, I believe.

SHERRY.—No, you fool—we ordered steaks! Steaks!

SLAKE.—Yes, sir—here's your bread.

SHERRY.—But I tell you . . .

CATHERINE.—(*In monotone*) I'll take the bread, I'll take the bread. You may have the steak when it comes, all the steak—all the steak.

SHERRY.—(*Fiercely*) Give me the bread! I'll eat the bread!

SLAKE.—(*Chuckles softly in background*)

CATHERINE.—(*Whining piteously*) Sherry! Give me half . . . give me half . . . Sher-ry . . . I'm hun-gry . . . so hungry. (*Her voice is now high-pitched, piercing*)

SHERRY.—It's mine . . . the bread is mine!

CATHERINE.—(*Whine mounts*)

MUSIC.—*Quick, dramatic progression of chords . . . the other voices are stilled.*

SHERRY.—It's mine! The bread is mine! The bread is . . . (*Break . . . pause . . . he gasps as he sinks back on couch . . . long pause*).
What—what a horrible dream! I thought I was in control. I was sure I was in control . . . but when I saw the bread . . . Oh, Cathy! I took the bread from you . . . I took the bread from Cathy! (*Tearfully*) Oh, Cathy, Cathy . . .

there won't be enough hours in a lifetime to make it up to you for all this torture I've let you endure.

(*A sudden painful thought*) It was a dream. It couldn't have been that . . . (*Confusion*) Oh, reality and thoughts are so tangled up together! . . . No—that wasn't the test. In the test my head will be clear . . . But what if I'm not in control of my behavior . . . what if I do as I did in that fantasm . . . that nightmarish terror! Oh, Cathy . . . give me strength!

MUSIC.—*Transition with clock motif . . . out behind.*

SOUND.—*Door opened . . . closed . . . away.*

SLAKE.—Well?

WARREN.—(*Off*) I'm going to get the broth.

SLAKE.—(*Angrily*) Don't walk away from me! (*Pause*)

WARREN.—(*In*) Well?

SLAKE.—What is their condition?

WARREN.—The man's a little stronger . . . but neither of 'em can walk.

SLAKE.—Can they talk?

WARREN.—If you can call makin' sounds talkin', the man can.

SLAKE.—Very well . . . you needn't bother to bring them broth, however. I have this to give them.

WARREN.—Bread!? But they haven't eaten anything for a week —you don't want to give 'em solid food.

SLAKE.—(*Unpleasantly*) When the test is completed they will be in your tender care, Miss Warren.

SOUND.—*Door opens.*

SLAKE.—Would you like to watch this?

WARREN.—(*Slightly off*) No . . . Yes, yes, I would. I might be needed.

SLAKE.—Come in, then . . . Yes, you might be needed.

SOUND.—*Door closes.*

SHERRY.—(*Off*) Food.

SLAKE.—Yes . . . you might be needed. In a previous test of this order, which took place in the sixteenth century, it was necessary for three strong men to tear the two lovers apart when bread was placed between them. They were locked in a death struggle . . . over a piece of bread probably not as large as this.

WARREN.—I don't like this.

SLAKE.—I believe your salary is sufficiently large enough to compensate for that.

WARREN.—If word of this ever got to the ears of the authorities . . .

SLAKE.—(*Interrupting*) It won't . . . will it, Warren?

WARREN.—No—no, sir. *Pause* . . . *off* No—no, sir.

SHERRY.—(*To self*) Food . . . Why am I so hungry?

SLAKE.—(*Slightly away*) Are you awake, Mr. Latimer?

SHERRY.—(*Aloud*) Food, please, food . . . (*To self*) That voice. I hate that voice.

SLAKE.—Yes, food—in just a moment, Mr. Latimer.

SHERRY.—(*To self* . . . *slavering*) I hate that voice? Who's voice is it?

SLAKE.—Don't you know me, Mr. Latimer?

SHERRY.—Who's he? He said Latimer—that's my name. (*Aloud*) Food.

SLAKE.—There's food on the floor. (*Pause*) There's food on the floor.

SHERRY.—Food . . . Where? He said there's food on the . . . (*Stops*) I . . . I'm weak . . . so weak. If I can prop myself up on one arm . . . that voice said there's food on the floor . . .

WARREN.—(*Off*) The girl hasn't moved.

SHERRY.—Girl? (*Exertion*) I'll get the food before those voices take it . . . If I can slide off this—this bed . . . I see it . . . bread . . . on the floor . . . just like the voice said. It's my bread . . . I'll . . . (*Stops* . . . *then fiercely*) Who's she? Woman . . . She's looking at my bread—*my* bread.

SLAKE.—(*Off*) Don't they remind you of starving animals, Warren?

SHERRY.—She's looking at me. Who is she? (*Exertion*) I'll get it before she can . . . slide down off this couch . . .

SOUND.—*Inert body slumping easily to floor.*

SHERRY.—I can get it—my bread . . . I . . . can . . . touch it . . . It's mine.

CATHERINE.—(*Off slightly . . . in weak sibillant whisper*) Sherwood. Sher-wood.

SHERRY.—That's *my* name—my name is Sherwood. She knows my name—but she won't get the bread.

CATHERINE.—Sherry! Oh, Sherry, dear!

SHERRY.—(*Sucks in saliva wolfishly*)

CATHERINE.—Sherry, dear . . . dear Sherry . . . I'm so *hungry* . . . I'm so hun-gry!

SHERRY.—(*Suddenly rational, albeit weak*) Catherine! Catherine! That's my Catherine! She's—she's hungry! I must feed her. She's hungry.

MUSIC.—*Softly behind.*

SOUND.—*Man crawling over bare wooden floor.*

CATHERINE.—(*In . . . softly*) Dear Sherry.

SHERRY.—Bread. Eat it. Bread—you eat.

CATHERINE.—No. You first—you're *hungrier.*

SLAKE.—(*Coming in . . . enraged*) Oh, pick the bread up, you babies—do you think I'm going to feed you? (*Pause*) Well, Warren, what's so funny?

WARREN.—Nothing, sir . . . It may take a bit of tuggin' to get them apart like you said, Mr. Slake—but that don't look like a death struggle to me . . . nothing like it.

MUSIC.—*Triumphant . . . up to conclusion.*

ANNOUNCER.—You have just heard the first presentation in the new NBC dramatic series, Authors' Playhouse. Tonight's story was Stephen Vincent Benét's "Elementals," especially

299

dramatized for Authors' Playhouse by Charles Gussman. Fern Persons was heard as Catherine Vane, John Hodiak as Sherwood Latimer, Arthur Kohl as John Slake, Michael Romano as Prince Alessandro, Nelson Olmsted as Antonio, Laurette Fillbrandt as Lucetta, Katherine Card as Miss Warren, and Bob Jellison as Renaldo.

The original musical score was written and directed by Rex Maupin.

Next week, a gripping story of the Southern swamplands by an American master of suspense and narrative power—"Snake Doctor"—by Irvin S. Cobb.

MUSIC.—*Theme . . . up and out.*

ANNOUNCER.—Authors' Playhouse has come to you from our Chicago studios. This is the National Broadcasting Company.

MUSIC.—*Chimes.*

Vic and Sade

MUSIC.—*Theme.*
   (*Opening and commercial credits*)

ANNOUNCER.—Well, sir, it's almost 10 o'clock at night as our scene opens now, and here in the living room of the small house, halfway up in the next block, we find Mrs. Victor Gook and her Uncle Fletcher. Uncle Fletcher is speaking earnestly. Listen.

FLETCHER.—A 4-foot length of railroad track makes a fine door stop. An' I know where I can lay my *hands* on a 4-foot length of railroad track. Right down there at the C & A shops.

SADE.—(*Skeptical*) Wouldn't it be a terrible *heavy* thing?

FLETCHER.—Yes. Yes, it would. Gross around . . . well, let's see . . . railroad track runs a hundred an' ten pounds to the foot now-days. Usta be only 80 pounds to the foot when I was straw boss on the section gang there in Belvidere. But now they roll 'em a hundred an' ten pounds to the foot. A 4-foot length would be four times a hundred an' ten or . . . (*Brief pause while he calculates*) . . .

SADE AND FLETCHER.—Four hundred an' forty.

FLETCHER.—Yeah . . . four hundred an' forty pounds.

SADE.—(*Giggles*) My stars!

FLETCHER.—*Heavy*, all right. But you *want* a heavy door stop. A four hundred an' forty pound door stop would hold a door *open* or hold a door *shut*.

SADE.—(*Giggles*) *I'll* say it would.

FLETCHER.—Think Mis' Keller's *like* a door stop for her birthday?

SADE.—I . . . don't think she could *handle* all that weight.

FLETCHER.—Husky *woman*, Mis' Keller. Tips the scales at a hundred an' sixty-six. All beef.

SADE.—I *know*—but rasslin' four hundred an' forty pounds around . . .

FLETCHER.—Ya don't hafta pick a door stop *up*, ya know, Sadie. You just leave it on your front porch. Kick it with your *foot* when ya wanta move it.

SADE.—(*Giggles*) *I* wouldn't wanta kick a big hunk of iron with my foot that weighed a quarter of a ton.

FLETCHER.—Is four hundred an' forty pounds a quarter of a ton?

SADE.—(*Giggles*) Haven't the slightest idea. *Sounds* like it might be, though.

FLETCHER.—(*Judiciously*) Well, let's see . . . *I* can cipher that out. There's 2,000 pounds in a ton. Half a ton would be 1,000 pounds. Quarter of a ton would be half of that, or 500 pounds. Darn close *to* it, all right.

SADE.—(*Giggles*) Person might as well waltz up to the Peoples' *Bank* Building an' give it a kick.

FLETCHER.—(*Thoughtfully*) Uh-huh. Well, it was just a *notion*. Mis' Keller could *use* a good door stop, though.

SADE.—Ah . . . another thing . . . Would a chunk of railroad track be very *ornamental* on the front porch?

FLETCHER.—(*Confidently*) Oh, *sure*.

SADE.—(*Dubious*) Um.

FLETCHER.—Four-foot length of railroad track look *very* nice on the porch.

SADE.—Um.

FLETCHER.—Tell ya something *else* I thought of. A *shoe* scraper.

SADE.—(*Dubious*) Yes . . . uh-huh.

FLETCHER.—You take a good shoe scraper . . . it looks attractive screwed onto your back-porch steps, an' it's a mighty, mighty hand . . .

SADE.—One of my *boys* must of got home. Heard the kitchen door open.

FLETCHER.—Fine.

SADE.—(*Calls*) You, Willie?

302

RUSH.—(*In kitchen*) Both of us.

SADE.—(*To Fletcher*) *Well* . . . everybody puts in an appearance simultaneous.

FLETCHER.—Fine.

SADE.—(*Raises voice*) We got lovely *company*.

VIC.—(*Approaching*) Not Addison Sweeney, the noted high diver?

SADE.—(*Raises voice*) Uncle *Fletcher's* here with me.

VIC AND RUSH.—(*Approaching*) Hi.

FLETCHER.—(*To Sade*) They been to the moving picture show, likely.

SADE.—Vic's been to lodge meeting. Rush went down to the Y.M.C.A., where the fat men play handball. (*In low, amused tones, without malice*) *Told* you that three *times*.

FLETCHER.—Fine.

RUSH.—(*Coming up*) Greetings, Uncle Fletcher.

FLETCHER.—Hellow, Rush.

VIC.—(*Coming up*) Essex woppum, Uncle Fletcher. Tizzy feeker yowley veep.

FLETCHER.—Uh-huh. (*Chuckles*) Dropped in on Sadie here a while ago only intending' to stay 5 minutes an' been hangin' around for better'n an hour.

SADE.—I was real glad you did. Got to feelin' real lonesome.

FLETCHER.—Fine.

VIC.—Yashum tunk, Uncle Fletcher.

FLETCHER.—Uh-huh.

VIC.—(*Cordially*) Jeeler yushman vupple girp.

FLETCHER.—Yes, indeed.

VIC.—(*Cordially*) Howyah booger toko sleeb. Patch hokish uddle yickalorum goshly rex doppo . . .

SADE.—(*Low tones, giggles*) Oh, *stop* that.

VIC.—(*Innocently*) Beg pardon?

303

SADE.—(*Low tones, giggling*) It's *mean* to tease a person.

VIC.—(*Innocently*) I'm not teasing anybody. I'm just . . .

SADE.—Well, *quit* it. (*Louder*) Uncle Fletcher an' me been havin' a lovely chat.

VIC.—Really?

SADE.—Tomorrow's his landlady's birthday, an' he's tryin' to think of a present to give her.

FLETCHER.—How's that, Sadie?

SADE.—I was telling Vic about tomorrow bein' Mis' Keller's birthday.

FLETCHER.—*Yes*, Vic. My landlady's *birthday* tomorrow.

VIC.—How old will she be?

FLETCHER.—Fine. (*Chuckles*) *My* idea was a fancy *door* stop, but Sadie here pretty much threw cold *water* on it.

SADE.—(*Giggles*) So *heavy*. He wanted to get a big hunk of railroad track from the C & A shops. Four feet long. Weight almost 500 pounds.

VIC.—Five hundred pounds of steel outa hold a door open in good shape.

SADE.—Golly, *yes*. How's a person even get it *home* from the G & A shops?

VIC.—Put it in their vest pocket.

FLETCHER.—Moving picture show pretty good, was it, Rush?

RUSH.—I never went. Been down at the Y.M.C.A. watchin' the fat men play handball.

FLETCHER.—Uh-huh,—fine.

RUSH.—(*To his folks*) Pretty fast handball game, *too*, this evening. Mr. Cunningham an' Mr. Morris almost had a fight. I was in the society of Blue-tooth Johnson, Leland Richards, an' Smelly Clark, an' the four of us . . .

FLETCHER.—How would a *shoe* scraper be for Mis' Keller's birthday present, Sadie? (*Aside*) Excuse me for interruptin', Vic.

304

Vic.—(*Generously*) Perfectly all right.

Rush.—(*Low tones, chuckling*) *I* was the party *talkin'*.

Fletcher.—(*To Vic*) I was tellin' Sadie before you got here I was turnin' a *shoe* scraper over in my mind.

Vic.—Uh-huh.

Fletcher.—Shoe scraper screwed on your back-porch steps is a good *lookin'* contraption an' a *useful* contraption. Fella can pick one up at the hardware store for three . . . four dollars that'll last a lifetime. I saw some the other day with fancy *grill*work. Iron *angels* an' junk flyin' around, ya know. (*Importantly*) *Or* . . . if ya don't want *angels* an' junk . . . they got 'em with your *initial*. (*Quotes some initials at random*) G, W, K, P, S . . . *any* of them initials you can get.

Vic.—(*A few suggestions*) M, F, Y, C, J.

Fletcher.—Sure. (*A few more*) B, Q, L, E, S.

Rush.—(*Still more*) A, T, X, R, M, N, V, R . . .

Sade.—(*Giggles*) Oh, *stop* that.

Fletcher.—Yeah—*any* of them initials you can get. Mis' Keller's initials are G. L. K. Geraldine Laura Keller. I expect, though, if ya want all *three* initials on your shoe scraper, it'll run ya more money. Prob'ly hafta be made up special.

Vic, Sade, and Rush.—Um.

Fletcher.—(*Reminiscently*) A half-wit I usta know back in Belvidere bought a shoe scraper for somebody's birthday one time. Arnie Gupples. Don't s'pose you ever *knew* Arnie Gupples, Vic?

Vic.—*Name's* not familiar.

Fletcher.—Sadie?

Sade.—Uh-uh.

Fletcher.—Arnie Gupples worked in a *shoe* store there in Belvidere years ago. *I've* bought shoes off'n Arnie. Far as that goes, I could name you off a *dozen* parties that bought shoes off'n Arnie. Hey, Sadie, your cousin Albert *Feeber* bought shoes off'n Arnie Gupples.

305

SADE.—Really?

FLETCHER.—(*Stoutly*) Your cousin Albert *Feeber* bought shoes off'n Arnie Gupples.

SADE.—Um.

FLETCHER.—I was with him when he *did* it. He said, "Rush, wherebouts in this town's a good place a man can buy a pair of shoes?" I took him over to the store where Arnie worked. Arnie sold him a pair of oxblood low-cuts for three dollars an' a quarter.

SADE.—(*Impressed*) *Well.*

FLETCHER.—Yes, sir, your cousin Albert Feeber.

SADE.—Um.

FLETCHER.—What I was gonna say about Arnie Gupples an' the shoe scraper, though, was he bought this shoe scraper for one of the Yowtch sisters, there in Belvidere, he was engaged to. *Gwendolyn* Yowtch. *Peaked* girl. Wouldn't weigh 70 pounds after the biggest supper she ever ate. Put on flesh in *later* years, though. *Recall* any of the Yowtch sisters, Sadie?

SADE.—I don't believe I knew anybody in Belvidere, Uncle Fletcher.

FLETCHER.—Fine. Well, there was Gwendolyn, Dorothy, Hazel, an' May. Dorothy an' Hazel married brothers. Ed an' Virgil Hashly. May died. *I* knew the whold *outfit.*

SADE.—Um.

FLETCHER.—(*Brief pause*) What was I talkin' about?

SADE.—(*Who's forgotten*) Ah . . . weren't you sayin' . . .

FLETCHER.—No. (*Thoughtfully*) It was something else.

RUSH.—The fella that give his girl a shoe scraper for her birth . . .

FLETCHER.—*Yeah.* Arnie *Gupples.* You're a good boy, Rush.

RUSH.—(*Little chuckle*) Um.

FLETCHER.—Arnie Gupples give Gwendolyn Yowtch this fancy shoe scraper for her birthday. They were engaged to be married at the time. Well, sir, first shot outa the box Gwendolyn went to scrape some mud off her shoes with that shoe scraper, twisted her ankle, had to have the doctor, got mad, an' give Arnie the mitten. Two months afterwards she married Art Hungle an' moved to North Dakota. Arnie felt so bad he quit his job at the shoe store. I heard afterwards he finally married a rich woman that made him learn to play on the cornet.

Vic, Sade, and Rush.—Um.

Fletcher.—(*Thoughtfully*) Stuff happens, don't it?

Vic, Sade, and Rush.—Um.

Fletcher.—(*Thoughtfully*) Way the world *goes*, I guess.

Vic, Sade, and Rush.—Um.

Rush.—Smelly Clark's Uncle Strap likes to talk about the peculiar junk that takes place in the Universe, an' he says he thinks that life is controlled by . . .

Fletcher.—Fine! What time's it gettin' to be, Sadie? Excuse, me, Vic.

Vic.—(*Generously*) Not at *all*.

Rush.—(*Low tones, chuckling*) *I* was the one *talkin'*.

Sade.—(*To Fletcher*) Quarter past 10, just about.

Fletcher.—*I* better head for *home*.

Sade.—(*Without conviction*) Oh—*early* yet, Uncle Fletcher.

Vic.—Stick *around*.

Rush.—*Yeah*.

Fletcher.—No, I better be gettin' along.

Vic.—Shank of the evening.

Fletcher.—Uh-huh. Picture show pretty good tonight, was it?

Vic.—I didn't attend. Went to lodge meeting.

Fletcher.—Uh-huh. (*Brief pause*) Yeah, Sadie, I could put my finger right *on* a 4-foot length of railroad track. Pretty well acquainted with Charlie Toss down at the C & A shops. *He'd* fix me up in a *minute*.

307

SADE.—Um.

RUSH.—(*Little chuckle*) How'd you get it *home* from the C & A shops?

FLETCHER.—Fine.   No, a 4-foot length of railroad track makes a good substantial door stop. Sadie an' I figured it out a while ago, Vic. A 4-foot length of railroad track'd gross a fella about a quarter of a ton.

VIC.—(*Little chuckle*) *That's* certainly substantial.

FLETCHER.—(*Chuckles*) Hold a *door* open without trouble, huh?

VIC.—You bet.

FLETCHER.—(*Chuckles*) Fella wouldn't wanta pick it up an' drop it on his *toe*.

VIC.—No, *sir*.

FLETCHER.—(*After a pause*) *Well*, Sadie.

SADE.—Um.

FLETCHER.—(*I'm going home*) Quarter past *ten*.

VIC.—Stick around, stick around.

RUSH.—*Yeah*.

SADE.—If he feels like he oughta go home to bed, he shouldn't be teased to stay an' lose out on good sleep an' . . .

FLETCHER.—*That's* right. No, I better trot along. Where's my coat an' hat?

SADE.—In the hallway. Rush, why don't you . . .

RUSH.—Sure. I'll get 'em.

FLETCHER.—*I* can fetch my own hat and coat.

RUSH.—(*Moving off*) Sit down.

FLETCHER.—YOU're a good boy, Rush.

RUSH.—(*Moving off, chuckling*) Uh-huh.

FLETCHER.—(*To Vic and Sade*) He's a good boy.

VIC AND SADE.—Um.

FLETCHER.—Enjoyed himself at the moving picture show tonight.

VIC AND SADE.—Um.

308

FLETCHER.—(*Thoughtfully*) Arnie Gupples. I bet this evening's the first time I've thought about Arnie Gupples in 20 years. Prob'ly if I met Arnie Gupples on the street I wouldn't even *know* him.

VIC AND SADE.—Um.

FLETCHER.—Your cousin Alfred Feeber bought a pair of shoes off'n Arnie, Sadie.

SADE.—(*Politely*) *Yes*, that's what you *said*.

FLETCHER.—I was with him when he *did* it. Bought a pair of oxblood low-cuts for three dollars an' a quarter. I remember . . . Thanks, Rush.

RUSH.—Not at all.

VIC.—Don't like to see you dash *off*.

FLETCHER.—I don't call quarter past *ten* dashin' off. No, time I went home an' hit the hay.

VIC.—Um.

FLETCHER.—Nice chat, Sadie.

SADE.—Enjoyed *so* much havin' you, Uncle Fletcher.

FLETCHER.—Uh-huh.

SADE.—An' will you tell Mis' Keller happy birthday for me?

FLETCHER.—Fine. Tomorrow morning, first thing, I believe I'll stroll down to the C & A shops an' see Charlie Toss about that 4-foot length of railroad track.

SADE.—Um.

FLETCHER.—Glad you had a dandy time at the moving picture show, Rush.

RUSH.—(*Little chuckle*) Thanks.

FLETCHER.—Well . . . see you all soon.

VIC.—Sure thing. Good night.

SADE AND RUSH.—Good night, Uncle Fletcher.

FLETCHER.—Good night.

ANNOUNCER.—Which concludes another brief interlude at the small house halfway up in the next block. (*Pause*)
(*Closing and credits*)

Lone Journey

MUSIC.—*Theme . . . up for 15 seconds and out.*

SOUND.—*Train whistle, as when it nears a crossing on a station
. . . heard as if sounding over great spaces, or from distance.*

ANNOUNCER.—The morning train from Harlowton, Montana, is
swinging down toward Lewistown, in the heart of Judith
Basin. Along the right of way, a cottontail rabbit sits up
alertly, shakes a long ear in the clear, cold air, and waits
for the silence to mend the streak of clattering, roaring noise
that cuts through the morning. Far away, a rancher and his
dog stop midway across their yard, turning to look for a
moment at the train. From the ranch-house chimney, full-
bodied smoke from a newly fed fire rolls cheerily into the day.

On the train, Wolfe Bennett looked out on the prairies and
the foothills against the horizon; he saw the rabbit, the
rancher, the dog. And even there in the coach, breathing its
stale, dusty ancient air, he knew what the Montana morning
smelled like, felt like, tasted like out there in the open.

WOLFE.—Hello, Montana. Hello, home! You, rabbit, there . . .
I know how it would feel to pick you up by those fine, thin
hind legs of yours, and smell the warm, living blood splashed
on your fur by a thirty-two. I know how a kid would love to
bring you home to show the family what a marksman he is
. . . and how empty the triumph can be if he lets himself
remember how you leaped and sprang, before the bullet
caught you. Hope nobody gets you, rabbit! If they don't,
how do you die? Hawk or eagle? Maybe old age. Keep clear
of that dog back there at the ranch house. Or maybe *he's*
old. He walked a little sedately. Turned his head slowly.
Probably the house dog now, and he just goes out to help
with milking for old time's sake. He can still lie inside the
barn door on a morning like this and daydream, listening to
the comfortable morning talk of the cows and the rancher
and the barn cats sitting in a half circle waiting for their milk.
Then back across the yard, into the warm kitchen for break-

310

fast. I can smell the coffee; hear the clank and slap of a big spoon in the jar of flapjack dough . . . There goes another big blob of it onto the pan . . . Hurry up, boys, there's the first stack, hot off the stove! (*Probably chuckles here or indicates pleasure, amusement*) Ah, it's good to be back! Good to look out on a world of peace and order and reason . . . far as you can see, you look on something that's sound and real and right, to the core. Would to heaven the rest of the world could find its way back to sanity like this . . . and soon . . . soon!

MUSIC.

ANNOUNCER.—When the train circled Lewistown and slipped into the familiar station, there was Mel Tanner, Wolfe's foreman at the Double Spear T and his good friend, waiting to bid him welcome. Mel had a few errands at the stores, the creamery, and lumberyard. They didn't take long, however —not more than an hour and he was ready to drive home before noon. But it got to be the middle of the afternoon before they started. Wolfe met so many friends and acquaintances in town that his progress down Main Street was slowed down to about a block an hour . . . half a dozen steps from visit to visit. Finally Mel thought up a little ruse. He got the car, drove it down the street to where Wolfe was talking to a rancher outside the Fergus Cafe, stopped the car, and told Wolfe to hop in. Now Mel had his man, and he drove straight out of town and headed for the mountains and home. They're rolling northward now past the fairgrounds . . .

SOUND.—*Subdued background of car heard from inside.*

MEL.—(*Fading on*) It was the same story at the creamery, but then that's nothing new.

WOLFE.—Say, wait a minute!

MEL.—What is it, Wolfe?

WOLFE.—It just dawned on me. I'm being shanghaied!

MEL.—Shanghaied!? Oh! (*Chuckling*) Well, you see, Wolfe, I was beginning to picture you making little speeches up and down Main Street till they pull in the sidewalks for the night.

WOLFE.—It's just as well that you got me away, Mel. I'm anxious to get out home and see everybody.

311

MEL.—No more anxious than everybody in the valley is to see you, Wolfe.

WOLFE.—Ach! Bet nobody even noticed I was gone!

MEL.—No? Well, I could name you offhand about a good big roomful of people that don't think the sun hangs at just the right slant when you're away.

WOLFE.—(*Laughing*) Say, what is this, anyway? Are you working up to some bad news you've got for me?

MEL.—No, by golly—haven't got any bad news; now what d'you think of that?

WOLFE.—I think that's swell. Got any *good* news, Mel?

MEL.—Nope—well, now hold on! Sure I have . . . small little piece of good news, anyhow. Got top price on those three bald-face steers.

WOLFE.—Well, good!

MEL.—Yep, got nine dollars and a half. Not bad, eh?

WOLFE.—No-o. What's their weight?

MEL.—One weighed a little bettern' eleven. The other two just a shade under twelve hundred.

WOLFE.—Hm-huh. Nine cents a pound. I saw some cuts of beef selling for 45 cents a pound in Chicago.

MEL.—Oh, I believe that, all right. You know, Wolfe, one of these days I'm going to sharpen me up a stack of pencils and figure her all out.

WOLFE.—What's that, Mel?

MEL.—Why, how come we spend three *years* shoveling high-price feed into making a steer to sell for 9 cents a pound, while the next fellow spends a few hours cutting up said steer to sell him for—say, an average of 20 cents a pound?

WOLFE.—Well, if you can figure that one out, Mel, I'll petition the country board to award you an especially shiny medal.

MEL.—Oh, I guess it wouldn't be so hard to figure out; doing something about it—that's where the going'd get tough.

WOLFE.—That's it, Mel. But, what the heck, let's talk about that tomorrow. How is everybody, that's what I want to know. How's Henry . . . and Sydney . . . Leila?

MEL.—Just the same. That's what I'm going to go to work and do . . . huh? What'd you say, Wolfe . . . oh! Why they're fine, just fine.

WOLFE.—I'll bet you haven't seen any of them since I left.

MEL.—Oh, is that so! Who do you suppose came down and helped me sort spuds 'couple days ago?

WOLFE.—Who, Tom McGee?

MEL.—No—old Henry Newman's niece!

WOLFE.—No kidding! She helped you *sort spuds!*

MEL.—She sure did; stuck with it pretty near a whole afternoon.

WOLFE.—Well, I'll be darned!

MEL.—She's all right, Wolfe; don't make any mistake about that.

WOLFE.—(*Light tone*) What d'you mean, don't make any mistake. I'll have you know I'm as fully aware of Sydney's intelligence and charm as you are, Mel.

MEL.—Yeah? Well, she seems to think pretty well of you, too.

WOLFE.—Oh, shucks! I would have to put that pipe tobacco in my suitcase . . .

MEL.—Well, here . . . here! (*As if hauling a tin out of his pocket*) Use some . . . of mine, Wolfe! There you are, help yourself.

WOLFE.—Thanks, Mel. Uhm. Pay Dirt brand; must be pretty fine stuff.

MEL.—Now, don't you go casting any asparagus at that tobacco; maybe it don't smell like a barbershop, but it's a smoke with a message—let me tell you.

WOLFE.—(*Sniffing*) Hm! I don't doubt it—maybe I'd better give you a last message before I tackle this stuff.

MEL.—All right, all right . . .

WOLFE.—Think maybe we'd better open some windows in this car before I light up?

313

MEL.—Go ahead open one . . . and . . . jump out of it, will you?

BOTH.—(*Laugh*)

MEL.—Did you hear me saying that Sydney's a good friend of yours, Wolfe?

WOLFE.—(*Slight pause*) Yes, I heard that, Mel. (*Louder tone*) Did Henry tell you what he wants to do with those trees of ours?

MEL.—(*Puzzled why Wolfe should change the subject*) Henry? Ah . . . why, no, no, don't believe he did.

WOLFE.—Wrote me about it; he said as long's they've got to be cut down, we can at least keep some of the lumber in the "family," as he put it.

MEL.—How's that?

WOLFE.—He proposed buying the lumber back from the mill and using it in his new house.

MEL.—Why, of course! How come somebody didn't think of that long ago?

WOLFE.—I don't know. Incidentally, we've got to get going on that house of Henry's; won't get the foundation in this year if we don't.

MEL.—That's a fact, too. We've had a couple good frosts already.

WOLFE.—Yes, I saw that in the Chicago papers.

MEL.—Oh . . . of course, it looks as though Henry won't have much use for a bigger house, after all.

WOLFE.—No . . . why not?

MEL.—The main reason he's been wantin' a new house's on account of Sydney, ain't it?

WOLFE.—Hm? Oh, I guess that's one reason, but he was pretty well set to build before she came on the scene. But what about Sydney?

MEL.—Unless I've been a reading the signs all upside down, that young lady'll soon be packing her suitcase and driftin' back to New York.

WOLFE.—(*Pause*) What makes you think that, Mel?

MEL.—As a matter of actual fact, she practically came right out with it, day she was helping me with the spuds.

WOLFE.—What'd she say?

MEL.—Oh, we were talking along . . . talking about you, mostly, and she got kinda absent-minded and threw the spuds in the wrong barrels, and when I kidded her about it she said she guessed she'd never make much of a ranch hand.

WOLFE.—(*Relieved tone*) Is *that* all? Nobody expected her to work at ranching.

MEL.—Now wait a minute . . . I didn't finish.

WOLFE.—Sorry.

MEL.—She said something about she wasn't going to be a parasite, and since she probably couldn't get a job out here, why she'd have to go back to New York. But I can't hardly believe that's really what's wrong.

WOLFE.—Why not? Why shouldn't that be it? She's a girl who's used to making her own way. *I* can certainly understand how she feels about it.

MEL.—Oh, sure, sure; so can I.

WOLFE.—All right, then.

MEL.—Yeah, but I've got a hunch—Sydney's a very beautiful girl. Smart, too, and interesting to talk to.

WOLFE.—So?

MEL.—Wouldn't it be mighty peculiar, Wolfe, if there wasn't some young feller waiting for her back there in the East somewhere; wouldn't it, now?

WOLFE.—Mm, yes, might be. But *that's* got nothing to do with it. She just wants to be independent and self-supporting. She'll get something to do out here . . . must be something we can find for her in Lewistown.

MEL.—Well, you'll have a chance to talk to her about it tonight. They're having a welcome home party for you, Wolfe.

WOLFE.—Huh? Who is?

315

MEL.—Why, Henry Newman and Sydney. Tonight.

WOLFE.—No kidding! Well, that's great! Now can you imagine them going to all that trouble!

MEL.—Oh, you bet I can. They haven't hardly been able to wait till you got back. They'll surely be tickled to see you got here today . . . Been kind of worried you *wouldn't* come back, you know.

WOLFE.—Anybody who'd stay away from here would have to be an awful chump, wouldn't you say so, Mel?

MEL.—Oh, I might, I might!

MUSIC.

ANNOUNCER.—At Henry Newman's, a little while later, Mr. Newman, on the front porch, scanning the landscape and offering in tribute one of his favorite songs . . .

HENRY.—(*Absently at first, then warming to it*)
Oh, beautiful, for spacious skies,
For amber waves of grain.
For purple mountain majesties,
Above the fruited plain
America, America, God shed His grace on thee,
And crown thy good, with brotherhood
From sea to shining sea.
(*Henry continues singing, perhaps starting to repeat chorus . . . then he hesitates and starts singing again, or sings softly, absently. He has heard the very distant sound of a car . . . not audible to the audience . . . and listens while still singing . . . then finally stops altogether*)

HENRY.—There she is! By golly, that's Mel's car I hear . . . just making the last turn into the valley. And high time they were getting back from town! Sydney! Oh, Sydney! I think the lone Wolfe has come back to the fold! Sydney!
(*Lead out*)

MUSIC.

ANNOUNCER.—Henry's voice echoed happily in the still, cold air. Sydney left her baking and came hurrying out of the house, and together they stood listening for the faraway sound of Mel's car. Soon, from the direction of the Double Spear T, came the signal of several short, cheerful blasts of the car horn.

316

Sydney and her Uncle Henry smiled and nodded quickly. Wolfe had come home. In a bare tree just beyond the porch, Mr. Olsen, the magpie, scolded in jealous annoyance at not being noticed. Sydney ran into the house and came back to give him an outrageously big helping of his favorite feed. Holiday warmth and excitement spread in great waves, from the oven within doors, to include the yard, the ranch, and the whole valley under the peaceful sky of a November afternoon.

Music.—*Theme.*

Against the Storm

ℓℓℓ

MUSIC.—*Theme.*

ANNOUNCER.—*Signature.*

MUSIC.—*Theme.*

ANNOUNCER.—Christmas morning was clear and bright in a European city. No one had remembered to order service discontinued on sunlight. It shone with its usual mellow winter calm on the steep roofs, the old meandering streets, and the wide boulevards; in the room of an improvised hospital, Christmas sunlight wakened a young patient.

MANUEL.—So. It is morning again. A sunny day out there. One of the nurses must have come in early, and very quietly, to pull aside the black curtain. Very kind of her. Did she know the sun would be out today? But, of course, Madeleine said she would put aside the curtain, because today would be . . . (*really realizes it now*) . . . today would be Christmas . . . Christmas morning . . . yes, the sunshine is right. It has a Christmas look. I can see what the city must look like, with snow on the roofs and the children blinking in the sunlight as they try their new sleds . . . people going to church . . . But where are the bells? They should be ringing for Christmas morning. "The Saviour is born, hallelujah, on earth, peace and good will to men."

The bells should be ringing out the melody . . . Ah, but church bells are made of what? Apparently of something for which we have a new use in the world today.

There are to be no bells this morning, then? Very well, that may be the general impression. For my part, I am certain there will be many bells, ringing clearly, safe beyond any danger of being silenced . . . or of being heard by any except oneself . . .

MUSIC.—*Fade in church bells from distance during following:*

ANNOUNCER.—Manuel closed his eyes on the sunlight of December 25, 1940, and he found it very easy to hear the church

318

bells of another city and another year, ringing with ancient authority. It was the second Christmas after he had met Kathy, and he had been invited by her grandfather, Dr. Reimer, to come to breakfast with the family. Afterwards, he and Kathy had gone for a walk down the Boulevard Frederick to a church where they knew the sexton, Herr Kampman, who rang the church bells.

He was an old man, proud of his profession, fond of the great bells so long entrusted to his care. It pleased him to have Manuel and Kathy stand by, so clearly aware of the privilege it was to be allowed here, at the very heart, the strong, earth-shaking heart of all the holiday spirit . . .

MUSIC.—*Bells up as loudly and resonantly as possible . . . we hear it toward close of the "Ringing."*

KAMPMAN.—(*Out of breath for a whole*) Now! So! . . . We have done.

KATHY.—It was beautiful, Herr Kampman!

MANUEL.—Almost better than last night!

KAMPMAN.—Oh, no! . . . I must disagree! . . . On Christmas Eve . . . that is the best! (*Quickly*) It is not for *myself* I speak, understand! I have very little to do with the matter. It is the bells themselves. The chimes of Christmas Eve they prefer to all the ringing they do throughout the entire year.

KATHY.—I don't blame them in the least.

MANUEL.—So they are temperamental, those bells up there.

KAMPMAN.—*In* the extreme. Excuse me, but I must wipe my forehead . . . This is very warm work.

MANUEL.—I should think it would be!

KATHY.—(*Looking up into belfry tower*) How many years have they rung, those bells, Herr Kampman?

KAMPMAN.—How many years, Fraulein? Ach, all of *my* years, and they are not few. All of my father's years, and his father's, and those of the father of my father's father. (*Chuckling*) And so on, Fraulein! Far, far back along the life of this city.

319

KATHY.—And they have *always* rung, all those many years, Herr Kampman?

KAMPMAN.—Mm, yes, with now and then an interruption. In the long stretch of the years, nothing serious. In *my* lifetime, the bells have always rung, in war or peace, under good rule or bad.

MANUEL.—That's quite a record, Herr Kampman. I hope it continues.

KAMPMAN.—Ach, who knows?

KATHY.—Herr Kampman, what do you *think* as you ring the bells?

KAMPMAN.—(*Musing*) What do I *think?*

MANUEL.—Such a question, Kathy!

KAMPMAN.—No, no! I understand what the Fraulein means . . . I know what she means . . . but can I *express* what I feel? It is difficult . . .

KATHY.—I should imagine it must make you feel glad, and proud, really. So many people hear the bells, and it is like a happy greeting to everyone who listens. It is the *voice* of the holiday.

KAMPMAN.—(*Thoughtfully*) Yes . . . yes, that is true. It gives me pleasure, too. I am glad when the sound is clear and good and the strokes fall as they should. Mistakes can happen: the air and the atmosphere also have their effect. But one forgets those occasions . . . I am really very fortunate to have been born into a family that has been . . . in a modest way, of course . . . known to have an aptitude for bell ringing. It is a tradition. One is comfortable in a *good* tradition. Best of all, one is comfortable in the work for which one has an aptitude and a liking. There would be very little trouble, I think, if everyone had an opportunity for that kind of contentment . . . Well! Frau Kampman is waiting at home with my Christmas coffee!

KATHY.—And we have been detaining you!

MANUEL.—Come, Kathy, we must go, too . . .

KAMPMAN.—You have not detained me. I am very glad you like to visit. Now I bid you good morning and a very happy day to you and Herr Doktor at home and everyone.

KATHY.—Thank you, Herr Kampman! We wish the same for you and Frau Kampman and your family!

KAMPMAN.—Thank you!

MANUEL.—Thank you for the music! (*Fading*) Merry Christmas, Herr Kampman!

KAMPMAN.—Merry Christmas (*fading*) Merry Christmas!

ANNOUNCER.—The morning sun of December 25th, 1940, shone now at such a slant that it reached across the hospital room in a city once very beautiful and touched Manuel's eyelids with a faint, soft warmth. But he kept his eyes closed and tried to make Herr Kampman's church bells ring in his mind again.

MUSIC.

ANNOUNCER.—Across the Atlantic, in the university town of Hawthorne, Kathy's first Christmas morning in America was to include attendance at the service at University Chapel with all the Allens, the Scotts, and her grandfather. But she and Siri went ahead of the rest, because they had promised to attend a program at the children's Sunday school. It was Siri's own secret idea that the busier she could keep Kathy today the better it would be for her spirits. Sitting now in the front row of stiff wooden chairs in the Sunday-school room, they have just heard a Christmas carol sung by the voices for whom it was written . . . clear, young, and forthright. Now a little girl in a neat velvet dress and brand new slippers is standing alone, in front of the enormous Christmas tree. It has been announced that she will recite a poem called "Christmas Morning," by Elizabeth Madox Roberts . . .

CHILD.—(*Reads with simplicity but with intelligence . . . no dramatic interpretation . . . over music?*)

> "If Bethlehem were here today,
> Or this were very long ago,
> There wouldn't be a winter time
> Nor any cold or snow.
>
> "I'd run out through the garden gate,
> And down along the pasture walk;
> And off beside the cattle barns
> I'd hear a kind of gentle talk.

321

"I'd move the heavy iron chain
And pull away the wooden pin;
I'd push the door a little bit
And tiptoe very softly in.

"The pigeons and the yellow hens
And all the cows would stand away;
Their eyes would open wide to see
A lady in the manger hay,
If this were very long ago
And Bethlehem were here today.

"And Mother held my hand and smiled—
I mean the lady would—and she
Would take the woolly blankets off
Her little boy so I could see.

"His shut-up eyes would be asleep,
And he would look just like our John,
And he would be all crumpled too,
And have a pinkish color on.

"I'd watch his breath go in and out,
His little clothes would all be white.
I'd slip my finger in his hand
To feel how he could hold it tight.

"And she would smile and say, Take care,
The mother, Mary, would Take care;
And I would kiss his little hand
And touch his hair.

"While Mary put the blankets back
The gentle talk would soon begin.
And when I'd tiptoe softly out
I'd meet the wise men going in."

Music.

ANNOUNCER
"I'd slip my finger in his hand
To feel how he could hold it tight.
And she would smile and say, Take care."

322

Gentle words, too soft to be heard above the roar of planes and the scream of bombs. But the quiet will return, and the words will ring out, and everything they mean, a song from heart to heart, as clear and as strong and as glad as the bells Herr Kampman used to ring. "These are thy brothers . . . take care, take care!"

Music.—*Theme.*
    (*Sign off*)

Music.—*Theme.*

Ma Perkins

MUSIC.—*Opening theme for 15 seconds.*

ANNOUNCER.—And now for Ma Perkins . . . brought to you by Procter and Gamble, the makers of Oxydol.
(*Opening commercial*)

ANNOUNCER.—And now here she is . . . Ma Perkins! Well, yesterday the folks heard Paul Henderson's last will and testament. It was a very short document, leaving everything to Fay. Paul's estate was a good one; so Fay's security and that of the child she is going to have are assured. But Fay doesn't care about that! Nor does she seem to care about the baby she's expecting . . . All Fay thinks about is Paul! (*Low*) Can Ma bring Fay through her grief and despair . . . make Fay see that life goes on, whether we will it or not? (*Tiny pause*) Well, right now Ma and Shuffle are walking home from the lumberyard through the October dusk. Rushville Center is peaceful and quiet as . . . listen!

SHUFFLE.—Tarnation, there's a real nip in the air tonight. Another couple of weeks and we'll be taking out the old ear muffs.

MA.—Oh, we'll have Indian summer first. This is the first real chilly day we've had since we got back.

SOUND.—*Jumping cue slightly . . . an automobile horn honks, not too intimate . . . the automobile is going fast . . . second honk fades . . . the sound of the car is barely audible.*

SHUFFLE.—Oh, there's Lonnie Konvalinka in his new car . . . (*Calls*) . . . evening, Lonnie!

MA.—(*Calling*) Hello, Mr. Konvalinka! (*A tiny pause . . . murmuring*) *She* sent Fay the sweetest note.

SHUFFLE.—*Mrs.* Lonnie?

MA.—Yes. She's *such* a nice person.

SHUFFLE.—Practically everybody in town must have sent Fay a note.

MA.—(*A sigh*) Yes. (*A tiny pause*)

SHUFFLE.—(*Very tenderly*) Come on now, Ma. It's a terrible thing, but you ain't going to let it color your whole life. You ain't going to let it discourage you.

MA.—It's going to color *her* whole life . . . Fay's. I guess on the day I die, Shuffle, I'll look back and I'll see how my life sort of divided itself up into three parts. The first was with Pa, till he . . . left us. The second part, with the children . . . getting Evey married, and Fay. And the third part . . . now. Fay being widowed, after less than a year of marriage. (*Dreamily*) Fay. Who'd ever thought that she'd be the one? The day she was graduated from grade school . . . all the little girls in their nice clean dresses . . . the day they was graduated from high school . . . why, she was the second youngest in her class, and now she's the one who . . . (*Practically a throw-away*) It's funny, it's funny.

SHUFFLE.—She'll come out of it, Ma. She'll get back into the scheme of things down here. Her friends . . . taking things easy . . . she'll be okay. Remember she's young, Ma, and youth ain't *never* sat down and cried and cried and never stopped crying. In a couple of weeks you'll be taking her down to buy some new dresses, and she'll look at herself in the mirror, and just by accident her eye'll fall on a new hat, and . . . say, you name one woman who can resist the temptation of a new hat, 'specially Fay. She always did have a weakness for the darnedest bonnets I ever saw!

MA.—(*Half laughing but a chiding note*) Well, Shuffle, I hope you're right. But you mustn't forget that we ain't *got* too long to wait while she recovers. (*Very sadly*) If she keeps on grieving and mourning through the next few weeks . . . she and her baby both will have a . . . well, Tom Stevens is worried already. (*Almost to herself, slowly*) No . . . the thing that's going to cure Fay is . . . is . . . *this*. (*A tiny pause*)

SHUFFLE.—(*Mildly surprised*) Eh? What are you waving your hand at . . . what do you mean, "this" . . . you mean old man Johnson raking up the leaves there on his front lawn? (*Calls without pause*) Evening, Mr. Johnson! (*A tiny pause*

325

. . . *murmuring with a smile*) Getting deafer 'n' ever, ain't he?

MA.—(*Hint of a laugh but an earnest note*) No, I don't mean Mr. Johnson, 'specially, but . . . yes, Mr. Johnson among other things. (*Sincerely*) Shuffle, if we'll only look around us, we'll see so much to . . . to take the sting out of our sorrows! That's what I meant when I waved my hand at *Rushville Center*. At Mr. Johnson raking his leaves. And the smell of the October leaves being burned on 20 lawns and the yellow house lights blinking on as folks like us walk home after a day's work. Living . . . I guess what I'm talking about is living. Taking the days as they come . . . the seasons . . . living for each day itself . . . just living! Putting up the screens in May and taking 'em down in September . . . doing your work, listening on an October night to the wild geese, as a mile over our heads they go on their wonderful and mysterious journey!

SHUFFLE.—Yep . . . that sure *is* a wonderful sound.

MA.—You know, Shuffle, when I was a little girl, my father used to stand with me outside our house, of an October afternoon, and show me the wild birds going south. Looked sort of like a smoky smudge. And one year, I must have been six or so, a gray goose feather fell right at my feet. And my father laughed and he said "hold on to that, young lady, the bird'll be back in the spring to get it, or maybe to drop you another feather!" And I asked my father . . . somehow it impressed me . . . "Year after year, will that same goose be flying right over our house?" He smiled sadly, and said, "If *you'll* be here to find the feather, the goose will drop it for you." (*A tiny pause*) I'm a woman grown, but I've never forgotten that little incident. And ever since I've *liked* the idea of year after year . . . the regularity of the seasons . . . the mysterious way of God, moving those birds across a thousand miles of day and night and empty air, and me standing there, a part of it, because I . . . well, because I'm a part of it. And that's what I'd like my children to know . . . especially Fay . . . I'd like *her* to see that if we'll only be there to find it, the gray goose feather will always come. Telling us that the world goes on, that all's right with the world. (*A tiny pause*)

SHUFFLE.—(*Quietly; he's deeply moved*) I guess that's the story of our lives, Ma . . . the lives of you and me and the rest of

us who stay in all the forgotten little villages, and let the rest
of the world go by. Except . . . *we* don't let the world go by
. . . it's the folks in a hurry who let it by. Us, we got time
to take it in.

MA.—(*Not much volume but very earnest*) Yes, Shuffle . . . that's
it exactly! And that's the secret of peace. Let each day come
. . . take it as it comes . . . take it for everything it has
. . . and when it goes, you've lived that day! Now if Fay
will only see that . . . (*A little catch . . . hint of a half
wistful laugh*) Yes, if Fay will only see it.

SHUFFLE.—(*Deep breath which comes out as a sigh*) Yep, yep, yep.
But Fay couldn't be in better hands, Ma, so don't you worry.
You got a good recipe for living, and if anybody can teach
it to her it's you. Just give her enough time and she'll come
through with flying colors.

MA.—(*A sigh*) Yes . . . if there'll be time enough. Well . . .
here we are. You said you're going some place for supper
tonight, Shuffle?

SHUFFLE.—I'm having a quick bite. Then I'm going to a meeting
of the volunteer fire department . . . I missed the last meeting . . . we're having a big discussion should we have a
bingo party for our annual blowout, or should we do like
they do in Three Rivers and give a masquerade and carnival.
Opinion is divided fifty fifty, and the arguments will be
coming thick and fast . . . Wouldn't miss it even for one of
your suppers, Ma.

MA.—(*Snickering*) And on which side are you going to throw the
weight of *your* opinion, Shuffle?

SHUFFLE.—Oh, whichever side needs a feller with a good loud
voice . . . I'm their man. (*They laugh*) Well, good night,
Ma . . .

MA.—Good night, Shuffle . . . see you tomorrow . . .

SHUFFLE.—(*Fading*) Yes, Ma. Night! And remember what I
said . . . don't worry!

MA.—(*Half calling*) I won't! And I think a masquerade would be
more fun than bingo!

SHUFFLE.—(*Fading, calling back*) Then I'm on the side of the
masquerade, and the bingo fellers ain't got a chance!

327

MA.—(*Laughing to herself, fondly, but throw away*) Shuffle, Shuffle.

SOUND.—*Her footsteps cross wooden porch . . . door opens and closes on*

GLADYS.—(*Off and fading in . . . take cue from door opening*) Yes, I can see that. Did somebody come in, Fay?

MA.—(*Surprised*) Who on earth . . .

FAY.—(*Fading in; quietly; neither happily nor unhappily*) Hello, Ma. Come in. Gladys Pendleton came over to pay us a call . . . We were waiting for you.

MA.—(*Astounded, but her pleasure grows through the speech*) Why . . . why, Gladys Pendleton! How nice of you, Gladys . . . I seen your mother downtown a couple hours ago . . . it was good of you to come, child!

GLADYS.—Good evening, Mrs. Perkins. I . . . I . . . I came over to tell Fay how I . . . well, I told her that she has my sympathy. I'm sorry. It was a terrible thing.

MA.—(*Gently*) Thank you, Gladys. Fay, wouldn't Gladys like some tea . . . or maybe she'd like . . .

GLADYS.—No, thank you . . . Fay's already offered me . . . I can't stay.

MA.—Well, you'll stay till I go up and wash my face and come down again. (*Fading*) We ain't seen you in a long time, Gladys. How've you been? You're looking real well!

GLADYS.—(*Raising voice very slightly*) Thank you . . . I've been fine. (*A little pause, half sulky, half nice*) Your sister told my mother this morning that Paul left a good estate. Are you planning on traveling?

FAY.—(*Quietly*) No. I'm going to have a baby, you know . . . I really haven't thought much beyond that.

GLADYS.—I'll tell you something, Fay. Don't let money matter too much. I know. It doesn't buy the things you want.

FAY.—(*Quietly*) I know that, Gladys.

GLADYS.—(*Half defiantly, half bitterly*) I was the only kid in our class who had a fur coat. I was the only girl in high school with a roadster. So what? When I met somebody I really liked I couldn't even keep him . . . he went and married somebody else.

328

FAY.—(*A bit flustered*) Gladys, you . . . you mean . . . Paul? But that was so long ago . . . I . . .

GLADYS.—(*A little burst*) Why do you think I came over here? Do you think I call on everyone I happen to have a nodding acquaintance with? I came because Paul . . . because I . . .

FAY.—(*Very gently but a bit breathless, a tone of wonder*) I guess I understand. Thanks . . . thanks for coming, Gladys. That's sort of . . . it's *very* nice of you. No, it's more than that . . .

GLADYS.—Oh, it's . . . well I don't . . . (*more rapidly, even more jerkily*) I think I'll be going now . . . If there's anything I can do for you let me know, Fay . . . Huh, that's a laugh! Maybe you're the one who should be doing something for me!

FAY.—I . . . I don't understand, No, don't go . . .

GLADYS.—I must. What don't you understand? Don't you know what I'm trying to tell you? Since I'm in the mood for confession . . . I'd trade places with you in a minute . . . You're better off than I can ever be. (*Fading without pause*) Don't bother to get up . . . In a day or two maybe we can have lunch together . . . Express my apologies to your mother . . . good night!

FAY.—But Gladys . . .

SOUND.—*Door opens and closes a bit off.*

MA.—(*Brightly . . . off and fading in*) Fay, did you say that you . . . (*Stops, surprised*) Where is she?

FAY.—(*Throw away, barely audible*) Gone. (*Marveling . . . to herself slowly*) She . . . she said that she'd . . . that she'd . . . she'd trade places with me in one minute. (*A little pause*)

MA.—(*Slowly*) Gladys said that? That . . . that was wise and good of her.

FAY.—(*To herself*) She must have meant . . . the baby . . . Even a few months with Paul being better than . . . than nothing. (*Little stronger tone of wonder*) She . . . why, she must have loved Paul all along.

MA.—(*Barely audible*) Yes. Maybe. (*A little pause*)

FAY.—(*For curtain*) I . . . I guess you're right, Ma. Maybe there are other people in the world besides me.

ANNOUNCER.—To which Ma might say, thankfully, "Yes, it's as I said. Live in the present and the future, Fay, because life does go on and we with it." Has Fay begun to live again . . . begun to feel herself a part of this world of ours again? Tomorrow Fay and Ma have some interesting visitors . . . old friends of ours . . . so be sure to listen again . . . tomorrow!

(Commercial)

ANNOUNCER.—So Gladys Pendleton says she'd change places with Fay in one minute, and Fay sees that perhaps she's not the *only* person in the world. Well, tomorrow Fay hears more advice, and soon we're going to hear more about Paul's will, so be *sure* to listen again!

This is Dick Wells speaking for the makers of Oxydol.

The Light of the World

MUSIC.—*Organ theme.*

SPEAKER.—(*Echo*) The Light of the World . . . the story of the Bible—an Eternal beacon, lighting man's way through the darkness of time!

MUSIC.—*Organ up full and out.*
> (*Commercial*)

MUSIC.—*Theme up.*

ANNOUNCER.—This is our day-to-day story of the Holy Bible—presented as a living, human monument to man's faith in God, reverently portrayed. The story is told in the language of today for clarity and understanding and to bring the greatness, the humanness of the Bible and its people to everyone, and to make those people as much alive today as the Book which houses them. And now, we continue the story of Joseph, character from the book of Genesis, Chapter 44, verse 4.

MUSIC.—*Church organ up.*
> (*Lead in*)

SPEAKER.—"And when they were gone out of the city, and not yet far off, Joseph said unto his steward, Up, follow after the men; and when thou dost overtake them, say unto them, Wherefore have ye rewarded evil for good?"

(*More intimate*) The day which Joseph has awaited with mingled hope and fear has arrived. He is ready, at last, to test the integrity of his brothers. The stage has been set for the moment which he has planned—the moment when he will know, beyond a shadow of doubt, whether his brothers will sacrifice Benjamin as they sacrificed him so many years ago! According to his orders, Joseph's brothers have been brought back to the palace in disgrace, and Benjamin has been accused of stealing a silver cup.

331

Now, as the brothers wait in the great reception hall, frightened and bewildered by this new development, Judah and Simeon stand apart from the others. Simeon speaks anxiously . . .

SIMEON.—(*Anxiously*) Judah . . .

JUDAH.—Yes, Simeon?

SIMEON.—(*Low*) Do you think we'll all be put into prison?

JUDAH.—(*Low*) I hope not. But . . . why couldn't the silver cup have been found in my grain sack . . . instead of in Benjamin's!

SIMEON.—Judah . . . we know Benjamin didn't take that cup!

JUDAH.—Of course he didn't. (*Sighs*) Simeon . . . I . . . I don't understand it . . . but . . . I'm sure that this is our punishment for what we did to . . . Joseph.

SIMEON.—(*Hopelessly*) Yes. I've always know that someday we'd be punished for selling him to the slave traders . . . and for lying to father . . . telling him Joseph was dead . . .

JUDAH.—(*Dully*) And now at last the time has come! We're in a foreign land . . . at the mercy of a pagan ruler!

SIMEON.—Yes. (*With sudden horror*) Judah . . . you don't think . . . Benjamin will be . . . will be . . . ?

JUDAH.—(*Sharply*) What?

SIMEON.—(*With horror*) You don't think he'll be . . . put to death?

JUDAH.—(*Hopelessly*) I don't know. (*With emotion*) Simeon . . . I can't let anything happen to Benjamin! I can never go back home . . . unless (*voice breaks*) Benjamin is with us!

MUSIC.

SPEAKER.—And while his brothers await his arrival with fear, Joseph stands by the window of his room. His fine, sensitive face is calm, but his eyes betray his emotion.

MUSIC.—*Behind following.*

JOSEPH.—(*With emotion*) Lord, God, I know that this is the most important day of my life! Everything that came before this . . . my brothers selling me into bondage . . . my being imprisoned . . . and then made governor of Egypt . . . were inevitable steps leading me and my brothers to this day. And in a little while, when I stand before them and accuse Benjamin of being a . . . a thief, I know that in that moment the whole future of our family will be at stake! If . . . if my brothers sacrifice Benjamin through jealousy and hatred, as they sacrificed me, I'll know you don't wish me to tell them that I am their brother. I'll . . . understand that for some reason you don't want me . . . ever . . . to see my father again. But please, Lord God of Abraham, give me wisdom . . . and strength.

MUSIC.—*Up and out.*

SIMEON.—(*Low*) Look, Judah, the guards are opening the doors.

JUDAH.—(*Low*) Yes. The governor must be coming!

GUARD.—(*Calling . . . off*) Make way for the governor of Egypt!

SIMEON.—(*Low*) There he is!

JUDAH.—(*Low*) Simeon . . . you and I will speak to the governor. Reuben or Dan or Levi or the others might lose their tempers.

SIMEON.—(*Low*) Yes . . . I think you're right, Judah. I'll tell them . . .

JUDAH.—(*Low*) I told Reuben before, Simeon. They understand . . .

SIMEON.—Oh. (*Change of tone*) Judah . . . he's taken his place upon the throne.

JUDAH.—Sssh . . . he's going to speak!

JOSEPH.—(*Calling*) You may come forward!

JUDAH.—(*Whispers*) We'll lead the way, Simeon.

SOUND.—*Footsteps on marble floor.*

JUDAH.—(*Humbly*) We kneel before you, my lord. (*Brief pause*)

JOSEPH.—(*Coldly . . . off slightly*) Please rise. I wish to talk with you.

SIMEON.—(*Whispers*) He's very angry!

JOSEPH.—(*Coldly . . . off slightly*) Come closer . . .

JUDAH.—Yes, O governor.

JOSEPH.—(*In . . . sternly*) In this country . . . there is no disgrace so great as a betrayal of hospitality!

JUDAH.—It is a disgrace in our country, too, my lord!

JOSEPH.—(*Sternly*) And yet . . . you have betrayed mine! I brought you to my palace. I honored you by having you dine with me today, and . . . and what have you done to repay me!

JUDAH.—(*Humbly*) We do not understand.

JOSEPH.—(*Sternly*) Let me speak! You know . . . there are few foreigners who have been treated so well! Do you realize how great an honor was bestowed upon you when you were invited to dine with me?

JUDAH.—Yes, O governor . . .

SOUND.—*Murmur of "Yes, my lord," etc. from brothers . . . off slightly.*

JOSEPH.—(*Sternly*) I was kind to you . . . I asked you about your home . . . your parents . . . I listened when you told me about your aged father . . . I gave you grain for your families . . . and I let you prove that you weren't spies! I believed your story . . . when you brought your youngest brother to Egypt!

JUDAH.—(*Humbly*) We told the truth, my lord. We are not spies!

JOSEPH.—(*Angrily*) I prefer a spy to a thief!

SIMEON.—My lord . . . our brother Benjamin did not steal the silver cup!

JOSEPH.—(*Sternly*) I have proof that he did! My steward Ahmed found the cup in his sack!

JUDAH.—(*Hopelessly*) We can't explain it, O governor.

JOSEPH.—Why not let the boy speak for himself?

JUDAH.—Please, my lord . . . let me speak for him! He is young. He's never been away from our home.

JOSEPH.—(*Sternly*) Well, then, what have you to say in his defense?

334

JUDAH.—(*Pleadingly*) Only that he did not take the silver cup, my lord! No member of our family could ever steal! You wouldn't understand about . . . our God . . . but no man of faith could ever turn thief!

JOSEPH.—(*Sternly*) Those are fine words, Judah. But if your brother Benjamin did not take the cup, who put it in his sack?

JUDAH.—We do not know! We must have an enemy in Egypt . . . someone who hates us . . .

JOSEPH.—(*Laughs scornfully*) Surely you don't think I'll believe that! No one in Egypt even knows you, no one but me . . . and my chief steward!

JUDAH.—(*Humbly*) Could your chief steward . . . ?

JOSEPH.—(*Sternly*) I'd trust Ahmed with my life!

JUDAH.—(*Pleadingly*) Then . . . I . . . I can't understand it . . . but . . . (*earnestly*) I swear that Benjamin did not take the cup! Won't you . . . please . . . believe me?

JOSEPH.—No! I do not believe you. But I won't hold you to blame, Judah, for your brother's crime.

SIMEON.—What!

JOSEPH.—You and your brothers may depart in peace, all but . . . Benjamin!

JUDAH.—And . . . Benjamin?

JOSEPH.—(*Sternly*) He must be punished!

SOUND.—*Horrified murmur from brothers.*

JUDAH.—(*Fearfully*) What will you do with him?

SIMEON.—Yes, how will you punish Benjamin?

JOSEPH.—(*Sternly*) Benjamin must stay here in Egypt . . . for life . . .

SOUND.—*Shocked murmur from brothers.*

JUDAH.—(*Shocked*) Oh, no!

JOSEPH.—He shall be my servant!

SIMEON.—(*Groans low*) Judah . . . this is indeed our punishment!

JUDAH.—(*Horrified*) You'll make Benjamin . . . your servant? He'd be no better than a . . . a slave!

335

JOSEPH.—(*Sternly*) Benjamin must be my servant . . . for life! That is my command! But the rest of you may go home in peace!

SIMEON.—No . . . no!

JUDAH.—May I speak, O governor?

JOSEPH.—There's nothing for you to say, Judah!

JUDAH.—Yes . . . there is, my lord. When we told you about our young brother Benjamin . . . on our first visit to Egypt . . . we told you that our father loved him best . . .

JOSEPH.—(*Coldly*) Yes . . . I remember!

JUDAH.—(*With emotion*) When we left our home with Benjamin, our father blessed us and charged us to protect him! Please, my lord, do not keep Benjamin here! If my father loses him now . . . (*voice breaks*) it will mean his death! He had one great shock many years ago, when he lost . . . (*voice breaks*) Joseph! He could not live through . . . another . . . shock!

SIMEON.—(*With emotion*) Judah is right, my lord! Forgive Benjamin. Let him return to Canaan.

JOSEPH.—(*Sternly*) My command has been given! You may go . . . all except Benjamin! He will be placed under guard!

JUDAH.—(*With emotion*) I swore that I would protect Benjamin with my life, O governor. I promised to return him to our father unharmed!

JOSEPH.—(*Coldly*) Yes?

JUDAH.—(*Pleadingly . . . with emotion*) Please . . . I beg of you . . . be merciful, O governor of Egypt! Keep me . . . instead of Benjamin!

JOSEPH.—What!

JUDAH.—(*Pleadingly*) Put me to death if you will . . . or let me stay here as your servant . . . but please. (*voice breaks*) let Benjamin return to Canaan! Let my father live his last few years . . . (*voice breaks*) in peace!

JOSEPH.—You really offer to stay here so that your youngest brother may go home to your father?

JUDAH.—(*Pleadingly*) Please . . . my lord!

336

SIMEON.—(*Low*) I think perhaps we would all choose to stay in Benjamin's place, O governor!

SOUND.—*General murmur of "Yes," etc. from brothers.*

JOSEPH.—(*With emotion . . . low*) Oh, Lord God of Abraham, I thank you for this day! I now know that I may reveal my true self to . . . my brothers!

JUDAH.—(*Pleadingly*) You'll let me stay . . . in Benjamin's place?

JOSEPH.—Do not be alarmed, Judah. Neither you nor Benjamin must stay!

JUDAH.—What!

JOSEPH.—(*With emotion*) I placed the silver cup in his sack to test you . . .

JUDAH.—(*Shocked*) To . . . test us?

JOSEPH.—(*With emotion*) Look, my brothers! I remove this hood . . . (*Brief pause*) Do you know me . . . now? I am your brother . . . whom you sold into bondage! I am your brother Joseph!

MUSIC.—*Organ.*
(*Lead out*)

SPEAKER.—And Joseph was reunited with his brothers, for as the book of Genesis tells us in Chapter 45, "Joseph said unto his brethren, Come near to me, I pray you. And they came near. And he said, I am Joseph your brother, whom ye sold into Egypt. And his brethren could not answer him, for they were troubled at his presence."

ANNOUNCER.—All dramatic material on this program is prepared in collaboration with nationally known biblical authorities of various faiths.

MUSIC.—*Organ.*
(*Commercial*)

ANNOUNCER.—The Light of the World . . . the day-to-day story of the Bible, currently the story of Joseph from the book of Genesis, will be continued tomorrow at this same time. Your announcer is James Fleming.

MUSIC.—*Theme.*

337

Justice Rides the Range

SOUND.—*Thunder . . . crackling and fade.*

ANNOUNCER.—Justice Rides the Range . . . transcribed and brought to you by Premium Quality Falstaff. Coming out of the old West with all the drama and romance of the cattle country!

MUSIC.—*"Half Past Four" . . . Eight bars . . . and fade to . . .*

ANNOUNCER.—Have you ever noticed the difference between a pretty good athlete . . . and a champion? *To come down to cases* . . . Like the difference between a good sand-lot shortstop and a big-leaguer? When you talk to big-leaguers, you realize that the expert in-fielders agree that there's a secret of playing any position.

Well, naturally, there's a secret in making beer, too. And the experts . . . the brew masters who know beer best . . . agree that the secret of fine beer flavor is in the yeast used in brewing. *Let's be reasonable about this.* Now, naturally, all brewers use yeast . . . but *only* Premium Quality Falstaff . . . only Falstaff is brewed with a Thorobred yeast actually insured for 1 million dollars. Now, you can see for yourself . . . to be so highly prized, Falstaff's Thorobred yeast *must* produce a grand flavor!

And that's right! But . . . judge Falstaff for yourself! Next time you're thirsty . . . step into your nearby Falstaff dealer's. Try the beer whose famous flavor is assured by a million dollar Thorobred yeast! Step up and say . . . make mine Falstaff!

MUSIC.—*First song.*
(*Lead in*)

RACE ROBBINS.—(*Slash B foreman*) Evenin', ladies and gents! My name's Robbins . . . Race Robbins. I'm the ramrod on the Slash B spread, hand-toolin' the outfit an' tryin' to make a showin' on the ranch books. But we got our troubles, 'cause we're carryin' a pretty heavy load o' steers . . . an' water

338

goin' to be shy, come summer . . . In the story, mebbe you recollect, Steve Gamble, the new man over on the Windmill, brought my boss's girl Polly back to headquarters in last night's roundup, and when he'd talked Dan Buckner out of makin' a gun play he rid off . . . with Calhoun Pope, of the Circle O, a-fannin' in . . . well, them two met out by the headquarters gate . . . and they made talk, with Mr. Pope sayin' . . .

SOUND.—*Horses coming in . . . stop.*

POPE.—(*Soft and deceiving*) Steady, Chombo! . . . Whoa! . . . Good morning!

STEVE.—(*Easy*) Howdy, Pope.

POPE.—I have to apologize on the business of your name. I'm afraid I'm a little careless that way . . .

STEVE.—Blazes, Mister Pope, you meet up with so many strangers here in the Grasslands, a man couldn't hardly expect you to remember 'em all! The name's Gamble.

POPE.—Of course! (*Two can play that game*) Perhaps your memory for names is better than mine!

STEVE.—I wouldn't make any claims. Mebbe the difference is . . . four or five folks here have made it a point to keep me from forgetting.

POPE.—(*Insolent*) My good friend Dan Buckner, for instance?

STEVE.—Well, I just met up with Mr. Buckner, but I can remember *him* . . . Then there's you . . . and your other good friend Yancey Gard.

POPE.—(*Is that a dig*) Yancey Gard is no friend of mine, sir!

STEVE.—No? Then mebbe the word is "hand"!

POPE.—(*Quieter . . . and therefore more dangerous*) Mistakes like that one could be dangerous, Gamble!

STEVE.—(*Guileless*) Oh! Thanks for telling me! Where I come from a man figures people by what they do . . . and not so much by what they *say*.

POPE.—(*Can stand just so much*) If you're trying to stir up a quarrel with me, you could make a short cut by calling me a liar!

339

STEVE.—(*Easy laugh*) Lord, Pope, I don't like quarrels well enough to go around stirring them up!

POPE.—(*Curt*) Then don't say things that can be too easily misunderstood!

STEVE.—(*Goes on*) But I was going to say . . . I never made it a rule to ride wide when quarrels are brought to *me!*

POPE.—(*Why waste time?*) I see . . . (*Up a little*) That habit you have of judging people by what they *do*, now . . .

STEVE.—It's the only way I know!

POPE.—Following it, *I* might remark on your making a friendly visit on the Slash B.

STEVE.—(*Laughs*) Oh, *that!* . . . Well, I don't know's Mr. Buckner would like you calling it friendly . . . Or mebbe it's a way you folks have over here . . . saying, "Glad to see you!" . . . and saying it with a *six gun!*

POPE.—(*Sharper*) Gamble, don't waste time trying to pull wool over *my* eyes. I know why you came into the Conejo! I know who paid you to come—and who's paying you to stay.

STEVE.—(*As grinning*) No! . . . Say, mister, you shore have got some news *for me there.*

POPE.—(*As shrugging*) All right, Gamble! . . . If Dan Buckner wants to bring hired gunmen into our fight . . . well, two can play at that game! The difference is . . .

STEVE.—You mean the difference between you and Mr. Buckner?

POPE.—(*Angry at last*) I mean the difference between his putting you up to this empty *claim* to Windmill Springs . . . this foolishness about your "*uncle*" . . . to cover up the fact that you've come here to make *his* fight . . .

STEVE.—(*Quiet*) I see now, Pope! (*Sighs*) Well, I never did see a man could be talked out of drawing to a bobtail flush if he had his mind made up to it! . . . So I reckon I'll be dusting along and . . .

POPE.—(*Control gone . . . up . . . but don't let him ham it!*) I have no idea of keeping you. But I want two things clear.

STEVE.—I reckon I can handle *two.*

340

Pope.—You need your wings clipped, Gamble! And one thing to remember is that I am going to make it my affair to tend to the clipping!

Steve.—(*Sighs*) Tally! I take that as a promise!

Pope.—(*Furious . . . but always down enough to be deadly*) It's a promise!

Steve.—(*Cheerful*) That's *one*. You said something about *two*!

Pope.—The other one is that I am . . . er . . . interested in Miss Polly Buckner! Come along, Chombo!

Sound.—*Hooves . . . fading.*

Pope.—Keep *that* in your mind, *all the time!* (*Out*)

Sound.—*Horse into hard run.*

Steve.—Hm-m-m! I never *did* see folks go on the prod easier than some of these here! (*Little laugh*) I get told *more* things *not* to do! . . . Come on, ridin' hoss!

Sound.—*Hoofs into shuffle . . . fade with*

Steve.—Somebody's goin' to tell me pretty soon I got to give up drinkin' an' rollin' smokes . . . an' 'bout *that* time, I'm goin' to get disagreeable!

Sound.—*Horse into lope . . . might pick up sound with music . . . might carry rhythm into hoofs of Pope riding in . . . off.*

Polly.—(*Letting down now*) Well, dad, they got away without pulling guns anyway!

Buckner.—(*Short*) That pair! Humph! You're almighty upset about this Gamble and Cal Pope fighting! They won't!

Polly.—(*Quick*) Dad, I thought at first that Steve Gamble had come into the Conejo to ride for Calhoun in the fight over Windmill Springs . . . I *told* you . . . I saw them having a confab the second day Gamble was in Conejo.

Buckner.—Pope lines out with the Gard gang; why wouldn't he send for another gun fighter?

Polly.—That's the way it looked. This morning, over at the Windmill, I charged him with it.

Buckner.—You didn't expect him to admit it!

POLLY.—I . . . No! . . . But what he said made me doubt it.

BUCKNER.—Humph! You better let *me* decide things like that, girl. You've got no truck with them!

POLLY.—(*Spirited*) Oh, don't treat me like a baby, dad!

BUCKNER.—(*She got it from him*) Damnation, I treat you the size you've grown up to! If you'd *act* like you had sense . . . !

POLLY.—(*Low and fast*) Wait! . . . Here comes Cal Pope! . . . Dad, those two men *may* have been side pardners. They're not *now!*

BUCKNER.—(*Gruff*) How in tophet are *you* to tell?

POLLY.—(*Fast*) Dad, it sounds silly . . . but it's *me!* Hush, now!

SOUND.—*The horse in . . . to stop*

POLLY.—(*Up*) Morning, Calhoun?

POPE.—(*Coming in*) Hello, Polly! Good morning, suh! . . . Steady, Chombo . . . (*Grunt*) There! Now *stand!*

SOUND.—*Spurs dragging gravel . . . in.*

BUCKNER.—(*Tart*) Pope, I thought I'd made it clear that the Slash B would manage to get along *some way* without you!

POLLY.—(*Low*) Oh, dad!

POPE.—(*Easy*) I'd certainly despise to go where I'm not wanted, suh! But this is a business call.

BUCKNER.—(*Smarting*) Business? . . . You've got one piece of business to do with me, Pope—and only one!

POLLY.—(*Mortified*) Oh, please . . . dad! I don't see why you can't disagree with a man without . . .

BUCKNER.—(*Explodes*) You keep out of this, Polly! When I disagree with a man . . . as you call it . . . I go the whole way! When Calhoun Pope gets ready to send Yancey Gard and his gunmen where they belong . . . over into the Fonda . . . and drops his dam fool fight for Windmill, we can get along. *Till* he does, we can't! Is that plain talk?

POPE.—(*As flushing some . . . but controlled*) I'm not responsible for the Gard gang, Mr. Buckner, nor for what they do, nor where they belong. As for the Windmill, it looks to me as if you had put a man on there yourself . . .

342

POLLY.—(*Laughs*) *That's* funny!

BUCKNER.—(*Blasting*) Why, rot you, Calhoun Pope, the man on Windmill is an upstart sheepherder from Nevada that I'm going to have the satisfaction of blasting *off* the Windmill if he don't take the hint and fan out! And *when* he's off . . .

POPE.—I don't want to say something, sir, that I'll regret . . . and I certainly ain't going to fight with you on your own place! . . . But . . . well, I'll let your statement pass.

BUCKNER.—(*Fuming . . . foaming*) You . . . you . . . . muddle-headed young fool! I can't talk to you! (*Fading*) Good morning, Pope! (*Up . . . off*) Polly, I'd like to talk to *you* about those colts, when you can get away! (*Out*)

SOUND.—*Door slams . . . off.*

POLLY.—(*Sighs*) Oh, Cal, what did you come here for today? Why can't you keep away from dad? If you'd let things ride . . .

POPE.—(*As smiling*) Why, Polly, honey, I guess you know the answer to that question.

POLLY.—Now, listen, Cal!

POPE.—I've come here before, even if I ain't welcome, to tell you that I'm going to marry you . . . when you get over being stubborn!

POLLY.—*That's* a waste of time! But I've told you that . . .

POPE.—Today I came because I'd heard that your Mr. Steve Gamble was headed this way with you.

POLLY.—Who told you *that?*

POPE.—Does it matter? The word got around!

POLLY.—(*Scornful*) One of your friends . . . the Gards, probably! Drifting around . . . riding the big circle . . . to see what they can pick up . . . !

POPE.—(*Quietly*) I'm going to let *that* pass, too, Polly . . . I'm trying to tell you that I came to see *that this man Gamble leaves you alone.* I've told him that . . . told him just now at the gate . . .

POLLY.—Oh, *you've* told him! Thank you *so* much for your interest! (*Fast and furious*) Now I'll tell *you* something, Mr. Calhoun Pope!

343

POPE.—What sort of stone you want in an engagement ring?

POLLY.—(*Swept along*) I'll tell *you* that Mr. Steve Gamble is *my* business! . . . And I don't want any interference from you between Steve Gamble and me *from this time on!* . . . Now, good morning . . . and a pleasant ride . . . wherever it is you're going!
(*Close*)

MUSIC.—*Song for* 8 *or* 10 *seconds.*

ANNOUNCER.—The other day a couple of us were sitting around, talking. And of course, I got to telling the boys about that mellow Falstaff flavor . . . about how downright satisfying that famous Falstaff flavor is. And one of the boys said, "Hey, when you mention a *flavor* . . . that's just one man's opinion!"

Well, I had the answer to that one, all right. Because every day a million bottles of Falstaff are served and enjoyed! That'll give you an idea how many folks know and appreciate Falstaff's famous flavor . . . the flavor created by the Thorobred yeast that's actually insured for one million dollars!

If you like good beer, you'll want to try that famous Falstaff flavor yourself. So next time you're thirsty for a cool, sparkling brew, step into your near-by Falstaff dealer's, and try Falstaff for yourself! You'll say it's swell . . . and *that's* a promise! Try Falstaff . . . soon!

MUSIC.—*Up to completion of number.*

RACE ROBBINS.—That's the way the story goes for now, ladies and gents . . . If you'd like to know how Calhoun Pope carried out the orders Polly Buckner give him . . . or what happened next in the fight for the Windmill Springs place . . . wall, *my* ad-vice is to pull your chairs up tomorrow night and listen when you hear the feller say, "Falstaff Beer *Pre*-sents . . . "!

MUSIC.—"*Half Past Four*" *for eight bars . . . fade for*

ANNOUNCER.—Justice Rides the Range is brought to you each weekday evening at this same time by your friendly Falstaff dealer and the Falstaff Brewing Corporation of St. Louis. Omaha, and New Orleans. This is Bill Adams speaking.

MUSIC.—"*Half Past Four*" *up and out.*

344